Envision It! | Visual Skills Handbook

Author's Purpose

Author's Viewpoint/Bias

Classify and Categorize

Cause and Effect

Compare and Contrast

Draw Conclusions

Fact and Opinion

Generalize

Graphic Sources

Literary Elements

Main Idea and Details

Sequence

Author's Purpose

Inform

Entertain

An author writes for many purposes including to inform, entertain, persuade, or express. An author may have more than one purpose for writing.

GET FIT

Persuade

Express

Author's Viewpoint/Bias

An author's viewpoint is the way that an author looks at the subject or ideas he or she is writing about.

Bias in writing shows strong feelings for or against something.

Classify and Categorize

When we classify and categorize, we look at how things are related based on their characteristics.

RECYCLING

MILK

GLASS

PAPER

KLEEN

CORN OIL

PLASTIC

Cause and Effect

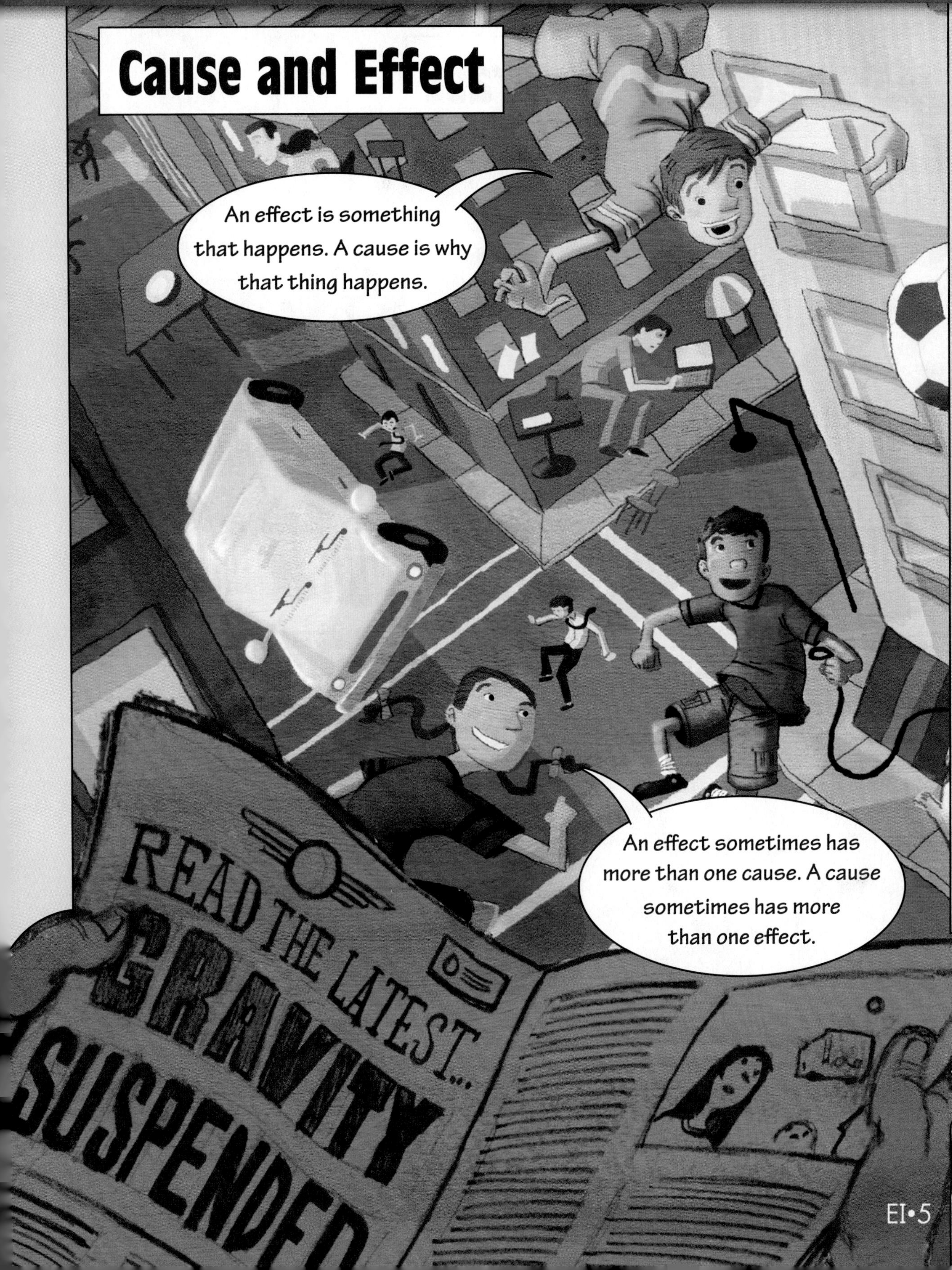

Compare and Contrast

To compare and contrast is to look for similarities and differences in things.

Draw Conclusions

When we draw conclusions, we make decisions or form an opinion about what we read.

Graphic Sources

A graphic source provides information visually, or in a way that the reader can see.

ANIMAL	ANIMAL FOOT PRINT	NUMBER OF SIGHTINGS
		3
		10
		6
		12
		9

Table

A table contains information in rows and columns. Tables allow you to compare facts.

NUMBER OF ANIMALS OBSERVED

Bar Graph

A bar graph arranges information so you can compare or rank it.

LAKE

W N E S

CAMPSITE

Map

A map is a drawing of a place that shows where something is or where something happened.

HOW TO MAKE A RAIN GAUGE

HANGER OR WIRE

BEND THE WIRE TO MAKE A HOLDER AND NAIL TO A FENCE

SCALE IN INCHES INSIDE OF CAN

STRAIGHT-SIDED CONTAINER FITS IN HOLDER

Diagram

A diagram is a drawing, usually with parts that are labeled.

Literary Elements

Understanding a story requires knowing the four main parts of a story: character, setting, plot, and theme.

Setting - the time and place in which a story happens

Character - a person or animal in a story

Plot - the pattern of events in a story

Rising Action

Climax

Conflict

Solution

Theme - the big idea of a story

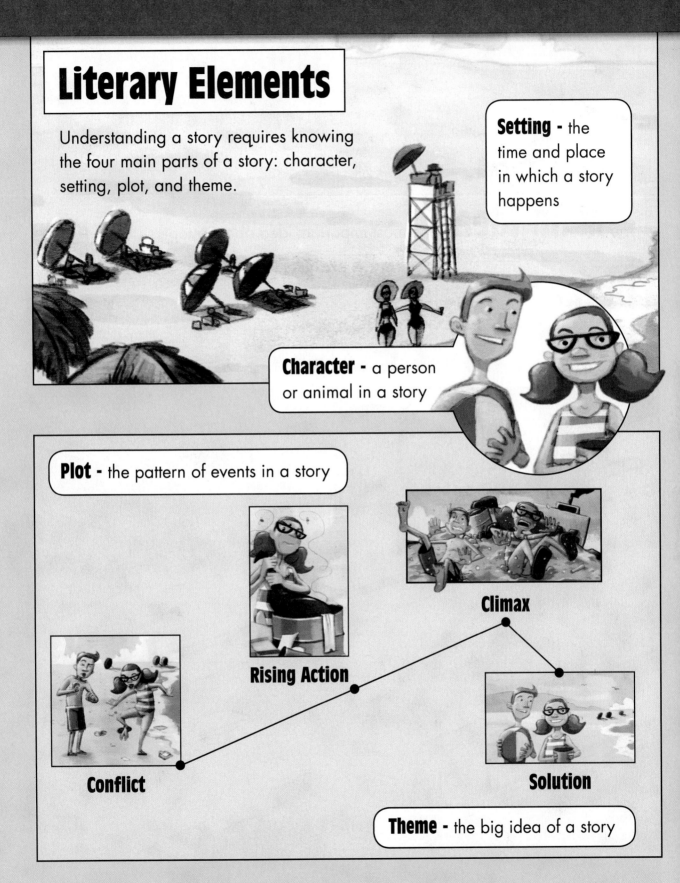

The **Main Idea** is the most important idea about a topic.

Details support the main idea.

Sequence

Sequence refers to the order of events in a text.
We use sequence when we list the steps in a process.

Envision It!

Visual Strategies Handbook

Background Knowledge

Important Ideas

Inferring

Monitor and Clarify

Predict and Set Purpose

Questioning

Story Structure

Summarize

Text Structure

Visualize

Background Knowledge

Background knowledge is what you already know about a topic based on your reading and personal experience. Use background knowledge before, during, and after reading to monitor comprehension.

To use background knowledge
- with fiction, preview the title, author's name, and illustrations
- with nonfiction, preview chapter titles, headings, captions, and other text features
- think about your own experiences while you read

> That reminds me of the time we went to the basement during the tornado warning.

Let's **Think** About **Reading!**

When I use background knowledge, I ask myself
- Does this character remind me of someone?
- How is this story or text similar to others I have read?
- What else do I know about this topic from what I've read or seen?

Important Ideas

Important ideas are essential ideas in a nonfiction selection. Important ideas include information and facts that provide clues to the author's purpose.

To identify important ideas
- read all titles, headings, and captions
- look for words in italics, boldface print, or bulleted lists
- look for signal words and phrases—*for example, most important,* and others
- use photographs, illustrations, or other graphic sources
- note how the text is organized—cause and effect, problem and solution, question and answer, or other ways

This must be an important idea.

Let's Think About Reading!

When I identify important ideas, I ask myself
- What information is included in bold, italics, or other special lettering?
- What details support important ideas?
- Are there signal words and phrases?
- What do illustrations, photos, diagrams, and charts show?
- How is the text organized?
- Why did the author write this?

Inferring

When we **infer**, we use background knowledge along with clues in the text to come up with our own ideas about what the author is trying to present.

To infer

- identify what you already know
- combine what you know with text clues to come up with your own ideas

> I see baking soda foam. Your volcano must have erupted!

SCIENCE FAIR

Let's Think About Reading!

When I infer, I ask myself

- What do I already know?
- Which text clues are important?
- What is the author trying to present?

Monitor and Clarify

We **monitor comprehension** to check our understanding of what we've read. We **clarify** to find out why we haven't understood what we've read and to adjust comprehension.

To monitor and clarify

- use background knowledge
- try different strategies: ask questions, reread, or use text features and illustrations

I don't remember if plants are a renewable or non-renewable resource.

Let's see...

EARTH'S RESOURCES

RENEWABLE RESOURCES | NON-RENEWABLE RESOURCES

AIR   WATER   COAL   OIL   NATURAL GAS

SCIENCE

Let's **Think** About **Reading!**

When I monitor and clarify, I ask myself
- Do I understand what I'm reading?
- What doesn't make sense?
- What strategies can I use?

Predict and Set Purpose

We **predict** to tell what might happen next in a story or article. The prediction is based on what has already happened. We **set a purpose** to guide our reading.

To predict and set a purpose
- preview the title, the author's name, and the illustrations or graphics
- identify why you're reading
- use what you already know to make predictions
- check and change your predictions based on new information

> I predict the locations of the state capitals are based on their populations.

Let's Think About Reading!

When I predict and set a purpose, I ask myself
- What do I already know?
- What do I think will happen?
- What is my purpose for reading?

Questioning

Questioning is asking good questions about important text information. Questioning takes place before, during, and after reading.

To question
- read with a question in mind
- stop, think, and record your questions as you read
- make notes when you find information
- check your understanding and ask questions to clarify

ARACHNID TARANTULA

What does *arachnid* mean? Where does it fit in a food chain? Do tarantulas have to adapt to their environment to survive?

Let's Think About Reading!

When I question, I ask myself
- Have I asked a good question with a question word?
- What questions help me make sense of my reading?
- What does the author mean?

Story Structure

Story structure is the arrangement of a story from beginning to end. You can use this information to summarize the story.

To identify story structure

- note the conflict, or problem, at the beginning of a story
- track the rising action as the conflict builds in the middle
- recognize the climax, the time when the characters face the conflict
- identify how the conflict is resolved

Problem/Conflict

Rising Action

Resolution

Let's **Think** About **Reading!**

When I identify story structure, I ask myself
- What is the story's conflict or problem?
- How does the conflict build throughout the story?
- How is the conflict resolved in the end?
- How might this affect future events?

Summarize

We **summarize** to check our understanding of what we've read. A summary is a brief statement—no more than a few sentences—and maintains a logical order.

To summarize fiction

- tell what happens in the story
- include the goals of the characters, how they try to reach them, and whether or not they succeed

To summarize nonfiction

- tell the main idea
- think about text structure and how the selection is organized

This blizzard is stalling rush hour traffic.

Let's Think About Reading!

When I summarize, I ask myself

- What is the story or selection about?
- In fiction, what are the characters' goals? Are they successful?
- In nonfiction, how is the information organized?

Text Structure

We use **text structure** to look for how the author has organized the text. Organizations include cause and effect, problem and solution, sequence, or compare and contrast. Analyze text structure before, during, and after reading to locate information.

To identify text structure

- before reading: preview titles, headings, and illustrations
- during reading: notice the organization
- after reading: recall the organization and summarize the text

First, teach your dog how to sit.

Then, teach him how to roll over.

Finally, teach him how to speak.

WOOF!

Let's Think About Reading!

When I identify text structure, I ask myself
- What clues do titles, headings, and illustrations provide?
- How is information organized?
- How does the organization help my understanding?

Visualize

We **visualize** to form pictures in our minds as we read. This helps us monitor our comprehension.

To visualize

- combine what you already know with details from the text to make pictures in your mind
- use all of your senses to put yourself in the story or text

PLUMES OF ORANGE AND BLUE SMOKE FILL THE AIR. THE GROUND RUMBLES LIKE THUNDER. SUDDENLY, YOU'RE FLYING ABOVE THE GROUND AND INTO **OUTER SPACE!**

Let's **Think** About **Reading!**

When I visualize, I ask myself
- What do I already know?
- Which details create pictures in my mind?
- How can my senses put me in the story?

SCOTT FORESMAN
READING STREET

GRADE 5

COMMON CORE ©

Program Authors

Peter Afflerbach

Camille Blachowicz

Candy Dawson Boyd

Elena Izquierdo

Connie Juel

Edward Kame'enui

Donald Leu

Jeanne R. Paratore

P. David Pearson

Sam Sebesta

Deborah Simmons

Susan Watts Taffe

Alfred Tatum

Sharon Vaughn

Karen Kring Wixson

Glenview, Illinois

Boston, Massachusetts

Chandler, Arizona

Hoboken, New Jersey

ALWAYS LEARNING

PEARSON

We dedicate Reading Street to
Peter Jovanovich.

His wisdom, courage,
and passion for education
are an inspiration to us all.

Accelerated
Reader®

Acknowledgments appear on pages 482–485, which constitute an extension of this copyright page.

ISBN-13: 978-0-328-72456-7
ISBN-10:   0-328-72456-4
10 11 12 13 14 15 16 17 18 V057 18 17 16 15

Reading STREET

Dear Reader,

Are you ready? You are about to take a trip along a famous street—*Scott Foresman Reading Street*. During this trip you will meet exciting people, such as astronaut Dr. Ellen Ochoa, the legendary King Midas, and a boy who creates his own world with its own language and customs. You will take real and imaginary journeys to the bottom of the sea and to the center of the Earth.

As you read selections about ghost towns, amazing bats, and insects that swell up to store food, you will gain exciting new information that will help you in science and social studies.

While you're enjoying these exciting pieces of literature, you will find that something else is going on—you are becoming a better reader, gaining new skills and polishing old ones.

Have a great trip— and send us a postcard!

Sincerely,
The Authors

Unit 4 Contents

Adapting

 How do people and animals adapt to different situations?

Unit 4 Contents

Week 6

Unit 4

Envision It! A Comprehension Handbook

Envision It! Visual Skills Handbook EI•1–EI•13

Envision It! Visual Strategies Handbook EI•15–EI•25

Words! Vocabulary Handbook W•1–W•15

Adventurers

Who goes seeking adventure and why?

Week 1

Let's Think About Reading!

humorous fiction • science

Unit 5 Contents

Week 4

Week 5

Week 6

Unit 5

Envision It! A Comprehension Handbook

Envision It! Visual Skills Handbook EI•1–EI•13

Envision It! Visual Strategies Handbook EI•15–EI•25

Words! Vocabulary Handbook W•1–W•15

Unit 6 Contents

The Unexpected

What can we learn from encounters with the unexpected?

Week 1

Let's **Think** About Reading!

expository text • science

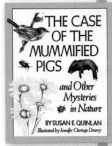

Unit 6 Contents

Envision It! A Comprehension Handbook

Envision It! Visual Skills Handbook EI•1–EI•13

Envision It! Visual Strategies Handbook EI•15–EI•25

Words! Vocabulary Handbook W•1–W•15

Don Leu
The Internet Guy

Right before our eyes, the nature of reading and learning is changing. The Internet and other technologies create new opportunities, new solutions, and new literacies. New reading comprehension skills are required online. They are increasingly important to our students and our society.

Those of us on the Reading Street team are here to help you on this new, and very exciting, journey.

See It!

- Big Question Video

- Concept Talk Video

- Envision It! Animations

- eReaders

Hear It!

- eSelections

- Grammar Jammer

- Vocabulary Activities

Concept Talk Video

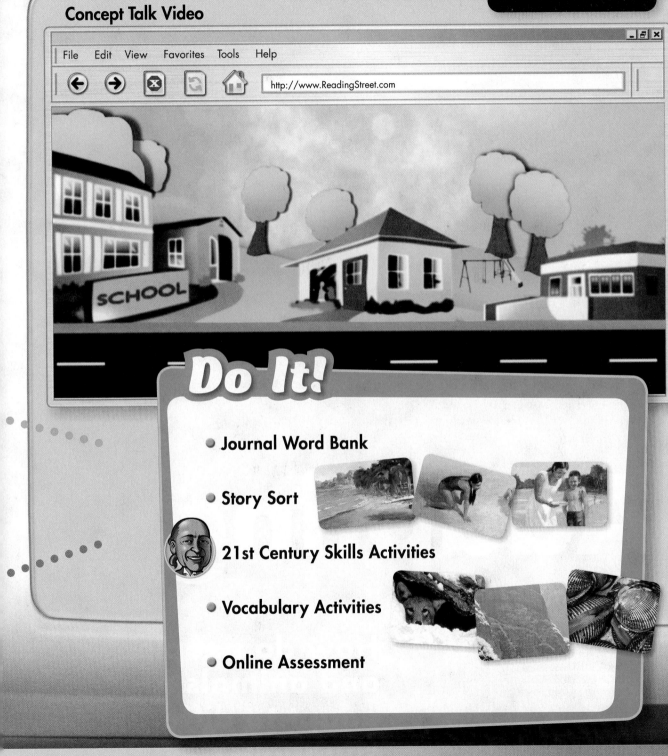

| File | Edit | View | Favorites | Tools | Help |

http://www.ReadingStreet.com

Do It!

- **Journal Word Bank**

- **Story Sort**

- **21st Century Skills Activities**

- **Vocabulary Activities**

- **Online Assessment**

Adapting

THE BIG ?

How do people and animals adapt to different situations?

Common Core State Standards

Language 6. Acquire and use accurately grade-appropriate general academic and domain-specific words and phrases, including those that signal contrast, addition, and other logical relationships (e.g., *however, although, nevertheless, similarly, moreover, in addition*).
Also Speaking/Listening 3.

Let's Talk About

People Adapting

- Share opinions about ways you have adapted.

- Listen to a classmate talk about adapting to situations.

- Determine your classmates' main and supporting ideas about adapting.

READING STREET ONLINE
CONCEPT TALK VIDEO
www.ReadingStreet.com

Envision It! | Skill Strategy

Skill

Strategy

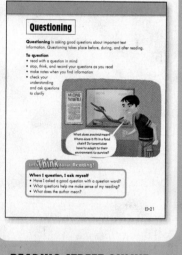

READING STREET ONLINE
ENVISION IT! ANIMATIONS
www.ReadingStreet.com

Comprehension Skill

Draw Conclusions

- A conclusion is a decision you make after thinking about the details of what you read.

- Your own prior knowledge can help you draw conclusions. When you draw a conclusion, be sure it makes sense and is supported by what you have read.

- Use the text and the graphic organizer to help you draw a conclusion about Jeff.

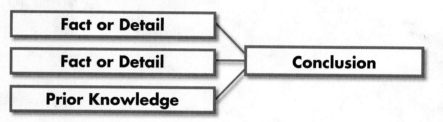

Comprehension Strategy

Questioning

As you read, it is important to ask questions. Begin reading with a question in mind before you read and make notes when you find information that answers your question. You can ask an interpretive question, which will help you explain something in a story or text. Your answers can help you monitor and clarify your comprehension of a story.

THE GO-CART

The summer had been downright boring. Nothing extraordinary had occurred. Then Jeff read an ad in the local newspaper: "Go-Cart Race Next Month! Win $1,000!" He decided that he *had* to enter the race.

"But Jeff, you don't own a go-cart," his father said.

The newspaper noted that the go-cart had to be homemade. Jeff had been saving his allowance, and he had enough money for the plans and parts for the go-cart.

"But Jeff, you've never built anything," his mother said.

Jeff set about his building task. He read the instructions that came with the go-cart kit carefully. If something was confusing or hard to understand, he called the hardware store and asked a clerk to explain. Every day he toiled on his go-cart, and every night it was that much closer to being finished.

Finally, the day of the race arrived. Jeff put on his helmet and revved his engine. The announcer roared, "On your mark! Get set! Go!" And Jeff, who had never raced a go-cart before, was off!

Skill Draw a conclusion about why you think Jeff *had* to enter the race.

Strategy What kind of person do you think Jeff is?

Skill Draw a conclusion about how you think Jeff felt as he revved his engine.

Your Turn!

⏸ **Need a Review?** See the *Envision It! Handbook* for additional help with drawing conclusions and questioning.

Let's Think About...

▶ **Ready to Try It?** Use what you have learned about drawing conclusions and questioning as you read *Weslandia*.

Weslandia

23

Common Core State Standards
Foundational Skills 3.a. Use combined knowledge of all letter-sound correspondences, syllabication patterns, and morphology (e.g., roots and affixes) to read accurately unfamiliar multisyllabic words in context and out of context. **Also Language 4.**

Envision It! | Words to Know

civilization

complex

fleeing

blunders

envy

inspired

rustling

strategy

Vocabulary Strategy for

🔍 Endings *-ed, -ing, -s*

Word Structure The Old English endings *-ed* and *-ing* may be added to verbs to change the tense, person, or usage of the verb. The *-s* ending has the same function. You can use endings to help determine the meaning of an unknown word.

1. Examine the unknown word to see if it has a root word you know.

2. Check to see if the ending *-ed, -ing,* or *-s* has been added to a base word. Remember that some base words drop the final *-e* before adding an ending. For example, *rustle* becomes *rustling.*

3. Reread the sentence and make sure the word shows action. (The ending *-s* may be added to nouns too.)

4. Decide how the ending changes the meaning of the base word.

5. Try the meaning in the sentence.

Read "Long-Ago Lives" on page 25. Look for words that end with *-ed, -ing,* or *-s.* Use the endings to help determine the words' meanings.

Words to Write Reread "Long-Ago Lives." Imagine that you are living in an ancient civilization. Write about what you see. Use words from the *Words to Know* list in your writing.

LONG-AGO LIVES

We do not usually have envy of the lives of people who lived thousands of years ago. We are likely to imagine them fleeing for their lives from enemies or wild beasts. Any civilization without excellent shopping, television, and computers seems far too primitive for us.

However, we have learned much about early cultures. What we have learned shows us that their world was often complex, not simple. They were not all that different from us. For example, two thousand years ago the Mayan people played a ball game. The game was played by teams on stone courts with special goals. Players needed great strength and skill. The strategy was to send a heavy ball through a high stone ring using only hips, knees, and elbows. Kings might play this game, for which the stakes were very high. No one wanted to make any blunders because the loser might lose his head!

This game may have inspired our modern game of soccer. Stand on one of those ancient ball courts and you can almost feel the excitement of the crowd or hear a feather headdress rustling.

Your Turn!

⏸ Need a Review?
For additional help with endings -ed, -ing, and -s, see Words!

▷ Ready to Try It?
Use what you've learned as you read Weslandia on pp. 26–37.

Fiction tells the stories of imaginary people and events. As you read, notice how the character makes up his own world.

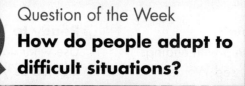

Question of the Week

How do people adapt to difficult situations?

Weslandia

by PAUL FLEISCHMAN   illustrated by KEVIN HAWKES

"Of course he's miserable," moaned Wesley's mother. "He sticks out."

"Like a nose," snapped his father.

Listening through the heating vent, Wesley knew they were right. He was an outcast from the civilization around him.

He alone in his town disliked pizza and soda, alarming his mother and the school nurse. He found professional football stupid. He'd refused to shave half his head, the hairstyle worn by all the other boys, despite his father's bribe of five dollars.

Passing his neighborhood's two styles of

Let's Think About...

Why does Wesley feel like an outcast?

🎯 Questioning

housing—garage on the left and garage on the right—Wesley alone dreamed of more exciting forms of shelter. He had no friends, but plenty of tormentors.

Fleeing them was the only sport he was good at.

Each afternoon his mother asked him what he'd learned in school that day.

"That seeds are carried great distances by the wind," he answered on Wednesday.

"That each civilization has its staple food crop," he answered on Thursday.

"That school's over and I should find a good summer project," he answered on Friday.

Let's Think About...

What do you think Wesley's project will be? **Predict**

Let's **Think** About...

What clues here tell you how Wesley's land was being planted? Reread to find out.
Important Ideas

As always, his father mumbled, "I'm sure you'll use that knowledge often."

Suddenly, Wesley's thoughts shot sparks. His eyes blazed. His father was right! He could actually *use* what he'd learned that week for a summer project that would top all others. He would grow his own staple food crop—and found his own civilization!

The next morning he turned over a plot of ground in his yard. That night a wind blew in from the west. It raced through the trees and set his curtains snapping. Wesley lay awake, listening. His land was being planted.

Five days later the first seedlings appeared.

"You'll have almighty bedlam on your hands if you don't get those weeds out," warned his neighbor.

"Actually, that's my crop," replied Wesley. "In this type of garden there are no weeds."

Following ancient tradition, Wesley's fellow gardeners grew tomatoes, beans, Brussels sprouts, and nothing else. Wesley found it thrilling to open his land to chance, to invite the new and unknown.

The plants shot up past his knees, then his waist. They seemed to be all of the same sort. Wesley couldn't find them in any plant book.

"Are those tomatoes, beans, or Brussels sprouts?" asked Wesley's neighbor.

Let's Think About...

Why does the neighbor think that Wesley's garden is full of weeds?

Questioning

"None of the above," replied Wesley.

Fruit appeared, yellow at first, then blushing to magenta. Wesley picked one and sliced through the rind to the juicy purple center. He took a bite and found the taste an entrancing blend of peach, strawberry, pumpkin pie, and flavors he had no name for.

Ignoring the shelf of cereals in the kitchen, Wesley took to breakfasting on the fruit. He dried half a rind to serve as a cup, built his own squeezing device, and drank the fruit's juice throughout the day.

Let's **Think** About...

How does the description help you visualize the fruit Wesley is eating? **Visualize**

Pulling up a plant, he found large tubers on the roots. These he boiled, fried, or roasted on the family barbecue, seasoning them with the plant's highly aromatic leaves.

It was hot work tending his crop. To keep off the sun, Wesley wove himself a hat from strips of the plant's woody bark. His success with the hat inspired him to devise a spinning wheel and loom on which he wove a loose-fitting robe from the stalks' soft inner fibers.

Unlike jeans, which he found scratchy and heavy, the robe was comfortable, reflected the sun, and offered myriad opportunities for pockets.

Let's Think About...

How did Wesley learn how to do all of these things?

Questioning

Let's **Think** About...

Do you think Wesley's relationship with his schoolmates will change? Why do you think that? **Predict**

His schoolmates were scornful, then curious. Grudgingly, Wesley allowed them ten minutes apiece at his mortar, crushing the plant's seeds to collect the oil.

This oil had a tangy scent and served him both as suntan lotion and mosquito repellent. He rubbed it on his face each morning and sold small amounts to his former tormentors at the price of ten dollars per bottle.

"What's happened to your watch?" asked his mother one day.

Wesley admitted that he no longer wore it. He told time by the stalk that he used as a sundial and

had divided the day into eight segments—the number of petals on the plant's flowers.

He'd adopted a new counting system as well, based likewise upon the number eight. His domain, home to many such innovations, he named "Weslandia."

Uninterested in traditional sports, Wesley made up his own. These were designed for a single player and used many different parts of the plant. His spectators looked on with envy.

Realizing that more players would offer him more scope, Wesley invented other games that would include his schoolmates, games rich with

Let's Think About...

Why do you think the number eight is important in Weslandia?

Questioning

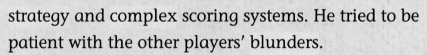

strategy and complex scoring systems. He tried to be
patient with the other players' blunders.

August was unusually hot. Wesley built himself
a platform and took to sleeping in the middle of
Weslandia. He passed the evenings playing a flute
he'd fashioned from a stalk or gazing up at the sky,
renaming the constellations.

His parents noted Wesley's improved morale.
"It's the first time in years he's looked happy," said
his mother.

Wesley gave them a tour of Weslandia.
"What do you call this plant?" asked his father.

Not knowing its name, Wesley had begun calling it "swist," from the sound of its leaves rustling in the breeze.

In like manner, he'd named his new fabrics, games, and foods, until he'd created an entire language.

Mixing the plant's oil with soot, Wesley made a passable ink. As the finale to his summer project, he used the ink and his own eighty-letter alphabet to record the history of his civilization's founding.

In September, Wesley returned to school...
He had no shortage of friends.

Let's Think About...

What do you think will happen to Weslandia when school starts again?
Predict

Common Core State Standards

Literature 1. Quote accurately from a text when explaining what the text says explicitly and when drawing inferences from the text. **Also Literature 2., Writing 9.**

Envision It! Retell

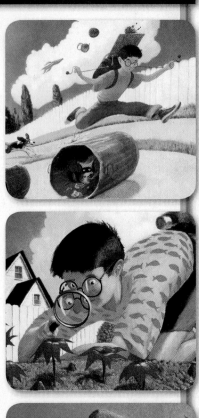

Think Critically

1. Would you like to live in Weslandia or in a land of your own making? Use details from the story to support your opinion. **Text to Self**

2. *Weslandia* shows that you can find a fun idea for a fantasy tale right outside your own back door. How can you tell that the author had fun inventing this story? Use examples from the text. **Think Like an Author**

3. Suppose you never read *Weslandia*. Look at only the illustrations, from start to finish. Then draw conclusions about the plot and characters. Use examples from the art to support those conclusions.
Draw Conclusions

4. Is Wesley a person you could admire? Support your answer with details from the story. **Questioning**

5. Look Back and Write Look at the picture on pages 36–37. Then read the story's final sentence. Explain how the words make a surprise ending to *Weslandia*. Provide evidence to support your answer.

Key Ideas and Details • Text Evidence

Meet the Author
Paul Fleischman

When he was asked if his childhood was like Wesley's in *Weslandia*, Paul Fleischman replied, "Yes and no. I felt different from my peers because I was so short— the shortest boy in my grade all the way through tenth grade. And like Wesley, my friends and I made up an alternate world—our own games, our own underground school newspaper." On the other hand, he says, "Unlike Wesley, I wasn't an outcast. I was president of my grammar school and had a great pack of friends."

Mr. Fleischman has received many awards for his books, including a Newbery Medal for *Joyful Noise: Poems for Two Voices*. He grew up in Santa Monica, California, where he listened to his father, well-known writer Sid Fleischman, read chapters of his books to the family. Paul Fleischman says, "We grew up knowing that words felt good in the ears and on the tongue, that they were as much fun to play with as toys."

Paul Fleischman's love for music has played a part in his writing. While growing up, he learned to play the piano. He also enjoyed listening to all kinds of music on the radio, from Beethoven symphonies to pop songs. Mr. Fleishman now lives on the coast in California with his wife, Patty. He has two grown sons.

Here are other books by Paul Fleischman.

JOYFUL NOISE
Poems for Two Voices
PAUL FLEISCHMAN
illustrated by Eric Beddows

LOST!
A Story in String
BY PAUL FLEISCHMAN
ILLUSTRATED BY C. B. MORDAN

Reading Log
Use the *Reader's and Writer's Notebook* to record your independent reading.

Common Core State Standards

Writing 3. Write narratives to develop real or imagined experiences or events using effective technique, descriptive details, and clear event sequences.

Also Writing 3.a., 3.b., Language 1.

Picture Book

A **picture book** tells a story with words and pictures. It can be a real story about something that happened to you or it can be fictional. The following student model is an example of a picture book page.

Writing Prompt In *Weslandia*, a boy decides to remake his world rather than accept it as it is. Think about someone you know who doesn't always follow the crowd. Now write a picture book, with your own illustrations, about that person.

Let's Write It!

Key Features of a Picture Book

- may tell a story or describe a true event
- often contains dialogue
- includes illustrations or art

READING STREET ONLINE
GRAMMAR JAMMER
www.ReadingStreet.com

Writer's Checklist

Remember, you should . . .

 write an imaginative story with a clearly defined focus.

 include dialogue that develops the story.

✓ use proper punctuation for quotations in dialogue.

✓ illustrate your story.

Where There's a Will, There's a Way

My older brother Will is strong and athletic. He used to like playing basketball. Because he was small, the other players on the team overshadowed him. They were taller and better at passing and making good shots.

One day, Will said, "I want to take gymnastics."

"Why?" I asked Will.

"Because," Will replied, "I think I will be good at it."

So Will took gymnastics. At first, some of the other boys laughed. Will kept at it. He took gymnastics year after year. Now they do not laugh at him. Will is one of the top gymnasts in the district.

Writing Trait Focus/Ideas
The introductory paragraph provides a clearly defined focus.

Subject and object pronouns are used correctly.

Genre
A **picture book** always tells a story with illustrations.

Conventions

Subject and Object Pronouns

Remember Pronouns take the place of nouns. A **subject pronoun** is used in the subject of a sentence (*I, he, she, we,* and *they*). **Object pronouns** are used in the predicate of a sentence after an action verb or with a preposition (*me, him*).

41

© **Common Core State Standards**
Literature 5. Explain how a series of chapters, scenes, or stanzas fits together to provide the overall structure of a particular story, drama, or poem. **Also Literature 4., Language 5.**

Social Studies in Reading

Genre
Poetry

- Poetry is meant to appeal to the senses, emotions, or mind.

- Sensory words in a poem help the reader understand what the writer smells, sees, hears, tastes, and feels.

- Sometimes, the poet uses rhyme scheme to reinforce the meaning of a poem.

- Read the two poems on these pages. Notice the rhyme scheme one poet uses, and how it reinforces meaning.

Under the Back Porch

BY VIRGINIA HAMILTON

Our house is two stories high
shaped like a white box.
There is a yard stretched around it
and in back
a wooden porch.

Under the back porch is my place.
I rest there.
I go there when I have to be alone.
It is always shaded and damp.
Sunlight only slants through the slats
in long strips of light,
and the smell of the damp
is moist green,
like the moss that grows here.

My sisters and brothers
can stand on the back porch
and never know
I am here
underneath.
It is my place.
All mine.

Keziah

BY GWENDOLYN BROOKS

I have a secret place to go.
Not anyone may know

And sometimes when the wind is rough
I cannot get there fast enough.

And sometimes when my mother
Is scolding my big brother,

My secret place, it seems to me,
Is quite the only place to be.

Let's Think About...

These poems follow rhyme scheme and use sensory images. How do these things reinforce the meanings of the poems? **Poetry**

Let's Think About...

Reading Across Texts How are Wesley and the poems' authors similar and different?

Writing Across Texts Write a poem about *Weslandia* that you think Wesley might write. Use evidence from the text.

Common Core State Standards

Speaking/Listening 4. Report on a topic or text or present an opinion, sequencing ideas logically and using appropriate facts and relevant, descriptive details to support main ideas or themes; speak clearly at an understandable pace. **Also Foundational Skills 3.a., 4., 4.b., Speaking/Listening 5., Language 4.**

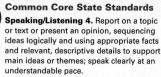

Let's Learn It!

READING STREET ONLINE
ONLINE STUDENT EDITION
www.ReadingStreet.com

Vocabulary

Endings -ed, -ing, -s

Word Structure You can use the structure of words to learn more about what a word means. The *-ed* and *-ing* endings are from Old English. The verb ending *-ed* shows actions. The ending *-ing* can show that a word is being used as an adjective. The noun ending *-s* shows that a noun is plural.

Practice It! Find at least three words in *Weslandia* that end with *-ing* or *-ed*. Find at least three nouns that end with *-s*. How does understanding the endings help you understand these words?

Fluency

Appropriate Phrasing/Punctuation Clues

When you read, phrasing and punctuation marks such as exclamation points, question marks, or dashes help readers interpret meaning. Punctuation marks also tell you which words in a sentence are grouped together, and where you should pause as you read.

Practice It! With a partner, practice reading from *Weslandia*, page 30, paragraph 2. One partner should read using punctuation clues and phrasing to interpret the meaning in his or her own way. Then the other partner should take a turn. Talk about the differences with your partner.

44

Listening and Speaking

When you demonstrate a skill, make eye contact to communicate effectively.

How-to Demonstration

In a how-to demonstration, you show how to do something step by step. At the same time, you explain what you are doing at each step.

Practice It! With a partner, demonstrate one of Wes's projects for the class. Try the project first to make sure it works. Make sure you have all the materials you will need for your demonstration. Break the project down into steps and prepare an explanation for each one. Then present it to the class, and restate the steps when necessary.

Tips

Listening . . .

- Pay attention and concentrate on the speaker's message and instructions.

- Ask questions as you follow the oral instructions.

Speaking . . .

- Face the audience and speak loudly and enunciate clearly.

- Hold up your visuals, and gesture as you show each step of the process.

Teamwork . . .

- Discuss the demonstration with your partner.

- Ask your partner questions and consider his or her suggestions and ideas.

Common Core State Standards

Language 6. Acquire and use accurately grade-appropriate general academic and domain-specific words and phrases, including those that signal contrast, addition, and other logical relationships (e.g., *however, although, nevertheless, similarly, moreover, in addition*). **Also Speaking/Listening 1.c.**

Let's Talk About

Overcoming Obstacles

- Share experiences of when and how you overcame obstacles.

- Listen to a classmate's experiences with overcoming obstacles.

- Ask a classmate questions about obstacles he or she overcame.

READING STREET ONLINE
CONCEPT TALK VIDEO
www.ReadingStreet.com

46

You've learned
1 6 0
Amazing Words
so far this year!

Common Core State Standards
Literature 1. Quote accurately from a text when explaining what the text says explicitly and when drawing inferences from the text.

Envision It! | Skill Strategy

Skill

Strategy

Comprehension Skill

Generalize

- To generalize is to make a broad statement or inference that applies to several examples.

- Active readers make generalizations about story characters as they read. They support their generalizations using evidence from the text as well as their own background knowledge.

- Use a graphic organizer like the one below to help you make a generalization about Victor's character and to use textual evidence to support your understanding about Victor.

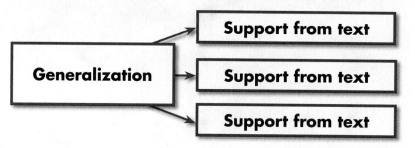

Comprehension Strategy

Predict and Set Purpose

As you read, it is important to make predictions. You can check your predictions during and after reading. Your predictions will help you set your purpose for reading as you read to see if you were right. This will help you recall and understand what you read.

The School Dance

Victor looked at himself in the mirror. He was wearing a sport coat and a new pair of shoes. "I think I look okay," he thought, "but what if the other kids don't think so?"

Victor was going to the Autumn Dance at school. He was looking forward to seeing his friends, but he was a little nervous about dancing. "What if I look goofy?" Victor worried.

Victor had asked his mother those questions. "You'll be fine," his mother said. "Just go and have fun."

At the gym, Victor saw that all the students were standing against the walls of the large room. Music was playing but no one was dancing. In fact, most kids were looking at their shoes. Then Victor spotted Nadia, his neighbor. He'd known Nadia since they were in second grade! At the same time, Nadia rushed up to Victor and said, "Let's dance! Someone's got to get things started."

Victor felt weird, but he and Nadia started dancing in the middle of the room anyway. Slowly, other kids came out to dance too. Soon everyone was laughing and having fun.

Skill What generalizations can you infer about Victor from what he says in the text?

Strategy What do you predict will happen to Victor at the dance?

Skill What generalization can you make about the other kids from the way they are acting?

Your Turn!

❚❚ **Need a Review?** See the *Envision It! Handbook* for additional help with generalizing and predicting.

▶ **Ready to Try It?** Use what you have learned as you read *Tripping Over the Lunch Lady*.

Common Core State Standards
Language 4.a. Use context (e.g., cause/
effect relationships and comparisons in
text) as a clue to the meaning of a word
or phrase. **Also Language 4.**

Envision It! | Words to Know

Dalmatian

frilly

promenading

sprained

substitute

Vocabulary Strategy for

🎯 Unfamiliar Words

Context Clues As you read, you will find unfamiliar words. See if you can use context clues to figure out the meaning of a new word. *Context* means "the words and sentences near an unfamiliar word."

1. Read the words and sentences around the unfamiliar word. Are there clues that help you determine the meaning of the unfamiliar word?

2. To help find context clues, you can look for a word or words set off by commas. Also look for examples, comparisons, or contrasts that suggest the meaning of the word.

3. Put the clues together and decide what you think the word means.

4. If you cannot find the meaning quickly, look the word up in a dictionary.

Read "Dogs on Parade" on page 51. Look for context clues that help you determine and clarify the meanings of unfamiliar words.

Words to Write Reread "Dogs on Parade." Imagine that you are writing an entry in your journal about the dog show. Use words from the *Words to Know* list in your journal entry.

Dogs on Parade

"Hello, everyone, and welcome to the third annual Westown Dog Show. I'm your radio host, Spot the Dalmatian. As you might guess, I got my name because I'm a white dog covered with black spots. And I usually compete in the dog show, but just last week I jumped down from a couch and injured my leg. The vet says I sprained it. Maybe that's why my owners tell me to stay off of the furniture. Anyway, I'm here today to bring you all of the action from the show.

"And here we go! The dogs have entered the building and are all walking in a line around the arena. I wish you could see them promenading around this big hall. They all look great!

"The first dog is my friend Dot. She's walking for me. Because of my leg, I needed a substitute, or someone to take my place, while my leg heals. And right behind her is Sandy the Cocker Spaniel. She looks so pretty with that frilly collar she wears. Just a piece of lacy white cloth can work wonders!

"Well, it's time to break for a commercial. Stay tuned, and I'll be back with you in sixty seconds!"

Your Turn!

⏸ Need a Review?
For additional help with context clues, see *Words!*

▶ Ready to Try It?
Use what you've learned as you read *Tripping Over the Lunch Lady* on pp. 52–67.

Tripping Over

Question of the Week

How do people overcome obstacles?

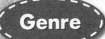

Realistic fiction deals with characters and actions that seem real but come from the author's imagination, sometimes in a humorous way. As you read, notice how the author makes the setting and humorous characters come to life.

the Lunch Lady

by Angela Johnson   Illustrated by Matt Faulkner

53

I'm never going to be a gymnast.

You know how people say that some folks can't walk and chew gum at the same time? Oh yeah, they were talking about me.

I fall down stairs and roll out of bed onto the floor. I drop things on my toes and get trapped in closets. I've broken my arm making cookies. Don't ask. I even got locked in my own locker once. I wanted to see what it was like inside, and had to stay there till the end of school for the janitor to let me out.

Do you know how embarrassing it is to be caught in a locker? Just ask me.

I'm especially not good with my feet *off* the ground. I was telling Mr. Deimeister just that, about the time I went flying off the trampoline over Tony Friedman's head yesterday and scared him so bad (he wasn't spotting for me but was talking to Gus Jackson about what they were going to do after school) that he choked on some gum he wasn't supposed to have in his mouth.

Right around the time he was having the Heimlich done on him and Gus was screaming to apply direct pressure (luckily we'd just had a first-aid class the period before gym), I realized that what everybody calls me is probably true.

Jinx.

That's how everyone refers to me. My own parents, even.

Mom thinks it's cute. My uncle Jeff began calling me Jinx when I started crawling backward as a baby and getting stuck in boxes, under tables, and even, the story goes, a pair of my dad's boots.

Dad pats me on the head like an old skunky stray and says Uncle Jeff was just like me.

Yeah, right.

Uncle Jeff drives a Porsche and lives in a cabin in the woods with a hot tub.

I'm too uncoordinated to ever drive a car, and I'm pretty sure a hot tub is just a bad accident waiting to happen. I love Uncle Jeff anyway, though. I guess he might have been a jinx back in the day. But hey, he must have grown out of it, which doesn't necessarily mean I will.

I'm never going to be able to keep my feet together and fly perfectly on the trampoline. I'm never going to be able to make a basket without breaking somebody's bones (the doctors did do a good job on Mr. Deimeister's nose, though). I'm never going to run like my sister or kick a soccer ball like my brother without falling, throwing up, or pulling a muscle on me or somebody else. My dad won't even let me use a steak knife. I still have to cut meat with one of those plastic picnic things that sort of look like a knife.

But a while ago everything changed—my whole life, even, because of something I saw on the Folk Arts Channel. A couple days after that, a picture in an album made it feel exactly right.

Yes, ladies and gentlemen, boys and girls, people I've run over, stepped on, and tripped up . . . I am going to be a square dance star.

The dancers on television floated over the floor, arm in arm. They smiled, laughed, and nobody fell into anybody else or sprained anything. They were all so happy and even seemed to really like each other. And then I saw this woman who looked just like my mom. She could have been my mom, she looked so much like her. Then in the middle of a swing around she looked the camera in the eye and smiled at me. Honest, it was as if she looked right at me to say: "You could be me, and look—I can do this."

Wow.

It was a couple of days later when a picture fell out of a photo album I'd just dropped in the fish tank (I rescued everything pretty quick, except now our goldfish hide when I come close to the tank), but there in living color was a picture of my mom arm in arm with this kid with hair way down his back—square dancing.

It was in my genes.

I knew then it was meant to be.

And not only am I going to be a star, I'm going to be the fifth-grade school gym square dance champ of the whole world. And nobody's going to stop me—ouch . . .

It's a hard thing to change people's minds about how things are done and to get them to do something new.

This is how it went with Mr. Deimeister when I went to his office and told him what might be the most wonderful thing since kneepads and bandages.

"What?" he said, sort of backing away from me like he always does.

"Square dancing, Mr. Deimeister. Square dancing. It's fun and it's good exercise for everybody. I saw it on the Folk Arts Channel and practiced with a huge stuffed teddy bear."

"What?"

"It was real cool the way the guys swung the girls and everybody skipped and twirled around the room. I think it would be good for us all to learn a new skill, learn to dance with partners ('cause usually the boys don't want to), and get a good workout."

"What?"

"We wouldn't have to wear the frilly dresses or bow ties like they did on TV. I think our regular gym clothes would be okay. Do you think they have square dance music in the band room?"

"What?"

I think a few more meetings with Mr. Deimeister will get him to come around to the square dance way. So later that day I dropped off some square dance music at his office. He wasn't there and I accidentally dropped a ten-pound weight I was moving off his desk onto a fishing pole that fell on the floor. There was a stuffed fish over his desk.

Scary.

I thought we'd be dancing by now, but days after my meeting with Mr. Deimeister we're still on the trampoline that decided a long time ago it didn't like me. Evil is what it is. Evil. And it won't even take pity on my poor classmates, who have to keep catching me and throwing me back on it.

Mr. Deimeister keeps yelling, "Spot Jinx, spot Jinx!"

I'm feeling like a clumsy Dalmatian with all the spot Jinx going on. And I'm thinking how happy I'd be if my two feet were safely planted on the wooden floor, promenading down the court. Square dancing would save me.

I'd be the world's best square dancer. Maybe I could even stop wars and hunger with square dancing. I'd go to other countries and dance with my square dance group that would not include any of the people who back away when I use a fork in the lunchroom or have their arms stretched out to catch me when I'm going down the stairs to art class.

Maybe I'd get some award for ending unhappiness in the world by spreading square dance love all over the planet.

Maybe I'd change the whole wide wor—

"*Spot Jinx!*"

And maybe I'll do that after I come back from the nurse's office.

"I don't really want to square dance, Jinx."

Victoria is my best friend and I was counting on her to help me in the gym square dance campaign. Anyway, she's a good dancer and hasn't broken Mr. Deimeister's nose.

"C'mon, Vic. You have to be with me on this. I'm sick of dodge ball and volleyball. I broke half the gym windows and knocked out two people before Mr. Deimeister sat me on the bench to watch the clock."

"I still don't want to square dance, Jinx. We'll look stupid. The boys won't do it and all the girls will end up dancing together with the boys laughing at us."

Victoria pulls her braids back and blows a big bubble. Señora Smith comes over and taps her on the shoulder.

"No gum in Spanish class. How can you learn a new language with Super Bubble in your mouth?"

When Vic swallows the gum, Señora Smith makes a face and goes back to teaching us how to ask for a bathroom in Spanish.

"So what if they laugh. It'll be fun. Our feet will be on the ground and there won't be any round hard balls to knock anybody down or break anything. Help me out. This could be great."

My best friend forever, Vic will be.

She's going to the gym during our free period to practice with me.

We'll be square dance champions of the world when we finish.

Square dancing forever.

I'll be carrying Vic's books for a few weeks to class for her.

Her foot cast is pretty cool, though. Bright purple and she let me draw orange daisies all over it already. Everybody is so nosy in this school. Within minutes everyone knew that we were square dancing under the basketball hoop when the broken foot thing happened. You'd pretty much think that would change my mind about square dancing, except technically it was Vic's fault.

We were doing just fine until she thought she heard people coming through the gym doors and turned to run.

Her feet got twisted up with mine. I still feel bad for her, though.

Oh, to be a square dancer.

But I've got a plan.

I printed out five hundred flyers that say SQUARE DANCE MANIA and taped them up all over the school to get people talking. But the next day everybody just looked confused when they read them, including Mr. Deimeister, who just shook his head and stared at me. And it didn't do anything to keep my feet from flying underneath me and the trampoline from smacking me in the face.

I'm so used to trampoline face by now.

I dreamed last night that all of Warren Harding Elementary School was square dancing through the streets. Everybody swung their partners do-si-do. Allemande right to the corners, then we all joined hands and circled to the left.

When I woke up, I was lying on the floor with a sore arm, probably from swinging my partners in my sleep. I guess my dreams of being a gym class hero in square dancing are pretty much squashed since now the whole school knows how Vic's foot got broken.

I spend the whole gym class with all of my friends and enemies skipping around me until Mr. Deimeister says, "The next person to skip around Jinx is running one hundred laps."

Bounce,
bounce,
bounce,
on the evil trampoline.

62

My mom says to give it up.

My dad just laughs.

My little sister sticks her tongue out at me and calls me doofus.

So I've been thinking, just thinking maybe, maybe square dancing isn't the thing. Maybe I can bring peace to the world and less bruises to myself with something else. Maybe jumping rope or jacks in gym might be ok . . .

But then, in gym, Mr. Deimeister says he wants to see me after class.

What's that about? It's been a couple of days since I hurt anybody, and the nurse even stopped me in the hall today to ask if I've been absent.

Anyway in the end I don't get to talk with Mr. Deimeister 'cause he's too busy getting some kid out of the basketball hoop who keeps yelling, "It was just a bet, it was just a bet."

I ate all my lunch today 'cause word got round that we didn't have the trampoline in gym class. I usually don't eat much on gym days. Not since that real bad tuna casserole day that my stomach just couldn't take. (Of course, there was also the unfortunate incident where I tripped over the lunch lady and landed in the sloppy joes . . . but let's not get into that.) Anyway, only saltines on gym day, that's my rule.

But what happened today was better than no trampoline.

It was better than no dodge ball or volleyball. It was better than no field trip to Ice-Skating World or the rock-climbing wall at the Wellness Center. The only thing better than none of these things was no Mr. Deimeister taking us to all those places.

Story is he had a nasty fishing accident over the weekend and he won't be back for a couple of weeks.

It's better than Halloween and summer vacation all rolled up in one. It's better than three desserts and no curfew. It's better than a water main break in school or a snow day that lasts a week.

What's really great is that there isn't a sub either. We all get to go to study groups. No sub gym teacher to carry on the trampoline evil.

Life is good—until I find out it's a lie in fifth period and I'm going to have to dress and head out onto the gym floor like every day before with a substitute teacher who will follow all the lesson plans that Mr. Deimeister left behind.

Vic, whose foot is still healing, limps out beside me.

"Sorry, Jinx, I know you were counting on study group."

"Yeah, I was. But I'll be all right. I've flown off the trampoline before. At least this teacher hasn't seen me do it before."

But then I began to hear something.

It started low as I got closer to the gym door. Then I heard it a little louder. I moved quicker than I ever had getting to gym class.

There was music coming out of the gym. There was music coming out of *my* gym class.

It was square dance music coming out of that gym class. And beside the boom box playing that music was a bright shiny new gym teacher who had never gotten her nose broken by me!

Everything was going to be different. That little accident with Vic didn't mean anything. I'd be the fifth-grade champ of the world. Just me—all by myself.

All I could do was smile as the substitute explained how we were to line up and which hands we had to grab of each other's to dance. I don't even remember her name, this wonderful teacher who brought square dancing to us.

She started the music up again and everybody started moving to the words she called out. All I remember is Josh running at me to swing me around. . . .

In a few minutes I didn't remember anything for a while.

65

They say I have a concussion and a sprained ankle. Josh only got a big bruise on his forehead.

I had to stay in the hospital for two days. I've had a lot of visitors, though. Most of my gym class came the second day and brought square dance music for me.

The nurses weren't happy.

I even got a visit from Mr. Deimeister, who was on the third floor and wheeled himself down to visit me. He smiled when he rolled himself into my room and heard the music.

"I thought you had a concussion, kid," he said, looking at my bandaged foot.

I shrugged. "How do you get hurt *fishing*?"

He shrugged back. "I didn't know my reel would snap. I must have broken it somehow and not known it. Anyway, I was reeling a big one in, and out of the boat I went. Just a few ribs and some cuts, a concussion and a collapsed lung. I'm okay."

Oh, no. A broken reel?

Naaah.

"So. How was it?"

"How was what?" I say.

"The square dancing. I called the substitute to suggest it. I take it you were the one who left the music in my office."

"Oh yeah, that was me."

"Well, it looks like you missed the square dancing. Sorry. I thought you'd be safe from the trampoline while I was gone."

"Mr. Deimeister, I didn't get here because of the trampoline."

The look on poor Mr. Deimeister's face made me laugh so hard, I almost fell out of the bed. The nurse came in and said she thought I'd had enough visitors, but I kept laughing because I knew then that I was never going to be a square dance champion.

So what else could I do but laugh?

Common Core State Standards
Literature 1. Quote accurately from a text when explaining what the text says explicitly and when drawing inferences from the text. **Also Literature 2., Writing 9.**

Envision It! | Retell

Think Critically

1. The main character is nicknamed Jinx by her family. You may have read other stories or seen a movie about someone who, like Jinx, has a nickname. Do you think being known by a nickname is a good thing? Why or why not? **Text to Self**

2. Why do you think the author chose to present the story through the voice of the main character? Do you think it was a good choice? Why or why not? **Think Like an Author**

3. Make a generalization about how the main character feels about herself. Use details from the story to support your ideas. **Generalize**

4. On page 57, Jinx says that she is going to be a square dance star. Based on the incidents in the story, what do you predict the chances of this happening are? **Predict and Set Purpose**

5. **Look Back and Write** Look back at pages 59–60 and pages 66–67. How do events described on pages 59–60 and pages 66–67 connect to each other? Provide evidence from the story to support your answer.
Key Ideas and Details • Text Evidence

Meet the Author

Angela Johnson

Angela Johnson was born in Tuskegee, Alabama. She is the author of more than forty children's books, many of them award-winning titles. Ms. Johnson's books often show how good friendships help people deal with difficult times.

Stories were a big part of Ms. Johnson's life growing up. Both her father and her grandfather were storytellers, and she always loved to read and be read to. In college, she wrote short stories and poetry, but it wasn't until she was taking care of the son of a children's author that she realized her future lay in writing children's books.

Ms. Johnson has won many awards for her books. In 2003, her importance as a writer was acknowledged when she won an award, the MacArthur Foundation's "genius award." The award was a surprise to Ms. Johnson, but not to those who read her books.

Here are other books by Angela Johnson.

Use the *Reader's and Writer's Notebook* to record your independent reading.

Common Core State Standards

Writing 3. Write narratives to develop real or imagined experiences or events using effective technique, descriptive details, and clear event sequences.
Also Writing 3.a., 9., Language 1.

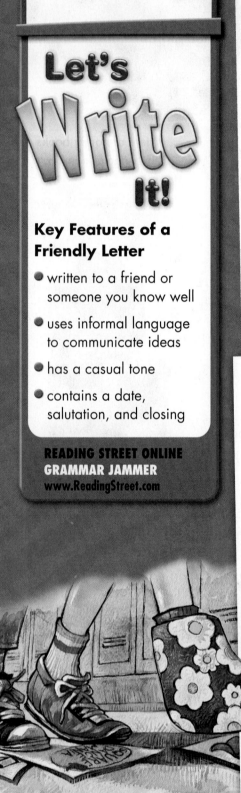

Let's Write It!

Key Features of a Friendly Letter

- written to a friend or someone you know well

- uses informal language to communicate ideas

- has a casual tone

- contains a date, salutation, and closing

READING STREET ONLINE
GRAMMAR JAMMER
www.ReadingStreet.com

Friendly Letter

A **friendly letter** is a letter to someone you know well. It uses informal language and has a casual, familiar tone. The student model on the next page is an example of a friendly letter.

Writing Prompt Write a letter from one character to another from *Tripping Over the Lunch Lady.*

Writer's Checklist

Remember, you should . . .

☑ use written conventions for informal letters correctly.

☑ communicate ideas using informal language.

☑ use both simple and compound sentences in your letter.

November 6, 20__

Hi Vic,

I know square dancing in gym class didn't work out that well, but now I have an even better idea—playing badminton. It seems like the safest sport around, even for someone as accident prone as I am.

Badminton is a fun sport. I played it last weekend when my family went to my uncle's birthday party. My cousins and I played badminton outdoors on the grass, and we had a great time. Grass is soft and springy. How can it hurt anyone?

Vic, will you support me when I present this idea to Mr. Deimeister? I'm afraid he will not like this idea, even though it is great. I need your support. Will you do this for me, please?

Your friend,
Jinx

Writing Trait Simple and compound sentences help the letter flow smoothly.

Pronouns and antecedents are used correctly.

Genre Friendly letters convey information in an informal way.

Conventions

Pronouns and Antecedents

Remember A **pronoun** takes the place of a noun or nouns. An **antecedent** is the word that a pronoun refers to. For example, **_Badminton_** is a fun sport. I played **_it_** last weekend.

Common Core State Standards
Informational Text 8. Explain how an author uses reasons and evidence to support particular points in a text, identifying which reasons and evidence support which point(s).

Genre
Persuasive Text

- A persuasive text tries to convince the reader to do or think something.

- The author of a persuasive text has a distinct point of view and position. Sometimes an author will repeat words or phrases to help support his argument.

- Persuasive texts may contain exaggerated, contradictory, or misleading statements.

- Read "Square Dancing: Good for the Heart and Mind." Look at elements that make this selection a persuasive text. What is the author's position or viewpoint?

Square Dancing:
Good for the Heart and Mind
by Victoria Barrett

All across the country, people of all ages are taking part in the best dance ever: square dancing! Square dancing is all about good music. Square dancing is all about exercise. Square dancing is all about a great time spent with friends and family.

Where else can you spin around with your partner to the accompaniment of a fiddle? Where else can you learn the do-si-do? These are just some of the reasons that the square dance is the best dance.

Square dancing has a long and very interesting history. Early European settlers brought with them their dances when they came to America. After farming all day, the settlers gathered in barns or fields to have a party. Over time, the dances changed as more steps were added.

As time passed, square dancing slowly moved westward. In places such as

Texas, square dancing became quite popular. Today, people can take classes or join square-dancing clubs. Square dancing is so popular in Texas that in 1991 it became the official state dance. Have you tried square dancing? If not, here are a number of reasons why you should:

☆ **Good exercise.** Square dancing requires dancers to spin, turn, and move their feet. All that movement keeps the heart and muscles in good shape. All doctors will agree that square dancing has plenty of health benefits. It's true!

☆ **It's good for your memory.** Circle to the left, bow to the corner, circle to the right, bow to your partner. Can you remember all of that? There are dozens of different square dances, and each dance has its own steps and movements. Remembering all the steps is great exercise for your brain.

☆ **It's fun!** Square dances are fantastic places to meet new people. You can come to square dances with your friends and family members. You can meet other people who like to dance. If you've never square danced before, you get the chance to try something new.

There are many reasons why people should try square dancing. It's good exercise, it helps your memory, and almost anyone can do it. Square dancing is the most fun you'll have in your entire life! All you need is a dance floor and some music, and you'll be doing the do-si-do before you know it.

Let's **Think** About...

How does the author use cause and effect in her argument?
Persuasive Text

Let's **Think** About...

Which sentences in the story are exaggerated, contradictory, or misleading statements?
Persuasive Text

Let's **Think** About...

Reading Across Texts Are any of the reasons Jinx gives to Mr. Deimeister for holding a square dance similar to the ones in this article?

Writing Across Texts Design a flyer for a square dance held at Jinx's school, including reasons why people should come to the square dance.

Common Core State Standards
Language 5.b. Recognize and explain the meaning of common idioms, adages, and proverbs. **Also Foundational Skills 4.b., Speaking/Listening 4., Language 4.a.**

Let's Learn It!

READING STREET ONLINE
ONLINE STUDENT EDITION
www.ReadingStreet.com

Vocabulary

Idioms

Context Clues An idiom is a phrase whose meaning cannot be understood from the ordinary meanings of the words that form it. For example, *hold your tongue* is an idiom that means "be quiet." One way to determine the meanings of idioms is to look for context clues.

Practice It! Look at the idiom "walk and chew gum at the same time" on page 54 of *Tripping Over the Lunch Lady*. Can you tell what this idiom means? Identify and explain ten other common idioms.

Fluency

Accuracy

Accuracy is being able to read and understand without having to stop to figure out words. One way to build accuracy is by rereading. Read a text several times and you will discover that each time you read, you will get better and understand more. You can also reread aloud to improve your fluency.

Practice It! With your partner, practice reading from *Tripping Over the Lunch Lady*. Practice pronouncing any difficult words first. Then read the paragraphs aloud three times. Take turns reading aloud and giving each other feedback.

Listening and Speaking

When you suggest a solution, be sure to explain both the problem and the solution.

Persuasive Speech

A speech is a formal talk given for a specific purpose. One purpose of a speech is to persuade listeners to do something.

Practice It! Prepare a speech to persuade listeners to make a change at school. Start by explaining what you think should be changed. Then give reasons for the change. Be sure to support each reason with facts and examples.

Tips

Listening . . .

- Pay attention to the speaker.
- Listen for supporting details as the speaker explains his or her main ideas.

Speaking . . .

- Use note cards to organize your ideas.
- Use language that helps you persuade.
- Make eye contact with your audience.

Teamwork . . .

- Listen to other opinions and discuss areas of agreement and disagreement.
- Ask for suggestions about your topic and consider other students' ideas.

MR. DEIMEISTER

Common Core State Standards

Language 6. Acquire and use accurately grade-appropriate general academic and domain-specific words and phrases, including those that signal contrast, addition, and other logical relationships (e.g., *however, although, nevertheless, similarly, moreover, in addition*). **Also Speaking/Listening 1.d.**

Oral Vocabulary

Let's Talk About

Adaptations

- Share what you know about ways animals adapt.

- Listen to and interpret a classmate's knowledge of adaptations.

- Determine main and supporting ideas in your classmates' messages about adaptations.

READING STREET ONLINE
CONCEPT TALK VIDEO
www.ReadingStreet.com

Common Core State Standards

Informational Text 2. Determine two or more main ideas of a text and explain how they are supported by key details; summarize the text. **Also Informational Text 1.**

Envision It! | Skill Strategy

Skill

Strategy

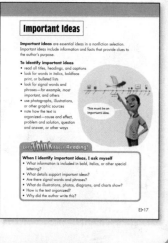

Comprehension Skill

🎯 Graphic Sources

- A graphic source, such as a picture, diagram, or chart, organizes information and makes it easy to see. Graphic sources help you understand what you read.

- Before reading, preview the graphic sources in a selection to help you gain an idea of the article's contents.

- As you read, compare the information in the text with the graphic source.

- Use a graphic organizer like the one below to help you use the graphics on page 79 to locate information and gain an overview of the contents in "Ant Facts."

Comprehension Strategy

🎯 Important Ideas

When you read you should always try to identify the important ideas of a selection. The important ideas are the essential information, facts, and details that help you understand what an author is writing about.

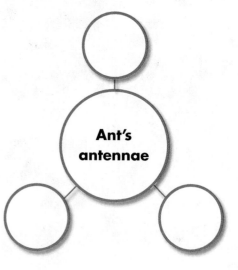

Ant's antennae

Ant Facts

Have you ever observed an ant crawling across a sidewalk lugging food back to its colony? To you, the food is the tiniest scrap. But to the ant, its size and weight are tremendous. Ants can carry objects that weigh several times more than they do. That is only one of the amazing facts about ants.

An ant's body is divided into three sections: the head, the thorax, and the abdomen. An ant's head is large with two antennae, which are used for smelling and feeling. Its mouth has two sets of mandibles. One set is for carrying. The other is for chewing. The thorax is the middle part of the ant. It's connected to the abdomen by a small, waistlike section. The abdomen is large and oval-shaped.

Skill Preview the title and the diagram below. Do they help you gain an idea of the article's contents?

Strategy What are some of the important ideas of this paragraph, and how do they connect to the topic of the article?

Skill How does this diagram help you locate information? What facts can you interpret from this diagram?

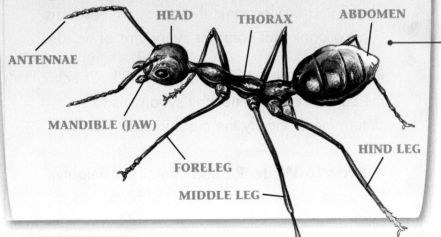

ANTENNAE · HEAD · THORAX · ABDOMEN · MANDIBLE (JAW) · FORELEG · MIDDLE LEG · HIND LEG

Your Turn!

Need a Review? See the *Envision It! Handbook* for additional help with graphic sources and important ideas.

Ready to Try It? Use what you have learned about graphic sources and important ideas as you read *Exploding Ants*.

79

scarce

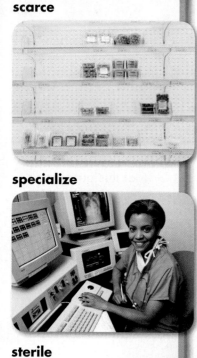

specialize

sterile

critical

enables

mucus

Vocabulary Strategy for

⟲ Synonyms

Context Clues Synonyms are different words that mean almost the same thing. For example, *cold* is to *freezing* as *hot* is to *boiling*. The words *cold* and *freezing* are synonyms. *Hot* and *boiling* are also synonyms. Complete this analogy: *scarce* is to *rare* as *expensive* is to _____.

Synonyms can sometimes be good clues when you find an unfamiliar word.

1. Read the words and sentences around the unfamiliar word. Is there a synonym you know nearby?

2. Use the known synonym in place of the unfamiliar word. Does the synonym help you determine or clarify the word's meaning?

3. If you need help, look up the word in a printed or electronic thesaurus. A thesaurus is a book that contains synonyms of words.

Read "Small but Mighty" on page 81. Check the context clues or nearby synonyms to determine or clarify the meanings of words.

Words to Write Reread "Small but Mighty." List some of the characteristics of bacteria and the ways bacteria can adapt. Use words from the *Words to Know* list in your writing and a thesaurus to find alternate word choices to make your writing lively.

Small but MIGHTY

Bacteria are made up of just one cell. However, they adapt just like all living things. In fact, their small size enables them to adapt quickly. We have medicines to kill harmful bacteria. However, bacteria have changed so that they can stand up to many medicines. Medicines that still work against them are becoming scarce, or rare. Doctors use these medicines less often so bacteria will not "learn" how to live with them.

Different bacteria specialize in different ways. Some live in your gut and help you digest food. Others are critical, or important, to the making of soil. They break down dead plant and animal matter.

Most bacteria are helpful, but a few can harm us. One kind causes a disease called pneumonia. The bacteria reproduce quickly inside the body. They give off poisons. The body fights back. It raises its temperature. It produces more mucus to protect the lining of organs.

It is best to keep surfaces as sterile as possible so you do not touch harmful bacteria.

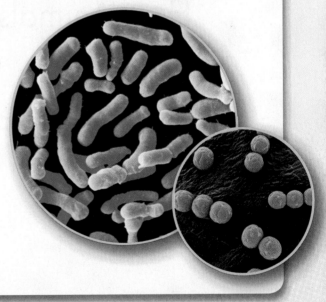

Your Turn!

⏸ **Need a Review?**
For additional help with synonyms, see *Words!*

▶ **Ready to Try It?**
Read *Exploding Ants* on pp. 82–93.

exploding ants

by Joanne Settel, Ph.D.

Amazing **Facts** About
How Animals Adapt

Genre

Expository texts explain what certain things are and how they came to be or behave. As you read, notice how the text's organizational pattern helps explain insect behavior.

Question of the Week
How do animals adapt to survive?

Why animals do gross things

Animals often do things that seem gross to us. They eat foods that people would find nauseating. They make their homes in disgusting places and feed on mucus and blood. They swell or blow up their body parts.

But while these behaviors are nasty to us, they are critical to life on earth. They make it possible for many kinds of living things to find food, shelter, and safety. Different species make use of every possible space and gobble down every nutritious crumb of food in the natural world. If every species of animal ate the same kind of food, or lived in the same place, there simply wouldn't be enough to go around. It would become impossible for all of the species to survive. So instead, animals specialize. One predator eats flesh, while another feeds on blood.

As a result, when it comes to eating, nothing is wasted. Almost every part of every living animal, from skin to dung to mucus, can provide food for some other species. All of these things contain good nutrients. An animal that has the right digestive organs and chemicals can easily break them down.

Similarly, when it comes to finding shelter, animals make use of any hole or space or building material that they can find. For example, the smelly, slimy holes and organs inside the body of a bigger animal can often provide a warm, protective home for small animals like insects.

Finally, animals often put their body parts to good use. Animals don't have bags to carry things around, tools to open things, knives to cut things, or weapons to defend themselves. Instead, they use their own bodies in ways that seem gross to us. By stretching, swelling, and bursting open, they can trick predators, store food, swallow big gulps, and defend their nests.

Swelling, expanding and exploding Bodies

Living honey jars

The swollen sacs of nectar that hang from the roof of a honey ant nest are actually alive. They're the fat bodies of ants that have turned themselves into living honey jars.

The "honey jars" are worker ants that store food and are known as *repletes*. Repletes spend their lives hanging upside-down from the roof of their nest waiting to feed or be fed. Their bodies provide sterile, airtight food containers.

It is when the colony has lots of extra food that the repletes get fed. Each replete receives regurgitated, or spit-up, food from hundreds of ordinary worker ants. The food consists of a golden liquid filled with a predigested mix of termite parts and plant nectar.

As they take in more and more food, the repletes swell. Soon their rear ends or abdomens are as large as small grapes. The swollen ants then climb to the roof of the nest and continue to eat. They remain on the roof for months, hanging by their claws, barely able to move. If for some reason a replete falls down, other workers must help drag its large, balloonlike body back up to the ceiling.

When food supplies outside the nest run low, the repletes become the feeders. Hungry nest mates now gather round for food. They touch the repletes' antennae with their own. The repletes then regurgitate big drops of golden honey.

The extra food provided by the repletes is important to the colony survival. Honey ants live in large colonies in dry desert regions of North America, Africa, and Australia, where food is often scarce. Storing food in their living honey jars enables the colony to make it through the hottest, driest desert seasons.

The sweet "honey" of the honey ant repletes is not only food for other ants, but also for some people. The aborigines in Australia consider the swollen honey ants to be sweet treats and pop them into their mouths like candy.

Soldier ants of the species *Camponotus saundersi* are designed to explode. These ants make themselves burst to defend their colony from other invading insects. When ants explode, they spray out a sticky chemical that kills or glues their opponents in place.

Camponotus ants manufacture their deadly chemicals inside their own bodies. The chemicals are stored in two big sacs called *mandibular glands.* These glands take up most of the ant's body opening, just under the mandibles, or jaws.

MANDIBULAR
GLANDS

EXPLODING
ABDOMEN

When an intruder approaches, the *Camponotus* ant will release small amounts of its special chemical to warn away the invader. If the intruder actually attacks, however, the *Camponotus* ant takes the next step. It violently contracts, or tightens, its muscles, bursting open and spewing out its deadly chemicals.

Camponotus ants aren't the only insect with this unusual behavior. It turns out that soldiers of the termite species *Globitermes sulfureus* are also exploders, bursting open when threatened and spraying a sticky yellow liquid all over their opponents.

Getting it down

A ball of bones

Every evening before it goes off to hunt, an owl spits up a few balls of fur and bones. The balls, or pellets, are what's left of the owl's last meal. An owl preys on small animals, such as mice, moles, shrews, birds, and insects. When the feathered predator captures its prey, it doesn't take the time to kill its victim and then pick out the fleshy, nutritious parts. It simply swallows the animal whole. Then the owl digests all the soft stuff, the muscles and organs.

The rest, the fur, feathers, teeth, and bones, are wastes. The owl gets rid of these by regurgitating a pellet.

Owls normally spit up two pellets a day. Over time the pellets pile up and form large heaps under the owl's roosting, or resting, site. By examining these

OWL PELLETS

pellets, scientists can learn all about an owl's diet. A pellet of a barn owl, for example, usually contains entire skeletons of two or three mammals, lots of fur, and insect parts. That means that a barn owl gulps down around six small mammals a day.

Six small mammals at two to six ounces each seems like a lot of meat for a bird that weighs less than one pound. The twelve-ounce owl, however, doesn't get fat on this feast. Most of its food is just the fur and bones that get chucked up as round pellets.

Big, big gulps

Gulping down a whole pig or chicken may sound like an impossible task for a snake. But it's no big deal for a twenty-foot python. In fact, many snakes often swallow food much bigger than their own heads. Even very small snakes may feast on mice, rats, birds, frogs, and whole eggs.

The snake's ability to swallow big prey results from the special design of its jaw. The bones of its mouth are loosely joined to its skull. A stretchy strip of tissue called a *ligament* holds together the two halves of the lower jaw. When the snake swallows its dinner, its mouth can stretch wide open. The lower jawbones spread apart and each bone moves separately to pull the prey into the mouth.

Snakes generally try to gulp down their food headfirst. This causes the prey's legs to fold back as the snake swallows. In addition, the snake's sharp teeth are curved

backward, preventing the squirming prey from wiggling back out. As the snake works its food down its throat, it pushes its windpipe out of its mouth. This means that it doesn't have to stop breathing as it swallows.

Because snakes eat such big meals, they don't need to eat every day. Most snakes only have to grab a meal once a week, and some only eat once every month. Large pythons hold the record, however. After feasting on a pig or chicken, these huge snakes can go for more than a year without any other food!

Common Core State Standards

Informational Text 1. Quote accurately from a text when explaining what the text says explicitly and when drawing inferences from the text. **Also Informational Text 2., Writing 8., 9.**

Think Critically

1. Think of wildlife shows you may have seen on television. How does the visual and written presentation of the facts in *Exploding Ants* compare to the visual images you have seen on television? Which way is more effective? Why? **Text to World**

2. *Exploding Ants* begins with a general idea: animals do gross things. Then the author gives specific examples to show why. Is this the way you would organize a selection like this, or do you have other ideas? **Think Like an Author**

3. The title of the selection includes the words "Amazing Facts About How Animals Adapt." Look at the illustrations and discuss how they explain the title. **Graphic Sources**

4. Reread the section "Getting It Down" on pages 90–93. Identify three important ideas from this section, and then explain why those ideas are important and how they are connected. **Important Ideas**

5. **Look Back and Write** Review the facts on pages 88–89. Exactly how do soldier ants operate? Provide evidence to support your answer.

Key Ideas and Details • Text Evidence

Meet the Author

Joanne Settel

How did Dr. Joanne Settel come to write *Exploding Ants*? She says, "I am a biologist with a specialty in zoology. I have been collecting journal articles with interesting animal facts for over thirty years. Every few years I pull out the ones that are the most interesting and put them together in a book. This time, I was particularly looking for items with a 'wow' factor. Things that would make kids go 'wow,' or 'gross,' or 'yuk.' I wanted a book that would stand out from the crowd."

She says that tracking down the photos was the most difficult part about writing this book, but it was also the most fun. She used the Internet to locate researchers.

Dr. Settel says, "I love making science exciting and accessible for others. There are so many amazing things going on in the natural world. It's tremendous fun letting people know about them."

Her advice to young people interested in writing is to pursue their passion. She says, "Talk to experts in the field. They will give you tidbits and unknown details that will make the writing interesting."

Here are other books by Joanne Settel.

Use the *Reader's and Writer's Notebook* to record your independent reading.

© **Common Core State Standards**
Writing 2. Write informative/explanatory texts to examine a topic and convey ideas and information clearly. **Also Writing 4., Language 1.**

Let's Write It!

Key Features of a Formal Letter

- has a purpose, such as asking for information

- includes a date, salutation, and closing

- includes an address for both the sender and the recipient

- uses polite and respectful language

READING STREET ONLINE
GRAMMAR JAMMER
www.ReadingStreet.com

Formal Letter

A **formal letter** is a type of letter with a polite, proper tone, often written to someone you do not know. Formal letters often request information or services; many formal letters are business letters. The student model on the next page is an example of a formal letter.

Writing Prompt Think about an interesting animal you would like to know more about. Write a letter to a local librarian asking where you might find more information about that animal.

Writer's Checklist

Remember, you should . . .

✓ use written conventions for formal letters correctly.

✓ communicate ideas using formal language.

✓ include important information.

✓ include a sentence that shows a sense of closure.

127 Willow Drive

Houston, TX 77073

October 3, 20__

Mrs. Chaves

Otto Middle School Library

12476 Thorne Blvd.

Houston, TX 77073

Dear Mrs. Chaves:

I am writing a research report on prairie dogs.

I would like to read a nonfiction book about a prairie dog and **its** habitat. I would also like to include a model or drawing of a prairie-dog city with **my** report. Therefore, I'd like to locate at least one resource with photos or a diagram of a prairie-dog city. Might you help me?

Thank you in advance for **your** wisdom and advice.

Sincerely,

Mikalah

Writing Trait Conventions include address, date, and salutation.

Possessive pronouns are used correctly.

Genre Formal letters often request help or information.

Conventions

Possessive Pronouns

Remember A **possessive pronoun** shows ownership, such as *my* book, *your* homework, *its* branch, or *their* bicycles. A possessive pronoun is just one word and does not need an apostrophe.

Genre
Expository Text

- Expository texts contain facts and information about different subjects.

- Some authors of expository texts use cause and effect to explain the relationships among ideas.

- Some authors of expository texts use graphics to illustrate information. These graphics can give you an overview of the contents.

- Read "The Art of Mimicry." Think about how cause and effect influences relationships among the ideas in the text. Use the heads and graphics to help you gain an overview of the text and locate information.

The Art of Mimicry
by Robert Kausal

Leaf-Mimic Mantis

Have you ever imitated the way a celebrity or a friend talks? Or maybe you can imitate the way your uncle Bob falls asleep while watching television. This is called mimicking. When we mimic, we usually do it to make other people laugh. But when animals mimic, it is often a matter of survival.

Many animals know that the best way to prevent becoming a predator's lunch is to appear as dangerous or unappetizing as possible. You may be surprised to learn that there are many animals that specialize in the art of mimicry.

Sticks and Stones

There is a critical difference between animals that use camouflage and animals that mimic. Animals that use camouflage try to "blend in" to their environments to avoid predators. Insects are especially good at this. There are insects that look like sticks, leaves, thorns, pebbles, and even bird droppings!

Animals that mimic model themselves after objects or other animals. Some of nature's best mimics of objects are insects. Many insects have adapted by making themselves look like other objects in their environments. They adapt by mimicking the sounds, movements, or behaviors of things or animals in their environments. Let's take a look at some of these animals that mimic.

A Master of Disguises

In the tropical waters of Indonesia lives the mimic octopus. This creature is a master of disguises. Most octopuses hide among reefs and rocky areas, but the mimic octopus's environment is muddy and sandy. Since places to hide are scarce, the mimic octopus has learned to trick predators into thinking it is another type of fish.

This flounder uses camouflage to blend into sand on the sea floor.

The flatfish is one of the mimic octopus's most successful disguises. The mimic octopus can change its shape and glide along the ocean floor just like a flatfish. Why a flatfish? For most ocean predators, eating a flatfish is like drinking sour milk. It tastes horrible! The amazing mimic octopus can also imitate a poisonous lionfish and a sea snake. Some divers believe the mimic octopus has other disguises as well.

Mimic Octopus

Let's **Think** About...

What causes animals to mimic? Provide a reason from the first page of this article.
Expository Text

Let's **Think** About...

How do the graphics on this page help you understand the information in the article?
Expository Text

It's a Dog—It's a Plane—No, It's a Lyrebird!

While many animals mimic other animals to fool predators, the male lyrebird of Australia mimics sounds to attract females of the species. This small brown bird clears a space in the forest, spreads its elaborate tail feathers, and begins a concert of sounds that amazes and fools any listener.

Lyrebird

Besides mimicking more than twenty different kinds of species, the lyrebird also imitates some unusual sounds. These include a chainsaw, a camera, a crying baby, a dog, a car alarm, and even musical instruments! This bird is like a one-man band!

Having a Hissing Fit

Snakes might look scary enough to you and me, but sometimes even they need a little help to keep enemies away. The hognose snake is a harmless snake found throughout the United States. However, its pattern of irregular dark spots enables the hognose to look like a venomous rattlesnake. When threatened, the hognose mimics the behavior of a

Hognose Snake

Let's Think About...

How does the graphic example at the bottom of this page help you understand the last paragraph?

Expository Text

rattlesnake. It coils up, hisses loudly, and strikes out at its predator, but this is all for show since the hognose doesn't have fangs or venom.

If acting like a venomous snake doesn't work, the hognose will roll over, stick out its tongue, release a foul smell, and play dead. So don't make the mistake of trying to pick up a dead hognose. It's not sterile!

The Last Resort

Sometimes the animal kingdom must rely on the ultimate survival tactic . . . playing dead. Many animals, such as bats, lizards, spiders, and toads, will play dead to fool their predators. This strategy works well. Many predators don't like to eat dead animals. This could be because there is no thrill in the hunt (or in a toad's case, because the animal's body is covered in mucus).

Not only weaker or smaller animals practice mimicry. Even predators get into the act. For example, some spiders behave and smell like ants. One type of spider even puts an ant on its back to disguise itself, like a wolf in sheep's clothing.

Many animals have learned to survive by practicing the art of mimicry. This form of deception won't get them an acting award, but it might help them live another day.

Let's **Think** About...

Why do animals play dead? Provide a reason from this page.
Expository Text

Let's **Think** About...

Reading Across Texts What can readers learn about the ways in which animals and organisms adapt by reading *Exploding Ants* and "The Art of Mimicry"? What can they learn by reading these two texts, and then "Small but Mighty"?

Writing Across Texts Write a paragraph that explains which of these adaptations you think is most useful and why.

Common Core State Standards

Language 5.c. Use the relationship between particular words (e.g., synonyms, antonyms, homographs) to better understand each of the words. **Also Foundational Skills 4.b., Speaking/Listening 6., Language 4.a.**

Let's Learn It!

**READING STREET ONLINE
ONLINE STUDENT EDITION
www.ReadingStreet.com**

Vocabulary

Synonyms

Context Clues You can figure out the meanings of unfamiliar words by looking at the words around them for clues. One kind of clue is a synonym, a word or phrase that means the same thing. Once you find a synonym that you know, try replacing the unfamiliar word with the synonym or producing an analogy to see if the sentence makes sense.

Practice It! Find the highlighted vocabulary words in *Exploding Ants*. Write synonym analogies using three of the words, for example, *Big is to tall as short is to* _____. Use a printed or electronic thesaurus if you need help.

Fluency

Rate

You can use different rates, or speeds, for reading depending on the type of reading you are doing. In a reading that has a lot of information, you may need to slow down when you come across unfamiliar vocabulary, such as scientific words or numbers.

Practice It! Practice reading *Exploding Ants* with a partner. Read the paragraphs aloud, and notice how you slow down if the information is difficult. Take turns offering each other feedback.

Listening and Speaking

Get Ready For Middle School

In a description, focus on vivid sensory words.

Description

A description is a spoken representation of a person, place, thing, or event. A description uses sensory words that tell what the subject looks like, sounds like, or feels like.

Practice It!

With a partner, present a description of an unusual animal. Study photos of your animal and brainstorm ways to describe the animal's physical features and other interesting aspects. Choose words that create vivid images.

Tips

Listening . . .

- Visualize what the speaker is describing.

- Ask questions to clarify understanding.

Speaking . . .

- Use vivid sensory language and correct grammar.

- Speak slowly and clearly.

Teamwork . . .

- Encourage group members to make suggestions.

- Share your ideas about animals with other group members.

Common Core State Standards

Language 6. Acquire and use accurately grade-appropriate general academic and domain-specific words and phrases, including those that signal contrast, addition, and other logical relationships (e.g., *however, although, nevertheless, similarly, moreover, in addition*).

Also Speaking/Listening 1.d.

Let's Talk About

Adapting to a New Place

- Discuss adapting to a new place.

- Listen to and interpret a classmate's messages about adapting to a new place.

- Determine main and supporting ideas in your classmates' messages about new places.

READING STREET ONLINE
CONCEPT TALK VIDEO
www.ReadingStreet.com

Common Core State Standards

Literature 1. Quote accurately from a text when explaining what the text says explicitly and when drawing inferences from the text. **Also Literature 5.**

Skill

Strategy

Comprehension Skill

Generalize

- To generalize is to make a broad statement or rule that applies to several examples.

- Active readers pay close attention to what authors tell them about story characters and make generalizations about those characters as they read.

- A generalization should be supported with evidence from the text.

- Use a graphic organizer like the one below to make a generalization about April. Use the story to back up your generalization.

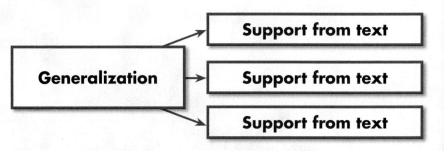

Comprehension Strategy

Story Structure

Active readers notice story structure. They note the problem characters face and the rising action, climax, and outcome. Generally, authors show the problem, or conflict, at the start. The characters work through the conflict as the action rises, and then solve it in the outcome.

First Day
Without Joy

The sunny morning seemed gloomy to April. Yesterday Joy had moved from the house next door. April was miserable as she imagined her first day of school without Joy.

Joy and April had been inseparable. They had studied together, walked to school together, and eaten lunch together. Today, April walked to school alone. Would she eat lunch alone?

At school the teacher introduced a new girl named Blanca. When the lunch bell rang, students rushed out the door. April was the last to leave. Her feet felt weighted as she moved toward the cafeteria.

In the cafeteria everyone was eating with a friend. Where would April eat? She spotted Blanca alone near the door. *She must feel alone* thought April.

"Will you eat with me, Blanca?" April asked. Blanca's face lit up, and they sat down.

"Where do you live?" asked April.

"My address is 128 Oak Street."

"That's down the street from me!"

The girls walked home together. "What a gorgeous, sunny day!" April said.

Skill Make a generalization about April's character. What supports your generalization?

Strategy What is the character's conflict? How do you think the character will resolve the problem?

Skill Make a generalization about the students at April's school. What supports your generalization?

Your Turn!

⏸ **Need a Review?** See the *Envision It! Handbook* for additional help with generalizing and story structure.

▶ **Ready to Try It?** Use what you've learned as you read *The Stormi Giovanni Club.*

The Stormi Giovanni Club

Common Core State Standards

Language 4.a. Use context (e.g., cause/effect relationships and comparisons in text) as a clue to the meaning of a word or phrase. **Also Language 4.**

cavities

episode

strict

combination

demonstrates

profile

Vocabulary Strategy for

◎ Unfamiliar Words

Context Clues You may come across an unfamiliar word in your reading. You can use the context, or the words and sentences around the word, to find clues that can help you determine and clarify the meaning of a word.

1. Reread the sentence in which the unfamiliar word appears. Try creating an analogy with the unfamiliar word and a possible synonym you know.

2. If not, read the surrounding sentences for context clues.

3. Put the clues together and decide what you think the word means.

4. Try the meaning in the sentence. Does it make sense?

Read "Trouble in TV Land" on page 109. Look for context clues that help you determine and clarify the meanings of unfamiliar words.

Words to Write Reread "Trouble in TV Land." Write a letter to your favorite fictional TV character about the way he or she solves a problem. State your opinions and give reasons to support them. Use words in the *Words to Know* list.

Trouble in TV Land

Can a TV show teach us how to win friends in the real world? Most sitcoms solve problems in thirty minutes flat, minus about eight minutes of commercials. They present an extremely simple and reassuring view of the world. A single episode demonstrates how to teach a bully the value of kindness, or how to overcome your worst fears. Nice-looking young people have a high profile in these shows, and they almost always solve their problems by the end. Plus, the commercials tell you things such as how to prevent cavities and whiten your teeth. These commercial messages claim they can save you from tooth decay and so much more. If you will only buy the right clothes and choose the right cell phone, everyone will love you and you will be happy.

In the real world, problems aren't so easily solved. Things you don't enjoy, such as having a strict teacher or parent, may actually be good for you. Everyone has problems. Some are as simple as forgetting a locker combination, but others are tough. You can't just make a wish and watch a failing grade go away, for example. To solve problems in the real world, you must be honest and willing to try hard, sometimes for a long time.

Your Turn!

⏸ **Need a Review?**
For additional help with context clues, see *Words!*

▷ **Ready to Try It?**
Read *The Stormi Giovanni Club* on pp. 110–125.

The Stormi Giovanni Club

by Lydia R. Diamond
illustrated by R. Gregory Christie

Genre

A **drama** is a story written to be acted out for an audience. As you read, imagine the actors speaking the lines and acting out the action.

Question of the Week
How do people adapt to new places?

Characters
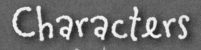

David

Hannah

**Stormi
Giovanni Green**

**Mom
Dad**

Marsha

Ajitha

Joseph

Penelope

Mrs. Moon

Class/Audience

SETTINGS: *The stage is divided into three areas. (1) Stormi's new home. (2) Stormi's new school: the classroom, Stormi's locker, the cafeteria. (3) Chicago, where Stormi's old friends live. Each area has a table and chairs and a computer.*

SCENE I

SETTING: *Stormi's new home. There are unpacked boxes everywhere.* MOM *holds Stormi's backpack.*

MOM: Stormi, hurry up.

STORMI *(off stage):* Coming, Mom.

MOM: You don't want to be late on your first day.

STORMI *(entering):* No. Wouldn't want that. *(to AUDIENCE)* I would rather not go at all.

MOM: Honey, don't frown. You've started at a new school before. It'll be OK.

STORMI: Yeah. *(to AUDIENCE)* OK like a book report due and you haven't read the book. OK like a trip to the dentist with five cavities. OK like walking over hot coals with bare feet.

(MOM hands STORMI her backpack and exits.)

113

SCENE II

SETTINGS: *In Stormi's new school,* STORMI *is in the classroom.* MOM *stands near her. In Chicago,* DAVID, PENELOPE, *and* MARSHA *stand around a table.*

STORMI (*to* AUDIENCE): Hi. I'm Stormi Giovanni Green. I'm named after Nikki Giovanni, the famous poet. I am not a happy camper! See, Mom and Dad move around a lot with their jobs, and since I'm the kid, I go too. They're college professors. Dad teaches philosophy. Philosophers try to figure out how you know what's true and what's not true, and why some things are right and some things are wrong. I only kind of understand. Mom teaches teachers how to teach. Oops, lost my train of thought. Mom says I'm distressed. . . .

MOM: No, Stormi, you've **digressed.**

(MOM *exits.*)

STORMI: **Digressed,** right. Got off the topic. OK. I just moved here from Chicago where I had great friends, played basketball, and was on the speech team. Moving is for the birds. So this time, no new friends. In fact, no anything that I'll just have to say goodbye to. From now on it's the Stormi Giovanni Club, and I'm the only member. When I told Marsha and Penelope I was moving they said:

MARSHA & PENELOPE: NOOO!!!!

STORMI: And I said, "Yes." And they said:

MARSHA & PENELOPE: NOOO!!!!

STORMI: And I said, "Yes." And they said:

MARSHA & PENELOPE: NOOO!!!

STORMI: And David said:

114

DAVID: Stop! Don't say "no" again. It'll be OK.

MARSHA: Sure, we can e-mail.

PENELOPE: And telephone.

DAVID: And send letters.

PENELOPE: But it won't be the same!

STORMI *(to AUDIENCE):* That didn't make me feel better.

(In Chicago, DAVID and MARSHA exit. In classroom, MRS. MOON enters.)

STORMI: So, here I am, in homeroom, on the first day of school, keeping a low profile.

MRS. MOON: Welcome, Stormi. Please tell us about yourself.

STORMI *(to CLASS):* I'm Stormi Giovanni. From Chicago.

MRS. MOON: Please tell us about Chicago.

STORMI: It's called the Windy City *(pause)* because it's windy.

MRS. MOON: All right. Let's welcome Stormi Giovanni, class. On the count of three. One, two, three . . .

(MRS. MOON gestures for the class to speak.)

CLASS: WELCOME, STORMI GIOVANNI!

(MRS. MOON exits classroom. STORMI sits at classroom computer.)

STORMI: Well, I lived through homeroom. Things were OK until study hall, when I went online to check my e-mail.

(In Chicago, PENELOPE sits at computer and types.)

PENELOPE: Dear Stormi, I miss you so much. Fifth grade is definitely better than fourth. Everyone says hi. Write to me about your new friends. Love, Penelope.

(In Chicago, PENELOPE exits. In classroom, HANNAH enters and stands behind STORMI. Pens stick out of Hannah's hair, from behind her ears, and hang on a string around her neck.)

STORMI *(typing):* Dear Penelope, FYI, I won't be making friends. Love, Stormi G.

HANNAH *(tapping STORMI on the shoulder):* Do you have a pen? Maybe a roller ball or a ballpoint? Black or blue is best. I don't really go in for the funky colors, you know, the greens and pinks.

STORMI: Oh, I'll look.

(STORMI searches through her backpack.)

HANNAH: We aren't allowed to use school computers for e-mail. Mr. Morgan is very strict about that. *(pause)* A mechanical pencil might be all right.

STORMI: I have a yellow #2 pencil.

HANNAH *(examining Stormi's pencil and frowning):* No, thanks. *(handing pencil back)* So, you're the new girl?

STORMI: I guess so.

HANNAH: What brings you here?

STORMI: I don't want to talk about it.

HANNAH: OK. *(pause)* My friends Ajitha and Joseph and I sit together at lunch. If you want, tomorrow you can—

STORMI: I always bring a book.

HANNAH: Oh. Don't let Mr. Morgan see you on e-mail— it's a guaranteed detention.

STORMI: Thanks. Gotta go.

SCENE III

SETTINGS: *STORMI is in her new home. In Chicago, MARSHA is at the computer with DAVID looking over her shoulder.*

STORMI *(to AUDIENCE):* Well, I made it through my first day. There's never much homework on the first day so I read a story in my creative writing class and made book covers. Marsha taught me this really cool way to make covers out of the funny papers. I finished and decided to check e-mail. I can go online for an hour after homework as long as Mom checks it first.

MARSHA *(typing):* Dear Stormi, Lunch was a drag without you. But David told us a stupid joke and before we knew it we were laughing anyway. Oh, wait, David wants to say hi.

DAVID *(typing):* Hey, what do you call a cross between a television and a pizza? A really bad idea. You can do it with any two things. Funny, huh? Get it? *(MARSHA pokes DAVID's shoulder.)*

MARSHA *(typing):* Me again. Isn't that the silliest thing? I bet you're making lots of new friends. OK. Later, Alligator.

(MARSHA and DAVID exit.)

STORMI *(typing):* Hey guys. I miss you. School is OK. *(to AUDIENCE)* OK like you forget your permission slip and miss the field trip. OK like your dad's playoff game's on TV the same night as the "to be continued" episode of your favorite show. OK like vegetarian meatloaf. *(typing)* Not much to write about. Bye.

(STORMI shuts off computer and sits on the floor, legs crossed, looking sad and lonely.)

STORMI: In my old house there was this little room under the stairs. Probably a closet, but it sloped down so there really wasn't enough room in it for anything. I hung a flashlight in there, and put a rug on the floor and made some pillows. I would go there anytime I was sad, or even just needed to think. Here I just have my room.

(DAD enters.)

DAD: How was school?

STORMI: OK I guess, Dad. *(to AUDIENCE)* OK like . . . never mind . . . you get it. It was not OK.

DAD: Make any new friends?

STORMI: No.

DAD: Could you try to make just one new friend? For me?

STORMI: You should make your own friends, Dad.

DAD *(laughs):* Could you try to make just one friend for *you*, then?

STORMI: I make no promises. Could you try to raise my allowance?

DAD: I make no promises, Pumpkin.

(DAD starts to leave.)

DAD: Take a look at the bay window in the living room. I thought we could hang a curtain from the ceiling and let that be your own private space.

STORMI: Thanks, Dad. I'll look at it.

(DAD exits.)

SCENE IV

SETTINGS: STORMI's *locker in the hallway of her new school. Later, the school cafeteria.*

STORMI (*to* AUDIENCE *while removing things from her backpack*): The second day was worse than the first. I lost the little piece of paper that had my locker number on it, and I had to go to the office to get a new one. Then I had to dump everything out of my backpack to find the other little piece of paper that had the combination on it. Then I had to figure out how to make the combination lock work.

(HANNAH, JOSEPH, *and* AJITHA *enter.*)

HANNAH: Do you always talk to yourself?

120

STORMI: I wasn't. I was just—

HANNAH: Whatever. I wanted you to meet Joseph. He talks to himself too.

STORMI: Hi.

JOSEPH: Hi. This is Ajitha. Ajitha, Stormi Giovanni.

AJITHA: After the poet?

STORMI (*surprised*): Yeah.

AJITHA: Are you having a hard time with your locker?

STORMI: We didn't have locks at my old school.

AJITHA: You don't have to lock it. I put tape on the side of mine to keep it open. Like this.

(*AJITHA shows STORMI.*)

STORMI: Cool. Hannah, did you find a pen?

HANNAH: I got a couple of interesting ones.

JOSEPH: Hannah collects pens.

HANNAH: I'm looking for the perfect pen.

STORMI: Why?

HANNAH: When I was little my grandpa gave me this old silver fountain pen. I wasn't supposed to take it out of the house, but I did, and I lost it. I keep thinking I'll find something almost as cool. It's my passion.

STORMI: That's cool. I have a friend who collects unicorns.

JOSEPH: Next period is lunch if you want. . . .

STORMI: I have a book.

(*STORMI exits.*)

121

AJITHA: That was audacious. *(pause)* Rude and bold.

HANNAH: She's OK.

JOSEPH: It would be hard to start a new school.

AJITHA: That's no reason to be rude. We were only trying to be hospitable and gregarious.

JOSEPH: I was just trying to be nice.

(They sit at a table in the school cafeteria and begin eating lunch. STORMI enters.)

STORMI *(to AUDIENCE):* Lunch at a new school is the worst. There's this awful time when you have your tray and you have to figure out where to sit. A book can really help. I sit alone and act like I'm reading. I have to act because it's hard to read in all of that noise. But today my plan didn't work. The cafeteria was packed.

AJITHA: Stormi, you can sit with us.

JOSEPH: What are you reading?

STORMI: *A Wrinkle in Time.*

AJITHA: That book is quite scintillating.

HANNAH: Don't mind her. She likes to use big words. She's not trying to make you feel stupid.

STORMI (*to* AJITHA): Do you write stories?

(AJITHA *pulls out a dictionary.*)

AJITHA: I try to learn a new word every day. (*reading from dictionary*) Scintillate: to sparkle, gleam.

JOSEPH: *A Wrinkle in Time* is sparkly?

HANNAH: You can sit here and read if you want to.

(STORMI *sits.*)

JOSEPH: I thought I would try out for the play.

HANNAH: If you do, I will too.

(STORMI *tries to look like she's reading but is drawn into the conversation.*)

HANNAH: It's *The Wizard of Oz*, right?

STORMI: We did that at my old school. I wanted to be the Lion so badly, but I was too small for the suit. I ended up designing the set.

AJITHA: I could enjoy that.

JOSEPH: I want to be the Scarecrow.

(JOSEPH *does a funny scarecrow imitation, with limp knees and wobbly head movements.*)

STORMI *(to AUDIENCE):* Lunch was almost as much fun as listening
  to David's lame jokes would have been. So, I've been thinking.
  You know how it is when you hurt your finger? Like maybe the
  pointing finger on the hand you write with. *(STORMI holds up
  finger and* demonstrates.) All of a sudden you notice all of these
  things you do with that finger. It hurts to put on a glove. It hurts
  to sharpen your pencil. It hurts to tie your shoe. And you think,
  I sure will be happy when this finger is better. Then one day you
  notice that it's better. You almost can't remember when it stopped
  hurting. You just didn't notice. It's the same with moving. You can't
  know when you will stop missing the last place so much it hurts,
  but you can't stop tying your shoes either. Hey, that sounds a
  little philosophical. My father would be proud.

(HANNAH steps forward.)

HANNAH: Look at this.

STORMI *(pointing to AUDIENCE):* I'm talking.

(HANNAH notices AUDIENCE for the first time.)

HANNAH: Oh. Hi.

AUDIENCE: Hi.

HANNAH: Look. *(She holds up a pen.)* A limited edition, 2001
  four-color, ballpoint gel ink pen, a rare and beautiful thing. . . .

(STORMI sits at the school computer.)

124

STORMI *(typing):* Hey, guys. I'm sorry I haven't had much to tell you. It's silly, but I thought I would feel better if I didn't make friends. I felt worse and I think people thought I was mean. Anyway, I've met some pretty interesting people. David, you'd like Joseph. He has this funny sense of humor and likes to act in plays. There's this really odd girl who I think is my favorite. She collects pens. Like your unicorns, Penelope. . . . And Ajitha uses all of these big words, but she isn't stuck up or anything. *(to* AUDIENCE*)* So, I've decided to let other members into the Stormi Giovanni Club. Really, it's better that way I think.

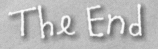

The End

Common Core State Standards

Literature 1. Quote accurately from a text when explaining what the text says explicitly and when drawing inferences from the text. **Also Literature 2., 5., Writing 9.**

Envision It! | Retell

Think Critically

1. Have you ever felt like a newcomer? How would you compare your feelings to Stormi's? **Text to Self**

2. Choose a scene and imagine playing a character. Decide how the playwright's dialogue makes it easy for you to "become" the character you are playing. **Think Like an Author**

3. Make a generalization suggested by the play about newcomers. Then look for details in the text that support this generalization. **Generalize**

4. Stormi acts differently at the start of the play than at the end. Think about the function of her character in the story. Discuss how she solves problems along the way. **Story Structure**

5. Look Back and Write Go back to scene 4 on pages 120–121. What is Hannah's passion and why? Provide evidence to support your answer.

Key Ideas and Details • Text Evidence

Lydia Diamond and R. Gregory Christie

Playwright Lydia R. Diamond said, "I think kids are a little more brave than adults sometimes." She was thinking about her own school days when she moved around a lot. The move from Mississippi to Massachusetts was especially hard. "It was cold in Massachusetts and warm in Mississippi, and that was strange. I made new friends quickly, though. I wasn't afraid." When she moves to new places now, with a husband and baby, it's different. "It's harder to leave friends when you're an adult. But my character Stormi Giovanni has taught me to have more faith, that I will make new friends, that it will be OK."

Lydia Diamond's plays have been performed in U.S. cities from New York to California. One of them, *Here I Am . . . See Can You Handle It*, is based on the writings of Nikki Giovanni. Ms. Diamond lives in Massachusetts with her husband and her son.

Illustrator R. Gregory Christie has won awards for his work on books of fiction and poetry for young people. One reviewer has said that his unique illustrations, which combine realism and exaggeration, "create harmony with the words."

Here are books you may be interested in.

KATHERINE PATERSON
Flip-Flop Girl

Flip-Flop Girl
by Katherine Paterson

A FAMILY APART
Joan Lowery Nixon

A Family Apart
by Joan Lowery Nixon

Reading Log

Use the *Reader's and Writer's Notebook* to record your independent reading.

Common Core State Standards

Writing 3. Write narratives to develop real or imagined experiences or events using effective technique, descriptive details, and clear event sequences.
Also Writing 3.b., 3.d., Language 1.

Let's Write It!

Key Features of Narrative Poetry

- tells a story
- often uses sensory details
- may include graphic elements

READING STREET ONLINE
GRAMMAR JAMMER
www.ReadingStreet.com

Narrative

Narrative Poetry

Narrative poetry refers to a poem that tells a story. The student model on the next page is an example of a narrative poem.

Writing Prompt The title character in *The Stormi Giovanni Club* struggles to adapt to life at a new school. Think about a situation that might come up for a student in a new school or place. Write a narrative poem about this situation.

Writer's Checklist

Remember, you should . . .

  use graphic elements, such as capital letters and varying line lengths.

  include sensory details.

  use figurative language, such as similes and metaphors.

  use and understand indefinite and reflexive pronouns.

At My New School

On the first day of school, I was blue.

I told **myself** that I wasn't whole

because I didn't know a soul.

On the second day of school, I was red.

I couldn't find the lunchroom,

I wanted to go to bed,

and I couldn't remember **anything** my teacher said.

On the third day of school, I was green.

Everyone was nice; they were **all** cool,

but I still felt like a fool

because I knew absolutely **nothing** about this school.

On my fourth day of school, I was tickled pink.

My smile reached **both** ends of the room,

and disappearing was my gloom:

I made a FRIEND that afternoon!

Writing Trait
The writer's **word choice** includes figurative language and sensory details.

Indefinite and reflexive pronouns are used correctly.

Genre
A **narrative poem** tells a story.

Conventions

Indefinite and Reflexive Pronouns

Remember Indefinite pronouns, such as *all*, *both*, *nothing*, and *anything*, refer to people, places, or things in a general, unspecific way. **Reflexive pronouns** end in *-self* or *-selves*, for example, *ourselves*, *itself*, *yourself*, *himself*.

129

Social Studies in Reading

Genre
Persuasive Text

- A persuasive text tries to convince the reader to do or think something.

- The author of a persuasive text has a distinct point of view and position. A point of view is backed up with evidence and by showing cause-and-effect relationships or comparisons.

- Persuasive text may contain exaggerated, contradictory, or misleading statements. The author may also repeat phrases in the text.

- Read "The Extra Credit Club." Think about the author's position. Look for any exaggerated, contradictory, or misleading statements.

The Extra Credit Club

The Extra Credit Club is the best club in school!

This brochure will tell you about everything The Extra Credit Club has to offer.

Join Now!

Meet us in room B-208 after school!

As the president and founder of The Extra Credit Club, I hope you will become a member. What is The Extra Credit Club? Simply put, it is a club for kids who want good grades. I noticed that some of my fellow students needed help in some subjects, so I started The Extra Credit Club. When you join The Extra Credit Club, you commit to working hard at school.

130

100% *of Extra Credit Club members get good grades!*

The Extra Credit Club is like a chess club, except that we do homework instead of play chess. With the support of your fellow Extra Credit Club members, you will achieve your goals. At club meetings, we help each other out. Let's say you need help with math. Well, a member who loves math (me!) will tutor you. Let's say you are great at science. You can tutor a member who needs help with science. Together, we help each other to get good grades. We guarantee it. How do I know? Well, I'm not just the founder and president of The Extra Credit Club. I'm also a member. See? Here's my membership card.

The Extra Credit Club

NAME: Eduardo Cabrera

MEMBER NO: 000001

Eduardo Cabrera,
Extra Credit Club
President and Founder

Let's **Think** About...

What is the author's viewpoint or position on The Extra Credit Club? How does he back up this position?
Persuasive Text

Let's **Think** About...

How does Eduardo use cause and effect to connect his ideas in his argument about his club?
Persuasive Text

131

Let's **Think** About...

Can you find a statement in the text that sounds contradictory or misleading? What is contradictory or misleading about the statement you have chosen?
Persuasive Text

Ever since I joined The Extra Credit Club, I have earned good grades. In fact, 100 percent of Extra Credit Club members have earned good grades since joining. Just look at my chart.

100%!

You are probably wondering: how many members are there in The Extra Credit Club? There are ten members, and they all agree that The Extra Credit Club is the most amazing thing that has ever happened to them. The Extra Credit Club is so much more than a club! It's a way of life.

You've made a fantastic first step just by reading this far. You're obviously a curious kid with a thirst for knowledge. You are perfect for The Extra Credit Club!

The Extra Credit Club will guarantee you a good report card. And so much more.

At The Extra Credit Club, members do extra credit homework. We think up difficult projects. Then we work together to complete them.

Last year, one member (me) tried to build a rocket. I wanted to make a rocket that would reach Mars. It took a lot of research. It took a lot of hard work in my family's garage. Eventually my mother found out and stopped me. But the point is: Extra Credit Club members aim for the stars. And in my case, even beyond the stars. Won't you join us?

Extra Credit Club members give back to society. That's why we have community projects. We visit retirement homes and read to elders. We volunteer at preschools. We teach toddlers how to read. We spend every moment of our day helping the community!

That doesn't sound like too much of a time commitment, does it?

To recap, **The Extra Credit Club** will:
- guarantee you a good report card.
- help you give back to the community.
- improve your life forever.

So tear off the application slip, fill it out, and return it to Eduardo Cabrera before the end of the week.

- -

NAME: _____

GRADE: _____

INTERESTS: _____

_____

SUBJECT(S): _____

Let's **Think** About...

Can you find an exaggerated statement in the text? How is it exaggerated?
Persuasive Text

Let's **Think** About...

Reading Across Texts Look back at *The Stormi Giovanni Club* and "The Extra Credit Club." Compare and contrast the two clubs.

Writing Across Texts Use details from *The Stormi Giovanni Club* and "The Extra Credit Club" to create your own new club. Write a letter to friends inviting them to join your club.

Common Core State Standards

Language 5.c. Use the relationship between particular words (e.g., synonyms, antonyms, homographs) to better understand each of the words. **Also Foundational Skills 4.b., Speaking/Listening 4., Language 4., 4.a.**

Let's **Learn** It!

READING STREET ONLINE
ONLINE STUDENT EDITION
www.ReadingStreet.com

Vocabulary

Unfamiliar Words

Context Clues You can use context clues to determine the meanings of unfamiliar words. Clues can include synonyms, antonyms, analogies, or explanations of the word.

Practice It! Write synonym analogies using these words from *The Stormi Giovanni Club*—*strict, creative,* and *gregarious. Famous is to well-known as average is to ordinary* is an example of an analogy. Use a printed or electronic thesaurus if you need help.

Fluency

Expression

When you read aloud, pay attention to how your tone of voice changes to reflect each character's feelings or personality. Notice how your voice changes when you read questions and exclamations.

Practice It! With your partner, take turns reading aloud a page from *The Stormi Giovanni Club.* Practice using different tones of voice to represent the way characters feel. Pay attention to different kinds of sentences.

134

When you give advice, remember your own experiences.

Give Advice

When you give advice, you suggest how to act in a situation. Advice is often based on experience and can help to solve problems.

Practice It! Prepare a speech for new students. Give them advice about how to adapt to a new place or situation. To make your advice easy to remember, think about examples from your own life and experiences.

Tips

Listening . . .

- Listen carefully to the advice.
- Ask questions to clarify the speaker's purpose.

Speaking . . .

- Enunciate and speak slowly.
- Use indefinite pronouns, such as *all*, *both*, *nothing*, and *anything*.

Teamwork . . .

- Identify where you agree and disagree with others.
- Elicit and listen to group suggestions.

Common Core State Standards

Language 6. Acquire and use accurately grade-appropriate general academic and domain-specific words and phrases, including those that signal contrast, addition, and other logical relationships (e.g., *however, although, nevertheless, similarly, moreover, in addition*).

Also Speaking/Listening 1.d.

Let's Talk About

Improving Ourselves

- Share your experiences about improving yourself.

- Listen to and interpret a classmate's ideas about improving ourselves.

- Determine main and supporting ideas in your classmates' messages about improving.

READING STREET ONLINE
CONCEPT TALK VIDEO
www.ReadingStreet.com

136

Common Core State Standards

Informational Text 1. Quote accurately from a text when explaining what the text says explicitly and when drawing inferences from the text.

Skill

Strategy

Comprehension Skill

Draw Conclusions

- A conclusion is a reasonable decision you make after you think about the facts or details you read.

- Drawing conclusions may also be called making inferences.

- You can also use your prior knowledge to help you draw conclusions.

- Use a graphic organizer like the one below to help you draw conclusions about the information the author presents in "The History of Gymnastics."

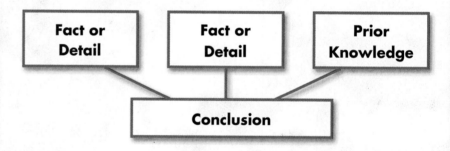

Comprehension Strategy

Visualize

Active readers visualize, or make pictures in their mind. Visualizing can help you understand a text. Look for details that will help you visualize what is happening.

The History of Gymnastics

Early Greek teachers were the first to teach gymnastics both for athletes and for everyone else. More than three thousand years ago, every Greek student would train in gymnastics. People thought that exercise taught the body and mind to work together.

Skill What conclusion can you draw about how Greeks thought about themselves and their bodies?

The Greeks taught three different kinds of gymnastics. One kind helped people stay strong and in good shape. Another helped people become strong and fit for sports. A third was used to train men for military service. Roman soldiers would also train in gymnastics.

Strategy How do the details in this paragraph help you visualize the information being presented?

Over time, people in Europe began to learn and enjoy gymnastics. During the 1970s, people all over the world watched the gymnasts at the Olympics.

At first, Americans did not enjoy gymnastics as much as the Europeans. They liked watching games instead, such as basketball or baseball. However, beginning in the 1970s, gymnastics became popular in the United States as well.

Skill Why do you think gymnastics started to become popular during the 1970s? Explain your conclusion.

Your Turn!

Need a Review? See the *Envision It! Handbook* for additional help.

Ready to Try It? Use what you have learned about drawing conclusions and visualizing as you read *The Gymnast*.

Envision It! | Words to Know

bluish

skidded

somersault

cartwheels   limelight

gymnastics   throbbing

hesitation   wincing

Vocabulary Strategy for

◎ Suffixes *-ion, -ish*

Word Structure A suffix is a syllable added to the end of a base word that changes the base word's meaning. The suffix may also cause a spelling change.

For example, when *-ion*, which means "the act or state of being," is added to *appreciate*, the final *e* is dropped: *appreciation*. Another example is the Old English suffix *-ish*, which adds the meaning "somewhat" or "like," as in *brownish*.

1. Look at the unknown word. See if you recognize a base word in it.

2. Check if *-ion* or *-ish* has been added.

3. Ask yourself how the suffix changes the meaning of the base word.

4. Try the meaning in the sentence.

Read "It's Easier in Daydreams" on page 141. Look for words that end with suffixes. Analyze words and suffixes to determine word meanings.

Words to Write Reread "It's Easier in Daydreams." Imagine that you are a sports writer. Write a paragraph about a sporting event you just watched. Use words from the *Words to Know* list in your paragraph.

It's Easier in Daydreams

I love to watch Olympic gymnasts. In fact, I hope to be one myself one day. In my daydreams, I am already a star. The audience roars as I step into the limelight. Without any hesitation, I somersault across the gym. I move with terrific grace and speed. The judges smile and nod and hold up cards with perfect 10.0's on them.

So you can understand why I was so upset after what happened. I signed up for a gymnastics class offered by the park district. The teacher showed us how to do cartwheels. *This is easy!* I thought, so I didn't pay attention. When it was my turn, I ran to the mat, closed my eyes, and threw myself at it. The next thing I knew, I was flat on my back. My head and knees were throbbing. I couldn't help wincing in pain as I got up. On the next try, I lost my nerve and put on the brakes. I skidded several feet into a wall and thumped my shoulder. There's a nice bluish bruise there to remind me. I have a long way to go to reach the Olympics.

Your Turn!

⏸ **Need a Review?**
For additional help with suffixes, see *Words!*

▶ **Ready to Try It?**
Read *The Gymnast* on pp. 142–151.

The Gymnast

by Gary Soto

Autobiography is the story of a person's life or
of major events in it, told by the person who lived
it. As you read, notice how the author looks back
at himself from a humorous point of view.

For three days of my eleventh summer I listened to my mother yap about my cousin, Isaac, who was taking gymnastics. She was proud of him, she said one evening at the stove as she pounded a round steak into carne asada and crushed a heap of beans into refritos. I was jealous because I had watched my share of *Wide World of Sports* and knew that people admired an athlete who could somersault without hurting himself. I pushed aside my solitary game of Chinese checkers and spent a few minutes rolling around the backyard until I was dizzy and itchy with grass.

That Saturday, I went to Isaac's house where I ate plums and sat under an aluminum arbor watching my cousin, dressed in gymnastic shorts and top, do spindly cartwheels and back flips in his backyard while he instructed, "This is the correct way." He breathed in the grassy air, leaped, and came up smiling the straightest teeth in the world.

I followed him to the front lawn. When a car passed he did a **back flip** and looked out the side of his eyes to see if any of the passengers were looking. Some pointed while others looked ahead dully at the road.

I . . . spent a few minutes rolling around the backyard until I was dizzy and itchy with grass.

But when I did a cartwheel, the shoes flew off, along with the tape.

146

My cousin was a show-off, but I figured he was allowed the limelight before one appreciative dog who had come over to look. I envied him and his cloth gymnast shoes. I liked the way they looked, slim, black, and cool. They seemed special, something I could never slip onto my feet.

I ate the plums and watched him until he was sweaty and out of breath. When he was finished, I begged him to let me wear his cloth shoes. **Drops of sweat** fell at his feet. He looked at me with disdain, ran a yellow towel across his face, and patted his neck dry. He tore the white tape from his wrists—I liked the tape as well and tried to paste it around my wrists. He washed off his hands. I asked him about the white powder, and he said it kept his hands dry. I asked him why he needed **dry hands** to do cartwheels and back flips. He said that all gymnasts kept their hands dry, then drank from a bottle of greenish water he said was filled with nutrients.

I asked him again if I could wear his shoes. He slipped them off and said, "OK, just for a while." The shoes were loose, but I liked them. I went to the front yard with my **wrists dripping tape** and my hands white as gloves. I smiled slyly and thought I looked neat. But when I did a cartwheel, the shoes flew off, along with the tape, and my cousin yelled and stomped the grass.

I was glad to get home. I was jealous and miserable, but the next day I found a pair of old vinyl slippers in the closet that were sort of like gymnastic shoes. I pushed my feet into them, tugging and wincing because they were too small. I took a few steps, admiring my feet, which looked like bloated water balloons, and went outside to do cartwheels on the front lawn. A friend skidded to a stop on his bike, one cheek fat with sunflower seeds. His mouth churned to a stop. He asked why I was wearing slippers on a hot day. I made a face at him and said that they were gymnastic shoes, not slippers. He watched me do **cartwheels** for a while, then rode away doing a wheelie.

I returned inside. I looked for tape to wrap my wrists, but could find only circle bandages in the medicine cabinet. I dipped my hands in flour to keep them dry and went back outside to do cartwheels and, finally, after much hesitation, a **back flip** that nearly cost me my life when I landed on my head. I crawled to the shade, stars of pain pulsating in my shoulder and neck.

My brother glided by on his bike, smooth as a kite. He stared at me and asked why I was wearing slippers. I didn't answer him. My neck still hurt. He asked about the flour on my hands, and I told him to leave me alone. I turned on the hose and drank cool water.

... and, finally,
after much hesitation,
a back flip that nearly
cost me my life ...

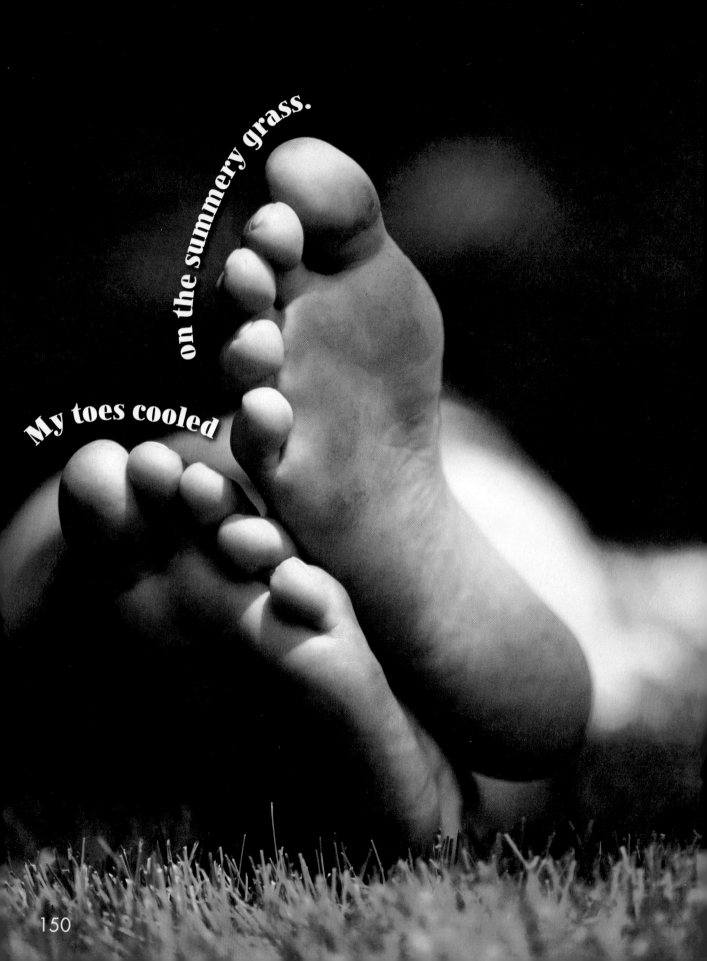

My toes cooled on the summery grass.

I walked to Romain playground where I played Chinese checkers and was asked a dozen times why I was wearing slippers. I'm taking gymnastics, I lied, and these are the kind of shoes you wear. When one kid asked why I had white powder on my hands and in my hair, I gave up on Chinese checkers and returned home, my feet throbbing. But before I went inside, I took off the slippers. My toes cooled on the summery grass. I ran a garden hose on my feet and bluish ankles, and a chill ran up my back.

Dinner was a ten-minute affair of piranha-like eating and thirty minutes of washing dishes. Once finished, I returned to the backyard, where I again stuffed my feet into the slippers and did **cartwheels by the dizzy dozens.** After a while they were easy, I had to move on. I sucked in the summer air, along with the smoke of a faraway barbecue, and tried a back flip. I landed on my neck again, this time I saw an orange burst behind my eyes. I lay on the grass, tired and sweaty, my feet squeezed in the vise of cruel slippers.

I watched the dusk settle and the first stars, pinpoints of unfortunate light tangled in telephone wires. I ate a plum and pictured my cousin, who was probably cartwheeling to the audience of one sleeping dog.

Common Core State Standards

Informational Text 1. Quote accurately from a text when explaining what the text says explicitly and when drawing inferences from the text. Also Writing 9.

Envision It! | Retell

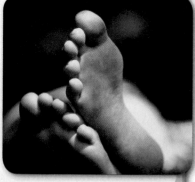

READING STREET ONLINE
STORY SORT
www.ReadingStreet.com

Think Critically

1. *The Gymnast* is an autobiography. Think of other autobiographies or biographies you have read this year. How does *The Gymnast* compare? How are other autobiographies different from *The Gymnast*? **Text to Text**

2. Gary Soto has taken an incident from his childhood and written an autobiography around it. Why do you think he wrote *The Gymnast*? What was his purpose for writing it? Provide evidence from the text. **Think Like an Author**

3. Young Gary draws the conclusion that his cousin, Isaac, is a show-off. Find details from the selection that support this conclusion. **Draw Conclusions**

4. Find passages that describe how Gary looks in his gymnastics outfit and how his cousin looks in his outfit. Discuss how the visual details help make Gary and his cousin two very different people. **Visualize**

5. **Look Back and Write** The dog in *The Gymnast* acts as an audience. Find the dog on pages 147 and 151. Why do you think the dog's reaction changes? Why are those details important in understanding *The Gymnast*? Provide evidence to support your answer. **Key Ideas and Details • Text Evidence**

Gary Soto

Gary Soto was born in a Mexican American community in Fresno, California. Although his writing comes from his experiences growing up in this community, not all his stories are based on actual events. His books show what it is like for a young Mexican American to grow up in the Central Valley of California.

School was not easy for Gary. He graduated from high school with "something like a 1.6 grade point average." However, it was in high school that he discovered he wanted to take writing seriously. He became fascinated by the works of poets, and eventually, he became a poet himself. His poetry has won several major awards and prizes.

Gary believes that reading is an important part of being a writer. He thinks that anybody who wants to be a writer should read books written by current authors as well as the old "masters."

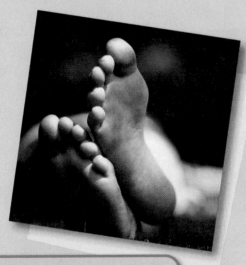

Use the *Reader's and Writer's Notebook* to record your independent reading.

153

Common Core State Standards

Writing 3. Write narratives to develop real or imagined experiences or events using effective technique, descriptive details, and clear event sequences.
Also Writing 3.a., 3.d., Language 1.

Let's Write It!

Key Features of an Autobiographical Sketch

- describes an event in the author's life

- may reveal the author's personality

- usually written in the first person

READING STREET ONLINE
GRAMMAR JAMMER
www.ReadingStreet.com

Autobiographical Sketch

An **autobiographical sketch** tells a true story about the writer's life. The student model on the next page is an example of an autobiographical sketch.

Writing Prompt *The Gymnast* is part of Gary Soto's autobiography. Think about an important time in your life. Write an autobiographical sketch about the experience.

Writer's Checklist

Remember, you should . . .

☑ write in the first person.

☑ tell about an experience in your life.

☑ communicate your thoughts and feelings about the experience.

Getting Ready to Dive

After I watched the 10-meter-tower divers in the Olympics, I decided I wanted to learn to dive off a tower, just like them. But since there were no 10-meter towers in my town, I settled on the 3-meter board on a raft in the middle of Lake Mystic.

On my first visit to the lake, whom did I ask if I could go out to the diving raft? I asked the lifeguards, of course. They wanted to know who had given me the deep-end test.

The deep-end test? Rats! I didn't know how to swim! Before I could dive, I would have to take swimming lessons.

I joined a swim class that met every day. After weeks of practice, an instructor gave me the deep-end test.

To pass, I had to swim from one dock to another and back. My mom, who had taken the test when she was young, told me that people often fail the first time they take it. However, whom do you think the instructor passed on the first try? Me, of course! I was tired, but happy. Finally I was ready for the diving board in Lake Mystic.

Writing Trait
The author's **voice** conveys thoughts and feelings about an experience.

Who and whom are used correctly.

Genre
An **auto-biographical sketch** tells about a true event from the writer's life.

Conventions

Using *Who* and *Whom*

Remember *Who* is a pronoun used as the subject of a sentence or clause. **Whom** is a pronoun used as the object of a preposition, or as a direct object. (To *whom* did you send a letter?)

Common Core State Standards

Informational Text 5. Compare and contrast the overall structure (e.g., chronology, comparison, cause/effect, problem/solution) of events, ideas, concepts, or information in two or more texts. **Also Informational Text 7.**

Online Reference Sources What is the first thing to do at a new Web site? Find out who wrote the information. Use the "About this site" button. Can you believe them?

- Online reference sources, such as dictionaries and encyclopedias, can be found on the Internet. They look like printed sources, and they are usually organized in a formal way.

- Some sites can give you different reference sources all in one place.

- Read "All About Gymnastics." Notice the search terms Alice used to find the Web pages. How is the information she finds different from information on television?

All About Gymnastics

After reading Gary Soto's *The Gymnast*, Alice decides she might want to do gymnastics. So she goes to an online reference Web site.

This site has four reference sources: an atlas, almanac, dictionary, and encyclopedia. When Alice types the keyword "gymnastics" into the search engine and clicks on "go," the site gives her a list of results that begins like this:

File   Edit   View   Favorites   Tools   Help

Search   "gymnastics"   GO!

Atlas
Almanac
Dictionary
Encyclopedia

Search Results: "gymnastics"

Gymnastics (Encyclopedia)
gymnastics, exercises for the balanced development of the body (see also *aerobics*).

File   Edit   Vi...

Alice clicks on this gymnastics encyclopedia link and gets an entry for gymnastics that ends like this:

Encyclopedia

gymnastics
Women compete in the vault, floor exercises, balance beam, and uneven parallel bars, as well as in rhythmic gymnastics and on the trampoline.

She wonders what these events are like, so she types "vault" into the search engine. The results include this dictionary entry:

Dictionary

vault

Pronunciation: (vôlt)—v.i.

In gymnastics, to leap over a vaulting or pommel horse, using the hands for pushing off.

This raises another question in Alice's mind: *What in the world is a pommel horse?*

   A dictionary search tells Alice that "pommel horse" means "a cylinder-shaped horse with handles near the center." Alice can't picture this, so she goes to another online reference site to find an image.

   Her search for "pommel horse" turns up images like these:

158

She returns to the first site and types "floor exercise" into the search engine and gets the dictionary definition:

Dictionary

floor exercise

Pronunciation: flôr ek′sər sīz

In gymnastics, a competition in which each entrant performs a routine of acrobatic tumbling feats and balletic movements without any apparatus on a specifically designated floor space, usually 12 m (39 ft.) square and having a matlike covering.

Alice continues searching until she finds out all she needs to know.

File   Edit   View   Favorites   Tools   Help

Common Core State Standards
Language 4.b. Use common, grade-appropriate Greek and Latin affixes and roots as clues to the meaning of a word (e.g., *photograph, photosynthesis*). **Also Foundational Skills 4.b., Speaking/Listening 1.a., Language 4.**

Let's Learn It!

READING STREET ONLINE
ONLINE STUDENT EDITION
www.ReadingStreet.com

Vocabulary

Suffixes -*ion*, -*ish*

Word Structure A suffix is a word part added to the end of a base word that changes the base word's meaning. The Latin suffix -*ion* means "the act or state of being," as in *graduation*. The Old English suffix -*ish* means "somewhat" or "like," as in *childish*. Recognizing a suffix can help you determine the meaning of an unknown word.

Practice It! Work with a partner to make a list of words ending in -*ion* and -*ish* from stories you've read. Use the meanings of these suffixes to determine the definitions of the words. You can use a printed or electronic dictionary or glossary for help.

Fluency

Appropriate Phrasing

Punctuation clues help to guide your voice as you read. Paying attention to punctuation marks and appropriate phrasing helps you better understand a story's meaning. Remember that phrasing describes how to pause while reading to interpret punctuation.

Practice It! Practice reading the first three paragraphs of *The Gymnast*. Pay attention to the commas and periods. Reread the section three times and pay attention to phrasing and pauses.

Listening and Speaking

Get Ready For Middle School

When you interview someone, make sure your questions are organized and clear.

Interview a Classmate

In an interview, one person asks another person questions about a specific topic or event. The purpose of an interview is to find out what the person being interviewed did or knows about.

Practice It! With a partner, conduct an interview. One person can act as Gary Soto while the other asks questions relating to what you read in *The Gymnast*. Write answers to your questions in a notebook. Then change roles, using another author.

Tips

Listening . . .

• Listen for key words and important details during the interview.

• Pay attention to the speaker's tone of voice, gestures, and facial expressions.

Speaking . . .

• Look at your partner as you speak.

• Speak clearly when you ask questions during the interview.

Teamwork . . .

• Answer interview questions with detail.

• Share your suggestions with a partner.

Common Core State Standards
Foundational Skills 4.b. Read on-level
prose and poetry orally with accuracy,
appropriate rate, and expression on
successive readings.
Also Literature 2., 5., 10.

Poetry

- Some poets use sound effects, such as internal rhyme and alliteration.

- Internal rhyme is rhyming that occurs within individual lines of a poem. Internal rhyme draws attention to certain words. It can reinforce a poem's meaning or make a poem fun to read.

- Alliteration is the repetition of consonant sounds at the beginning of words. The line "My shell still shows" from "Desert Tortoise" uses alliteration in the words "shell" and "shows."

- Read the poems and think about how sound effects add meaning and make the poems fun to read.

Desert Tortoise

by Byrd Baylor

I am the *old* one here.

Mice
and snakes
and deer
and butterflies
and badgers
come and go.
Centipedes
and eagles
come and go.

But tortoises
grow old
and stay.

Our lives stretch out.

I cross
the same arroyo
that I crossed
when I was young,

returning to
the same safe den
to sleep through
winter's cold.
Each spring,
I warm myself
in the same sun,
search for the same
long tender blades
of green,
and taste the same
ripe juicy cactus fruit.

I know
the slow
sure way
my world
repeats itself.
I know
how I fit in.

My shell still shows
the toothmarks
where a wildcat
thought he had me
long ago.
He didn't know
that I was safe
beneath
the hard brown rock
he tried to bite.

I trust that shell.
I move
at my own speed.

This
is a good place
for an old tortoise
to walk.

Camel

by Lillian M. Fisher

A camel is a mammal,
A most extraordinary animal
Whose appearance is a wee bit odd.
His body is lumpy,
Knees calloused and bumpy,
And his feet are naturally shod.
His humps are fantastical,
His manner bombastical,
Due to his proud ancient past.
He feasts upon brambles
And ploddingly ambles.
His gait is not very fast.
But he carries great loads
On long dusty roads
Where many a beast cannot.
He's a tireless walker
And goes without water
In weather increasingly hot.
This strange-looking beast
Who resides in the East
And in far-off places West
Is found at the zoo
Where he's happy, it's true,
But—
Deep inside—desert is best.

Let's **Think** About...

How does the alliteration in "Desert Tortoise" reinforce the poem's meaning and important ideas?

Let's **Think** About...

Do you think the internal rhyme in the first line of "Camel" adds to the meaning or makes the poem fun to read?

Which Lunch Table?

by Kristine O'Connell George

Where do I sit?
All my friends
from last year
have changed;
my world is
   fractured,
   lopsided,
   rearranged.

   Where do I fit?
   Nothing is clear.
   Can already tell
   this will be
   a jigsaw year.

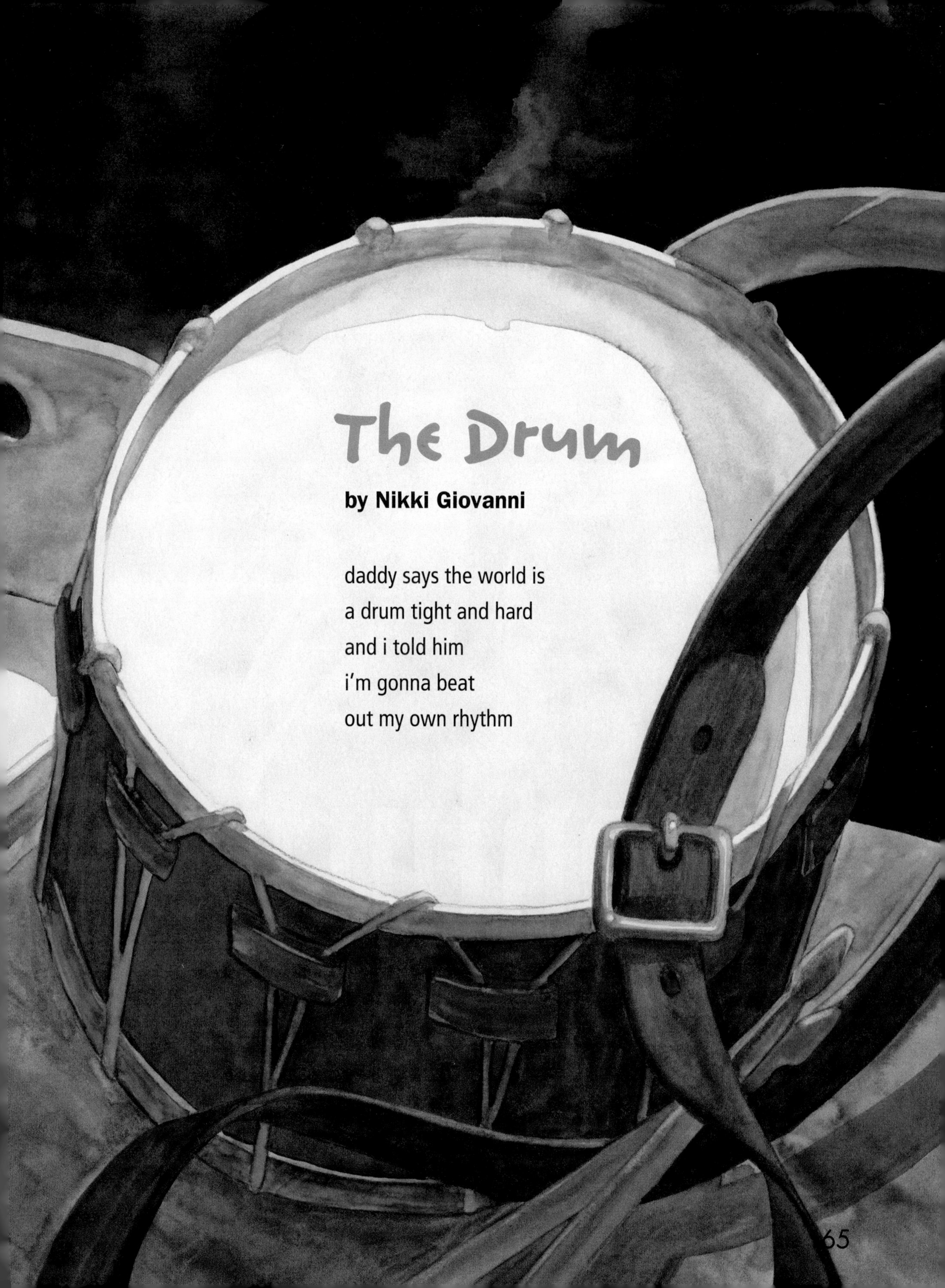

The Drum

by Nikki Giovanni

daddy says the world is
a drum tight and hard
and i told him
i'm gonna beat
out my own rhythm

Adventurers

THE BIG ?

Who goes seeking adventure and why?

Common Core State Standards

Language 6. Acquire and use accurately grade-appropriate general academic and domain-specific words and phrases, including those that signal contrast, addition, and other logical relationships (e.g., *however, although, nevertheless, similarly, moreover, in addition*).
Also Speaking/Listening 1.c.

Let's Talk About

Everyday Adventures

- Describe adventures you have every day.

- Listen to others talk about everyday adventures.

- Ask questions to clarify classmates' messages.

READING STREET ONLINE
CONCEPT TALK VIDEO
www.ReadingStreet.com

You've learned
2 0 0
Amazing Words
so far this year!

Common Core State Standards

Literature 2. Determine a theme of a story, drama, or poem from details in the text, including how characters in a story or drama respond to challenges or how the speaker in a poem reflects upon a topic; summarize the text. **Also Literature 3.**

Envision It! Skill Strategy

Skill

Strategy

Comprehension Skill

Literary Elements: Character and Plot

- The plot is the pattern of events in a story. It includes conflict, rising action, a climax, and a resolution.

- Characters are people in a story. Characters show you their traits, or qualities, by what they say and do.

- Use a graphic organizer like the one below to help you list a character's traits. Then explain the character's role and function in the plot, relationships, and conflicts in "The Day of Two Adventures."

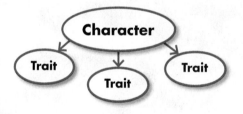

Comprehension Strategy

Background Knowledge

Active readers use what they already know to understand what they read. As you read, think about what you already know about people and events from your own life that are similar to those in the story.

THE DAY OF TWO ADVENTURES

Gram played tennis. She had frown lines from squinting against the sun to see the ball. Gramps's wrinkles were from smiling. "Games aren't for me," said Gramps.

Saturday morning, Gramps didn't want to climb Mt. Baldy with us.

"What a great adventure!" said Gram.

It was hard to keep up with Gram. "Gramps likes to go slow and enjoy the scenery," I panted.

"Three hours!" said Gram at the summit. Then she sat down suddenly, looking pale.

"Are you all right?" I asked.

"Climbing used up my energy, but lunch will fix that." Gram opened her pack. "Oh, no! I left our lunch at home."

I looked down the trail and saw Gramps approaching. "When did you leave home?" I asked when he arrived.

"Right after you," said Gramps. "I saw your lunch."

"What's that smell?"

"I decided to have my own adventure." Gramps took some muffins out of his pack. "I had never baked before, so I tried baking muffins."

Skill How does the relationship between Gram and Gramps contribute to the story's plot?

Skill Explain how Gram's character traits contribute to the conflict in this story.

Strategy Do you know someone like Gram? How does having this knowledge help you understand her character?

Your Turn!

⏸ Need a Review? See the *Envision It! Handbook* for additional help with character, plot, and background knowledge.

Let's Think About...

▶ Ready to Try It? Use what you have learned as you read *The Skunk Ladder*.

171

Common Core State Standards

Language 4.b. Use common, grade-appropriate Greek and Latin affixes and roots as clues to the meaning of a word (e.g., *photograph, photosynthesis*).

bellow

feat

savage

abandoned

attempt

cavern

immensely

Vocabulary Strategy for

🎯 Greek and Latin Roots

Word Structure Greek and Latin roots are words or parts of words from the Greek and Latin languages. For example, *excavation* comes from the Latin prefix *ex-,* meaning "out of," the Latin root *cave,* meaning "hollow," and the Latin suffix *-ation,* meaning "act or process of." *Excavation* means "the act or process of hollowing out."

Look at the word *archaeology*. Then follow these steps:

1. Look for a root in the word. See if you recognize the root. Do you know another word that has this root?

2. See whether the root meaning of the known word gives you a clue about the meaning of the unknown word.

3. Then check a dictionary to see if this meaning makes sense.

Read "The Cave in the Cliff" on page 173. Look for Greek and Latin roots and affixes you can use to determine the meanings of words such as *prehistoric, antitourist,* or other unknown words.

Words to Write Reread "The Cave in the Cliff." Write a paragraph about discovering a cave. Use words from the *Words to Know* list in your paragraph.

The Cave in the Cliff

Ryan reached a ledge on the cliff and looked down at the height he had scaled. "What an amazing climbing feat!" he said to his father. He was immensely proud of himself.

Then Ryan turned around to notice a large cavern opening in the side of the cliff. "Look, Dad. A cave!" he said.

Dad clambered up onto the ledge. "Let's inspect it," he said, and he and Ryan entered the cave. "I see signs of excavation near the back," Dad commented. "Somebody was digging, probably in an attempt to make the cave deeper. The dig was apparently abandoned years ago, though."

"Somebody has drawn on the wall," said Ryan. He pointed to a picture of a prehistoric, savage-looking beast.

They heard a loud bellow from the bottom of the cliff. Ryan could not distinguish the individual words, but he guessed that his brother was calling them to dinner.

They got ready to climb down.

"Shall we tell people about this cave?" asked Ryan.

"No, people might come and spoil it. I don't mean to be antitourist, but let's leave it as is," said Dad.

Your Turn!

⏸ **Need a Review?** For additional help with Greek and Latin roots, see *Words!*

▶ **Ready to Try It?** Read *The Skunk Ladder* on pp. 174–187.

Genre

Humorous fiction has characters and action that make you laugh. As you read, notice how the author creates humor out of two boys' boredom.

The Skunk Ladder

by Patrick F. McManus
illustrated by Richard Johnson

Let's **Think** About Reading!

Let's **Think** About...

How does what you know about planes and submarines make this paragraph humorous?

⊙ Background Knowledge

My friend Crazy Eddie Muldoon and I were sitting on the Muldoon corral fence one summer afternoon, trying to think of something to do. This was shortly after I had nearly drowned in the creek while testing Eddie's deep-sea diving apparatus, and after we had crashed in our homemade plane during takeoff from the roof of the Muldoon barn, and after our submarine had failed to surface with us in the pond, but before Mr. Muldoon started being treated by old Doc Mosby for a mysterious nervous condition. I recall mentioning to Eddie that his father seemed to be awfully jumpy that summer, and Eddie said he had noticed it, too, and wondered if it might not be caused by eating vegetables.

Even as we sat on the fence, Mr. Muldoon came by on his tractor and stopped to study us suspiciously. "What are you two up to now?" he demanded.

"Nothin', Pa," Crazy Eddie said. "Just trying to think of something to do."

Mr. Muldoon shuddered. "Well, when you think of it, you let me know before you start to do it, you hear?"

"Sure, Pa," Eddie said. "I guess what we'll do is go dig in the dirt. We've been talkin' about doin' that."

"Okay," said Mr. Muldoon, shifting his tractor into gear. "Just don't build nothin'!" Then he drove off.

"What kind of hole are we going to dig?" I asked Eddie.

He stared off into space, his face enveloped in that dreamy expression that always accompanied one of his wondrous new ideas. "A big hole," he said. "A real big hole."

Using what you already know about the characters, what can you predict about Eddie's new idea?

Predict and Set Purpose

177

Let's Think About...

Why do you think the narrator goes along with the plan?
Questioning

Digging the hole occupied us for most of a week. One of the problems with digging a big hole is that it is difficult to know when it is big enough and deep enough. There are basically two kinds of holes dug in the ground: (1) applied holes, such as for posts, wells, mines, etc., and (2) holes for holes' sake. Eddie and I were digging one of the latter. Eventually, the hole was so deep we could barely heave shovelfuls of dirt up over its sides. At that point, Eddie judged it to be finished.

Since Eddie had insisted that we keep the sides of the hole squared up, we had to pull ourselves out of it on a rope, one end of which was tied to a pile of stumps nearby. The stump pile also served to screen our digging activities from the view of Mr. Muldoon, who was cutting hay in a field on the far side of the farm. As Eddie often pointed out, any kind of engineering feat should be screened from the eyes of the engineer's parents. That way you could concentrate on your work and didn't have to be answering a lot of dumb questions all the time.

We were immensely proud of the hole, and I still don't believe I've ever seen a nicer one. It was so nice, in fact, that Eddie abandoned his view of it as purely an aesthetically pleasing hole and began trying to think of it as practical.

"You know what we could do with this hole?" he said. "We could make a wild animal trap out of it, you know, like Frank Buck does in Africa. We could cover it up with branches and leaves and grass, and wild animals would come along and fall into it. Then we could tame them and teach them to do tricks."

Eddie fairly glowed with enthusiasm as his idea began to take shape. "And then we could start our own circus," he went on. "We could charge people to see our animals do tricks. We might even get rich. Gosh, I bet we could catch a deer or an elk or a bear or a mountain lion, or. . . ."

Let's Think About...

What do you think the boys will do with the hole?
Predict

"One of your father's cows," I put in.

Eddie's glow of enthusiasm faded. "Yeah," he said. "I never thought of that."

Both of us stood there silently for a moment, thinking of Mr. Muldoon staring down into the hole at one of his milk cows. It was unpleasant to think about.

"Tomorrow we'd better fill the hole back in," Eddie said.

"How about tonight? Maybe a cow will fall in tonight."

Eddie pondered this possibility for a moment. "I got it," he said. "There's a big ol' door out behind the barn. We'll drag that down here and put it over the hole." And that is what we did, before knocking off work for the day, secure in the knowledge that the door would save us from the uncomfortable experience of watching his father undergo one of his fits of hysteria.

Early the next morning, Eddie and I headed for the big hole, prepared to start the tedious task of undigging it. As we approached the excavation, a familiar odor reached our nostrils.

"Must be a skunk around here someplace," Eddie said.

"Maybe it's in the hole," I said.

"Couldn't be. We covered it with the door."

Nevertheless, the skunk was in the hole. He had apparently found an open space under the door, slipped in for a look around, and plummeted the eight feet or more to the bottom of the hole.

Let's Think About...

What has happened so far that made Eddie decide to cover the hole with a door?
Summarize

Let's Think About...

What do you know about skunks that makes the story humorous?
Background Knowledge

Oddly, he did not seem to be frightened of us. Even stranger, for we did not know that skunks were great diggers, he had hollowed out a huge cavern under one side, in an attempt to dig his way out of the hole.

"We can't fill in the hole with the skunk in there," I said. "How are we going to get him out?"

"Maybe one of us could drop down in the hole, grab him real quick before he sprays, and then throw him out," Eddie said. "I'll yell real loud so he'll look at me and won't notice when you jump in and grab him and. . . ."

"I don't like that idea," I said. "Think of something else."

"I got it!" Eddie exclaimed, snapping his fingers. "We'll go up to my dad's shop and build a ladder. Then we'll stick it down the hole and hide someplace while he climbs the ladder. A skunk should be able to figure out how to climb a ladder."

Eddie and I were working on the ladder when his father walked into the shop. "I thought I told you not to build anything," he growled. "What's that?"

"Just a skunk ladder," Crazy Eddie said.

Let's **Think** About...

Would a skunk realistically be able to climb a ladder?
Questioning

182

"Oh," his father said. "Well, don't build nothin' else unless you tell me first."

Eddie and I went back out to the hole and stuck the ladder in it. The skunk showed no inclination to climb it, choosing instead to hide in the cavern it had hollowed out. Just then we heard Eddie's father yelling at us: "What did you mean, *skunk ladder?*" We peeked out around the stump pile, and there was Mr. Muldoon striding across the pasture toward us.

"Quick," said Eddie. "Help me put the door back over the hole!"

We threw the door over the hole, neatly hiding it from view. Before we could think of a good explanation for a big pile of dirt out in a corner of the pasture, Mr. Muldoon charged up.

"Now what?" he cried. "Where did that dirt come from? What's my door doing out here?"

Let's Think About...

Think of adventures you've read or know about. Are you surprised that Eddie's father acts the way he does?

Background Knowledge

183

Let's **Think** About...

How do you know that something unexpected is going to happen?
Inferring

Let's **Think** About...

The events on this page happen in a humorous way. Does this remind you of other books you've read or TV shows you've seen?
Background Knowledge

Let's **Think** About...

What details would you include to summarize these events?
Summarize

He reached down and grabbed the edge of the door. "Stop, Pa, don't!" Eddie yelled, rushing forward.

From that point on, the actions of the parties involved all blurred together. It is difficult to recall the exact sequence of action, but I will try.

Mr. Muldoon grabbed the door and flipped it off the hole. Then he said, "Smells like a skun . . ." at which time he shot out of sight, leaving his straw hat suspended in the air for perhaps a quarter of a second. (Later, I deduced that Mr. Muldoon had stepped on the edge of the hole, beneath which the skunk had hollowed out its cavern.) A cloud of dust puffed up out of the hole when Mr. Muldoon hit the bottom. Then he yelled several serious colorful words with the word "SKUNK!" mixed in with them. Next there were a lot of earthy scrabbling sounds, and Mr. Muldoon came clawing his way up the side of the hole, but the dirt gave way and he fell back in, saying something like "Ooofff!" It is important, perhaps, to realize that all the activity so far had taken place in a span of no more than four seconds. Eddie had meanwhile charged forward, yelling, "Pa, Pa, don't hurt him!" He was standing at the top of the ladder when the skunk rushed up that contrivance and emerged from the cloud of dust. Startled, and not wanting the skunk to reverse ends and spray him, Eddie grabbed the little animal by the head. The skunk started scratching and biting, so Eddie threw it back down in the hole, where its arrival was followed by a savage bellow from Mr. Muldoon, who, to our surprise, then came racing up the skunk ladder himself.

Let's **Think** About...

Why might Eddie's mom be angry about the skunk ladder? **Inferring**

This was the signal for Eddie and me to start running, which we did, and we continued running until the thunderous sounds of Mr. Muldoon's clodhopper boots faded behind us, and still we ran on, finally outdistancing even the nostril-searing smell of Eddie's father.

Eddie eventually made his way home and placed himself under the protective custody of his mother, until Mr. Muldoon's rage subsided into the odd little facial tic that was to remain with him for several months.

In the ruckus at the skunk ladder, Eddie had been hit in the face with a slight charge of skunk spray. Worried at first that the spray might have affected his brain, Mr. and Mrs. Muldoon finally assumed there would be no lasting ill effects. Twenty years later, however, Crazy Eddie became a Ph.D. in chemistry.

Let's Think About...

How does what you know about chemistry make Eddie's career choice humorous?

ⓢ **Background Knowledge**

Common Core State Standards

Literature 1. Quote accurately from a text when explaining what the text says explicitly and when drawing inferences from the text. **Also Literature 2., 3., Writing 8., 9., 9.a.**

Envision It! | Retell

Think Critically

1. What did you think of Eddie's solution to the problem of the skunk in the hole? Have you ever had a solution to a problem that didn't work out the way you had wanted? What did you learn from that experience?
   Text to Self

2. Why do you think the author included details about past incidents in the first paragraph? How do these details help explain what happens in the rest of the story?
   Think Like an Author

3. Describe the role and function Crazy Eddie plays in the conflicts and relationships in *The Skunk Ladder*. Use evidence from the text to support your answer.
   Literary Elements: Character and Plot

4. Think about how parents respond to their children's adventurous ideas. Which words or actions of Mr. Muldoon seem realistic? Which seem exaggerated?
   Background Knowledge

5. **Look Back and Write** Go back to the story's ending, when the boys are running away from Eddie's father. Do you think the boys will continue to have similar adventures like the one they just had? Write your opinion. Provide evidence to support your answer.
   Key Ideas and Details • Text Evidence

Meet the Author

Patrick F. McManus

Patrick F. McManus grew up on a farm in Idaho. This upbringing helped shape the writing of many of his books. His outdoor adventures as a child and his love for nature are topics that show up in his stories. Many of his writings are filled with humor, and the characters in his books often find themselves stuck in embarrassing situations in the great outdoors.

Mr. McManus had an unusual elementary school experience growing up. The school that Mr. McManus attended had only one teacher—his mother! The mountain valley where Mr. McManus lived was so remote that the schools there were small, and usually had only one room. He remembers spending a lot of time painting and drawing during elementary school, which helped pave the way to writing. He says, "There isn't too much difference between painting with paints and painting with words, except the latter is a lot less messy."

Mr. McManus lives in Spokane, Washington, with his wife and four daughters.

Reading Log

Use the *Reader's and Writer's Notebook* to record your independent reading.

Common Core State Standards

Writing 3. Write narratives to develop real or imagined experiences or events using effective technique, descriptive details, and clear event sequences.

Also Writing 3.d., Language 1., 5.

Rhyming Poem

Rhyming poems use rhyme to show feelings and ideas. They may also use figurative language and sensory details to richly capture a moment, an idea, or an observation. The student model on the next page is an example of a rhyming poem.

Writing Prompt In *The Skunk Ladder,* a somewhat ordinary task becomes a humorous adventure. Think about other funny adventures one might have. Write a rhyming poem about it, using figurative language.

Let's Write It!

Key Features of a Rhyming Poem

- contains rhythm and rhyme
- often uses poetic techniques and figurative language
- may include sensory details or vivid words

READING STREET ONLINE
GRAMMAR JAMMER
www.ReadingStreet.com

Writer's Checklist

Remember, you should . . .

- ☑ tell about a funny adventure.
- ☑ include rhyming words.
- ☑ use figurative language, such as similes and metaphors.
- ☑ use graphic elements, such as capital letters.
- ☑ use poetic techniques, such as alliteration and onomatopoeia.

Going for a Ride

I am a sloth in the back of the car,

until a bee flies in from afar.

And buckled in like a suitcase,

fear comes across my face.

I struggle and squirm,

I swat and I churn.

I **can't** get away

from the BUZZING ballet.

"**Don't** panic! Roll your window down,"

says Mom, with a frown.

I jab at the button with my thumbs;

like a bee the window hums.

And finally, that trapped and angry bee

gets the chance to escape from ME!

**Writing Trait
Word Choice**
Rhythm and rhyme convey ideas and mood.

Contractions and negatives are used correctly.

**Genre
Rhyming poems** tell a story using a rhyming pattern.

Conventions

Contractions and Negatives

Remember A **contraction** is a shortened form of two words. An apostrophe is used to show where one or more letters have been left out (*I + will = I'll*). Some are formed in special ways (*will + not = won't*). **Negatives** are words that mean *no* or *not*.

191

Common Core State Standards

Informational Text 5. Compare and contrast the overall structure (e.g., chronology, comparison, cause/effect, problem/solution) of events, ideas, concepts, or information in two or more texts. **Also Informational Text 2., Language 3.**

Genre
Autobiography

- An autobiography is the story of a person's life written by the person who lived it.

- Autobiographies are written in the first person, using *I*, *me*, and *my*.

- The events in an autobiography are actual events and experiences in a person's life. The author may use literary devices, such as conflict or dialogue, to present events.

- Read "Books and Adventure." Look for literary language or devices the author uses to present events in his life.

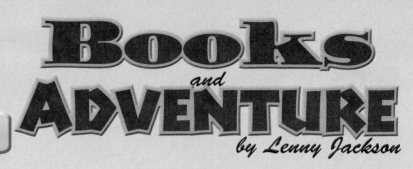

Books and ADVENTURE
by Lenny Jackson

My name is Lenny Jackson, and I was born on March 28, 1973, in Cleveland, Ohio. While most of the kids in the neighborhood spent their summers playing baseball or soccer, I spent my summers reading in my room. To me, reading books about knights and secret agents was always more exciting than chasing some ball across a field.

You can imagine my horror when my parents decided to send me to Camp Caribou for an entire summer. Camp Caribou wasn't just a regular camp either. Not only was the camp filled with forests, lakes, hiking trails, and fields, but it also had a soccer field, a basketball court, and a diving board. Basically, it was filled with all the things I never wanted to do.

The first person I met at Camp Caribou was Danny Tomzak. Back then, Danny was a tall, skinny, redheaded kid with freckles. I remember he had a shock of red hair that hung down over his eyes. When I walked in, he was standing next to a bunk in the corner of the cabin.

"Hi, I'm Danny," he said, sticking out his hand. "Nice to meet you. I'm your bunkmate."

"I'm Lenny," I answered, and then started unpacking my suitcase. Danny stood over me as I put away my shorts and T-shirts. I didn't say anything at first. Like I said, I was a shy kid and wasn't used to meeting new people.

Then I opened up my backpack and took out some of my books. I knew kids were supposed to spend summer camp hiking through the hills and singing camp songs, but that didn't mean I still couldn't enjoy my favorite hobby.

As I pulled out my books one by one, I noticed Danny's eyes light up with excitement.

"Robin Hood?" he exclaimed excitedly. He picked up a book and stared at the cover. "I love this book!"

"Really?" I remember asking in surprise. I didn't know anyone else who had read it.

"Sure! It's one of my favorites." Danny sat down on the bunk next to me. "Let's see what else you brought!"

And that's how my first day at Camp Caribou began. Danny and I spent the next hour talking about our favorite books. It turned out we liked the same types of books too. We both liked science fiction and adventure books. The rest of the campers came into the room and unpacked their suitcases, but we barely noticed them. Danny and I were too engaged in talking about space adventurers, robots, and spies.

Something else happened to me that day too. It turned out I made friends with the most adventurous kid on the planet. Sure, Danny liked to read, but he also loved to spend time outdoors. Looking back, I realize that it was Danny that brought me screaming out of my shell. If I heard Danny say "This is an adventure" once, I heard it a million times that summer.

Let's Think About...

Which words tell you that this selection is written in the first person?
Autobiography

Let's Think About...

What literary devices does Lenny use to present major events that happen to him at camp?
Autobiography

Let's **Think** About...

What literary language shows that the events described in the story actually happened?
Autobiography

For example, there was the time Danny talked me into jumping off the high-dive at the lake. My parents took me to swimming classes when I was a little boy, so I wasn't scared of the water. However, I *was* scared of heights. The thought of standing on a ladder, much less a high dive, made my knees tremble.

"This is an adventure," I remember Danny saying. "Now watch. Nothing's going to happen to you." To prove it, he ran to the edge of the diving board, bounced once, and dove into the lake. Maybe it was my imagination, but I thought I saw a huge smile on his face right before he hit the water.

I remember looking down at the lifeguard sitting in her chair. *I hope you're paying attention*, I thought. A few seconds later, I took a deep breath and jumped. I hit the water like a bowling ball. The water was freezing cold, but as soon as I broke the surface, I was laughing too hard to care.

194

Danny and I had a lot of other adventures that summer too. We watched a colony of ants build an anthill. We fished in Lake Anaconda and caught a snapping turtle that nearly ate Danny's fishing rod. We hiked into the hills. We went kayaking down the Caribou River. When we weren't outside, Danny and I sat on our bunks and read books.

When the summer was over, Danny and I went our separate ways. We wrote each other letters every other week. We wrote about all the interesting things we were learning in school, what movies we watched, and what new books we were reading. I remember writing Danny a letter telling him I even earned a spot on my school's swim team!

That was more than twenty years ago. Now, Danny and I e-mail each other. We write about our lives since we met that summer so long ago. But most of the time, we remember that first summer at camp, when books and adventure brought us together.

Let's Think About...

Reading Across Texts Compare and contrast *The Skunk Ladder* and "Books and Adventure." How did the authors write each story? How are the two selections similar and different?

Writing Across Texts Imagine that Eddie Muldoon went to Lenny's camp. Write a journal entry for Eddie about his camp experience.

195

© **Common Core State Standards**
Language 4.b. Use common, grade-appropriate Greek and Latin affixes and roots as clues to the meaning of a word (e.g., *photograph, photosynthesis*).
**Also Literature 7.,
Foundational Skills 4.b.,
Speaking/Listening 1.**

Let's Learn It!

READING STREET ONLINE
ONLINE STUDENT EDITION
www.ReadingStreet.com

Vocabulary

Greek and Latin Roots

Word Structure Many English words contain roots, or word parts, from Greek or Latin. You can use these roots to find the meanings of English words.

Practice It! The Greek root *dem* means "people." The Latin root *leg* means "law." Find and define words from stories you've read that have these roots. Can you think of English words with roots from other languages, such as Spanish?

Fluency

Expression

Partner Reading Reading with expression can bring the characters in a story to life. Use your voice to show the characters' feelings and personalities.

Practice It! With your partner, practice reading a page from *The Skunk Ladder*. One partner reads Eddie's lines, and the other reads the narrator's lines. Try to show what each character is like as you read. Then switch roles and reread the page.

Listening and Speaking

Get Ready For Middle School

When you participate in a performance, enunciate your words and speak loudly.

Dramatization

A dramatization is a version of a story that is performed for an audience. Dramatizations focus on using dialogue to show what happens in the story.

Practice It! Work with a group to dramatize a scene from *The Skunk Ladder*. Create a script and assign roles to group members. Rehearse your dramatization and then present it to the class. When you're finished, discuss with the class the similarities and differences between your drama and the original *The Skunk Ladder*.

Tips

Listening . . .

- Listen attentively to each speaker.
- Pay attention to facial expressions to help interpret the speaker's message.

Speaking . . .

- Make eye contact with the audience.
- Speak loudly and enunciate clearly to communicate well.

Teamwork . . .

- Participate in discussions by asking for and considering suggestions from others in your group.
- Talk about how you agree and disagree with your group.

Common Core State Standards

Language 6. Acquire and use accurately grade-appropriate general academic and domain-specific words and phrases, including those that signal contrast, addition, and other logical relationships (e.g., *however, although, nevertheless, similarly, moreover, in addition*).

Let's Talk About

Technology and Adventurers

- Share ideas about the importance of technology.

- Express opinions about technology and adventure.

- Listen to classmates' messages about technology.

READING STREET ONLINE
CONCEPT TALK VIDEO
www.ReadingStreet.com

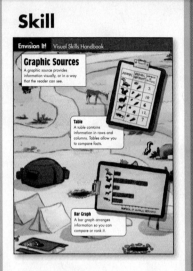

Envision It! Skill Strategy

Skill

Strategy

Comprehension Skill

🎯 Graphic Sources

- Graphic sources include charts, tables, graphs, maps, illustrations, and photographs.

- They can give you an overview of a text's contents. You can also use graphics to locate information.

- Use a graphic organizer like the one below to list details about the important information you locate in the selection's graphic sources.

Comprehension Strategy

🎯 Inferring

When you infer, you combine your background knowledge with evidence in the text to support your understanding about what the author is trying to present. Active readers often infer about the ideas, morals, lessons, and themes of a written work.

Queenstown Southampton

Cherborg

New York

41043'57" N, 49056'49" W

Shipwreck

For many years, people have spent their lives trying to find certain sunken ships. Why do they try to do this? There are several reasons.

Skill How do the title and the map give you an overview of the text's contents?

Some people want to find shipwrecks to learn exactly what caused the ships to sink. If they find out the cause of a shipwreck, they may be able to prevent the same kind of accident from happening again.

Some scientists and explorers search for shipwrecks to learn more about the past. They want to find out how old ships were designed. They also want to see the tools people used on those ships. The study of shipwrecks is called *nautical archaeology.*

Strategy What can you infer about why it is important to learn about the past? Use textual evidence to support understanding.

Once people find a sunken ship, they mark its location on a map. The map here shows approximately where the ocean liner *Titanic* went down. This map will help other people locate the shipwreck for years to come.

Skill How does the map help you understand where the *Titanic* sank?

Your Turn!

⏸ **Need a Review?** See the *Envision It! Handbook* for additional help with graphic sources and inferring.

▶ **Ready to Try It?** Use what you have learned about graphic sources as you read *The Unsinkable Wreck of the R.M.S.* Titanic.

TITANIC

Common Core State Standards
Language 4.c. Consult reference materials (e.g., dictionaries, glossaries, thesauruses), both print and digital, to find the pronunciation and determine or clarify the precise meaning of key words and phrases. **Also Language 4.**

Envision It! | Words to Know

debris

robotic

sonar

cramped

interior

ooze

sediment

Vocabulary Strategy for
🎯 Unknown Words

Dictionary/Glossary Sometimes a writer doesn't include context clues in the sentences surrounding an unknown word. In this case, you have to look up the word in a dictionary or glossary. Follow these steps.

Choose one of the *Words to Know*.

1. Look to see whether the book has a glossary. If not, use a dictionary. You can use a printed or electronic dictionary.

2. Find the word entry. If the pronunciation is given, read it aloud. You may recognize the word when you hear yourself say it.

3. Look at all the meanings listed in the entry. Try each meaning in the sentence that contains the unknown word.

4. Choose the meaning that makes sense in your sentence.

Read "In the Ocean Deeps" on page 203. Use a dictionary or a glossary to determine the meanings of words you cannot figure out from the text.

Words to Write Reread "In the Ocean Deeps." Write a paragraph about a similar scientific experiment. Use words from the *Words to Know* list in your paragraph.

IN THE OCEAN DEEPS

What lies in the ocean deeps and who lives there? Scientists work hard to answer those questions. The ocean floor is miles deep in many places. It is very cold and dark down there. The pressure of so much water would crush divers instantly. How can they get down there to find answers?

Scientists use high-tech machines. A sonar system sends out beeps of sound that bounce off the ocean floor. Computers can use the beeps to make maps. Scientists look at the maps for areas that interest them. Then they send down submersible vehicles that can withstand the high pressure. Many of these vehicles are robotic. They carry cameras and other equipment to record what it is like down there. At great depths, they may show an ooze of melted rock coming from deep inside the Earth. They may show a "desert" of sediment or a mountain range.

Some of these deep-sea machines carry divers. The interior of one of these machines is small, so scientists are cramped. But that is a small price to pay to be able to see for themselves the wonders of deep-sea life. Strange and wonderful plants and animals have been discovered far below the surface. Sadly, debris, trash, and damage done by pollution have also been found.

Your Turn!

❚❚ Need a Review?
For additional help with using a dictionary or glossary, see *Words!*

▷ Ready to Try It?
Read *The Unsinkable Wreck of the R.M.S.* Titanic on pp. 204–215.

THE UNSINKABLE WRECK OF THE R.M.S.
TITANIC

from *Ghost Liners: Exploring the World's Greatest Lost Ships*

BY ROBERT D. BALLARD AND RICK ARCHBOLD
ILLUSTRATIONS BY KEN MARSCHALL

Genre

Expository text tells the true story of an event. As you read, notice how the author tells why a ship sank and how he explored its wreckage.

APRIL 10, 1912, 12:00 NOON

Tugboats help the *Titanic* pull away from the Southampton pier.

APRIL 14, 1912, 11:39 P.M.

As the liner enters an ice field, a large iceberg lies directly in its path.

APRIL 14, 1912, 11:40 P.M.

The iceberg scrapes along the *Titanic*'s starboard side.

nside the cramped submarine, all I could hear was the steady pinging of the sonar and the regular breathing of the pilot and engineer. I crouched on my knees, my eyes glued to the tiny viewport. The pings speeded up—that meant the wreck was close—and I strained to see beyond the small cone of light that pierced the endless underwater night.

"Come right!" I was so excited I was almost shouting, even though the two others with me inside *Alvin* were so close I could touch them. "Bingo!"

Like a ghost from the ancient past, the bow of the Royal Mail Steamer *Titanic*, the greatest shipwreck of all time, materialized out my viewport. After years of questing, I had arrived at the ship's last resting place.

Effortlessly we rose up the side of the famous bow, now weeping great tears of rust, past the huge anchor and up over the rail. We were the first in more than seventy years to "walk" on the *Titanic*'s deck! The giant windlasses used for raising and lowering the anchor still trailed their massive links of chain, as if ready to lower away. I felt as though I had walked into a dream.

◄ Our little submarine *Alvin* rests on the *Titanic's* portside boat deck while the underwater robot *Jason Junior* explores the ship's B-Deck promenade.

A 1912 poster from England advertising the new White Star Liner, *Titanic*

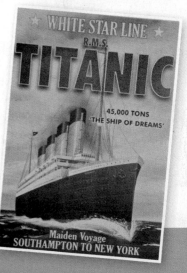

APRIL 15, 1912, 1:40 A.M.

Two hours after the collision, the bow of the *Titanic* is underwater.

APRIL 15, 1912, 2:17 A.M.

The *Titanic* breaks in two and the bow section begins its final plunge.

In 1912, the *Titanic* had set sail on her maiden voyage,
the largest, most luxurious ship the world had ever seen.
On board were many of the rich and famous of the day.

Then, on the fifth night out—tragedy. An iceberg, seen too late. Too few lifeboats. Pandemonium, and over 1,500 dead out of the more than 2,200 people on board.

Now the sub sailed out over the well deck, following the angle of the fallen foremast up toward the liner's bridge. We paused at the crow's nest. On the fateful night, lookout Frederick Fleet had been on duty here. It was he who warned the bridge: "Iceberg right ahead." Fleet was one of the lucky ones. He made it into a lifeboat and to safety.

The pilot set *Alvin* gently down on the bridge, not far from the telemotor control—all that remained of the steering mechanism of the ship. It was here that First Officer William Murdoch, desperate to avoid the mountain of ice that lay in the *Titanic*'s path, shouted to the helmsman, "Hard a-starboard!" Then Murdoch watched in excruciating agony as the huge ship slowly began to turn—but it was too late and the iceberg fatally grazed the liner's side. I thought of Captain E. J. Smith rushing from his cabin to be told the terrible news. Thirty minutes later, after learning how quickly water was pouring into the ship, he knew that the "unsinkable" *Titanic* was doomed.

We lifted off from the bridge and headed toward the stern. Over a doorway we could make out the brass plate with the words: 1st Class Entrance. In my mind's eye I could see the deck surging with passengers as the crew tried to keep order during the loading of the lifeboats. The broken arm of a lifeboat davit hung over the side. From this spot port-side lifeboat No. 2 was launched—barely half full. Among the twenty-five people in a boat designed to carry more than forty were Minnie Coutts and her two boys,

(Above) *Alvin* investigates the bow section of the *Titanic* wreck. The stern lies in the distance. (Below left) The telemotor control that once held the ship's wheel; (middle) the A-deck promenade; (right) a section of bow railing.

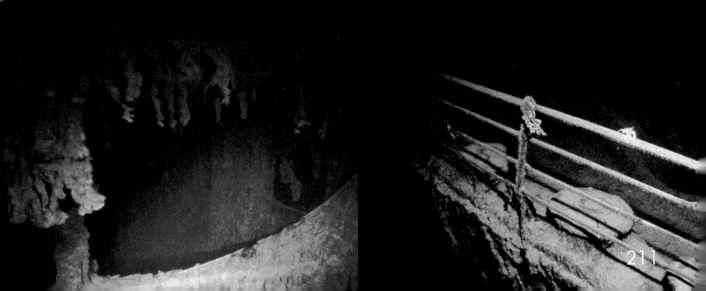

Willie and Neville. They were among the relatively few third-class passengers to survive the sinking.

As our tiny submarine continued toward the stern, we peered through the windows of first-class staterooms. The glass dome over the first-class grand staircase was long gone, providing a perfect opening for exploring the interior of the ship. But that would have to wait for a later visit, when we would bring along our robotic "swimming eyeball," *Jason Junior.* As we continued back, I wondered what we would find. We already knew the ship lay in two pieces, with the stern nearly two thousand feet (six hundred meters) away. Suddenly the smooth steel subdecking contorted into a tangle of twisted metal where the stern had ripped free. Beyond it hundreds of objects that had spilled out when the ship broke in two were lying on the ocean floor.

◄ *Jason Junior* explores the remains of the grand staircase.

NEARLY LOST BECAUSE OF A HAT

Willie Coutts's hat nearly cost him his life. When the *Titanic* hit the iceberg, his mother, Minnie, roused eleven-year-old Willie and his baby brother Neville (right), got them dressed, and put on their lifebelts. Through the swirl of panicking passengers, Minnie led her children out of third class toward what she hoped was safety. One officer handed his own lifebelt to Minnie, saying, "If the boat goes down you'll remember me." Another crewman led them to the boat deck. Minnie and Neville got in one of the last boats—but the officer in charge held Willie back. The rule was women and children first, and the hat Willie was wearing made him look too old. Willie's mother insisted but the officer refused again. Finally, good sense prevailed and Willie, too, stepped to safety.

As we floated out over this debris field, I found it hard to believe that only a thin film of sediment covered plates and bottles that had lain on the bottom for seventy-four years. One of the ship's boilers sat upright on the mud with a tin cup resting on it, as if set there by a human hand. Champagne bottles lay with their corks still intact. A porcelain doll's head stared at us from its final resting place in the soft ooze. Had it belonged to little Loraine Allison, the only child from first class who didn't survive that night? Most haunting of all were the shoes and boots. Many of them lay in pairs where

HAUNTING MEMENTOS

Unlike its fairly intact bow section, the ***Titanic***'s stern (page 214) literally blew apart on hitting the bottom. In the debris field between the bow and stern we saw hundreds of touching reminders of the tragedy. A porcelain doll's head (above right) is all that remains of an expensive French doll (inset). It may have belonged to Loraine Allison of Montreal (above middle with her baby brother), the only child from first class who did not survive. A tin cup (above left) has come to rest near the round furnace door of one of the ship's huge boilers.

bodies had once fallen. Within a few weeks of the sinking, the corpses had been consumed by underwater creatures and their bones had been dissolved by the cold salt water. Only those shoes remain—mute reminders of the human cost of the *Titanic* tragedy.

After only two hours on the bottom, it was time for *Alvin* to begin the long ascent back to the surface ship, two and a half miles (four kilometers) above. As we headed back to the surface, I was already impatient to return to the *Titanic*. We had only begun to plumb its secrets.

Common Core State Standards

Informational Text 1. Quote accurately from a text when explaining what the text says explicitly and when drawing inferences from the text. **Also Writing 8., 9.**

Envision It! Retell

READING STREET ONLINE
STORY SORT
www.ReadingStreet.com

Think Critically

1. In the early 1900s cruise liners like the *Titanic* were the only mode of transportation available between the United States and Europe. The journey could take weeks in some cases. How has transportation changed since then? **Text to World**

2. Like snapshots, words show you objects in the ruins: *tin cup, doll's head, shoes,* and *boots*. Find other snapshotlike words that the author uses to reveal the wreck.

Think Like an Author

3. Sometimes graphic sources can present information in a concise way. Look at the account of the *Titanic* tragedy on the bottom of pages 206 and 207. Why is this graphic source helpful to understanding the events? **Graphic Sources**

4. The author, Dr. Robert Ballard, does not explicitly reveal his feelings about the *Titanic* tragedy. As a reader, you need to infer them. How do you think the author feels about the tragedy? Use evidence from the text to support your inference. **Inferring**

5. Look Back and Write Go back to page 213 and reread the section about Willie Coutts. Write a brief diary account told in a first-person voice that describes how Willie was feeling at the time, as he struggled to get on the rescue boat. Provide evidence to support your answer.

Key Ideas and Details • Text Evidence

Meet the Author

DR. ROBERT BALLARD

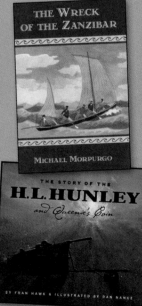

Dr. Robert Ballard was born in Wichita, Kansas, but grew up in San Diego, California, near the water. He says that growing up he always wanted to be Captain Nemo from Jules Verne's science-fiction novel *20,000 Leagues Under the Sea*.

Dr. Ballard has led or taken part in more than one hundred deep-sea expeditions. Another of his accomplishments is founding the Jason Foundation for Education. He did this in response to the thousands of letters from schoolchildren wanting to know how he discovered the R.M.S. *Titanic*. The goal of the Jason Foundation is to help teachers, students, businesses, government, and schools work together to inspire students to use exploration and discovery in their pursuit of learning.

Here are other books about famous ship disasters.

The Wreck of the Zanzibar by Michael Morpurgo

The Story of the H.L. Hunley and Queenie's Coin by Fran Hawk

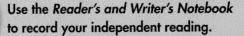

Use the *Reader's and Writer's Notebook* to record your independent reading.

Common Core State Standards
Writing 8. Recall relevant information from experiences or gather relevant information from print and digital sources; summarize or paraphrase information in notes and finished work, and provide a list of sources.
Also Writing 2.a., Language 1.

Let's Write It!

Key Features of Notes

- include important facts

- restate information in one's own words, noting any direct quotations

- cite, or name, original source(s)

READING STREET ONLINE
GRAMMAR JAMMER
www.ReadingStreet.com

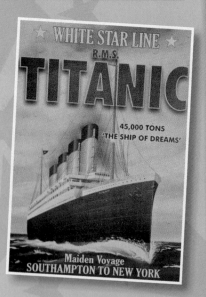

Notes

When you take **notes,** you write down the most important and interesting information on the topic. It is helpful to restate information in your own words to make sure you understand and remember it. The student model on the next page is an example of note taking.

Writing Prompt Choose several paragraphs from *The Unsinkable Wreck of the R.M.S.* Titanic and take notes on the most important facts and ideas.

Writer's Checklist

Remember, you should . . .

✓ include important facts, such as dates and names.

✓ use your own words to restate information.

✓ include interesting details.

✓ use adjectives and articles correctly.

✓ capitalize initials and titles.

The Titanic Sinks

The R.M.S. <u>Titanic</u> with Captain E.J. Smith

- giant passenger ship — 2,200 people aboard
- entered icy waters in the middle of the ocean
- April 14, 1912 at 11:30 P.M.

Frederick Fleet

- lookout in the crow's nest; saw an iceberg
- called to the bridge, "Iceberg right ahead!"

The First Officer William Murdoch

- ordered the ship to be steered hard to the right
- "Hard a-starboard!" he shouted; too late
- iceberg scraped the right side of the ship

Water poured into the ship

- within two hours the front of the ship was underwater
- people loaded into lifeboats
- not enough lifeboats
- more than 1,500 people died

Recently found along the ocean floor are cups, boots, and a French doll, probably lost by a young passenger.

Writing Trait Focus/Ideas Good notes help writers paraphrase information in expository compositions.

Adjectives and articles are used correctly.

Genre Notes help writers organize information and remember important facts.

Conventions

Adjectives and Articles

Remember A descriptive **adjective** answers these questions: What kind? How many? Which one? (e.g., a *French* doll; *2,200* passengers; *that* iceberg) **Articles** are special adjectives (such as *the, a, an*) that appear before nouns or other adjectives.

219

Common Core State Standards

Literature 2. Determine a theme of a story, drama, or poem from details in the text, including how characters in a story or drama respond to challenges or how the speaker in a poem reflects upon a topic; summarize the text. **Also Literature 1., 10.**

Social Studies in Reading

Genre
Historical Fiction

- Historical fiction is a story set in a particular historical period.

- In historical fiction, the background of the story is based on fact, but the story itself is fiction. Often the story will revolve around important changes or movements from history.

- Historical fiction is often written with a third-person point of view, employing words such as *he*, *she*, and *they*.

- Read "Shipwreck Season." Think about or explain how historical events or movements affect the theme of the story.

SHIPWRECK SEASON

BY DONNA HILL

It is 1880 on Cape Cod, Massachusetts. Sixteen-year-old Daniel is spending time at the lifesavers' station with the surfmen, who risk their lives to save people lost in shipwrecks along the rocky coast. Daniel has led a quiet life up until now, with very little adventure. He has rowed boats on calm rivers, never on a rough ocean. Now, with his dog, Truehart, Daniel watches from the shore as the surfmen conduct a practice lifeboat drill in the pounding seas.

Let's Think About...

How does the author show that boating was important during the 1880s?
Historical Fiction

The men ran along shore until the captain called, "Stop!" They sped the boat to the surf, lifted it off its carriage, and got the carriage back up on the beach. They took life belts from the boat and strapped them on. The captain put the steering oar in place. The surfmen grasped the gunwales on either side of the boat and waited tensely.

Daniel took his place at the stern beside the captain. As something on which to launch a boat, the ocean was different from what Daniel had known as a child, playing in the surf. Great mounds of water roared in toward the beach, crested, tumbled over, and came one after another in wild surges of power before turning into foam. The captain was studying the sea so intently that Daniel wondered if he were doubtful about launching today.

"Rough, isn't it, sir?"

"Not bad."

"What are we waiting for?"

"The slatch." The captain did not break his attention. "Slack water followed by a backwash to sea, usually the seventh wave after the biggest."

Now Daniel saw that waves were not all the same size. Big ones rolled in one after another, then a small one followed and crested. The captain shouted, "Now!"

The men rushed the boat into the sea, with Daniel and the captain shoving from the stern. They all ran out waist deep. As each section of the boat swept free, a man scrambled aboard facing the stern and wrestled his oar into place.

The sea rose up and took the boat. The captain leaped in over the stern and seized the long steering oar.

"Pull!" he cried. "Pull!"

The boat lunged through the water. Daniel fell back. He slipped in the pushing waves but kept his eyes riveted on the rowers, their huge arms and shoulders pulling in mighty strokes as they concentrated on the captain.

The captain was standing upright at his oar in the stern. Foam crashed over his back. Spray flew high overhead. Daniel saw him steer away from the biggest

Let's Think About...

How do you know that this story takes place during a different time in the past?

Historical Fiction

Let's Think About...

Why do you think the surfmen were important to the boating industry during the 1880s?
Historical Fiction

waves until they broke, but when one came that he could not avoid, he called for speed and sent the boat head on. A great sea broke over the bow and drenched the men. They did not falter or even wince.

Daniel was astounded by the surfmen's skill, power, and daring, and by the beauty of the white surfboat flying through glittering spray. He cheered, prancing, sloshing, and waving. A roaring mountain of sea came at him, ready to break over him. He saw it just in time, turned, and plunged toward shore.

The dog ran up and down the beach barking exuberantly as Daniel came splashing through the surf. She rushed at him, tail pumping madly, and nuzzled her cold nose into his hand.

"So you think I'm all right after all, do you, old girl?" Daniel laughed, roughing up her shaggy head.

Together they patrolled the beach, watching the surfboat. Out past the breakers, the boat capsized. The men bobbed in the sea. The dog stiffened and stared out intently. She did not relax until the boat was righted and the crew back at their oars.

"Ready to go to the rescue, right, old girl?" Daniel asked. He told her she was a noble dog.

Coming back with the boat looked even more hazardous than launching. The boat flew in ahead of a great swell, the captain standing in the stern, spray breaking around him.

Any oarsman, even the athletes of Daniel's club, would be impressed by this crew. The rowing Daniel and his friends did on a calm river, with nothing to think about but stroke and speed, was mere play compared to the efforts of these mighty oarsmen, which were not for sport, but in preparation to save lives.

It was no small thing to be a surfman, Daniel decided. It would be no small thing to be counted as one among them.

Let's Think About...

Even though there is a third-person narrator, we see a lot through Daniel's eyes. How does Daniel feel about what he sees?
Historical Fiction

Let's Think About...

Reading Across Texts Look back at *The Unsinkable Wreck* and "Shipwreck Season" and make a list of potential dangers at sea. Be sure to provide evidence from the texts.

Writing Across Texts Write a list of safety tips for people who are planning on taking an ocean voyage. Base your tips on your list of dangers.

Common Core State Standards

Language 4.c. Consult reference materials (e.g., dictionaries, glossaries, thesauruses), both print and digital, to find the pronunciation and determine or clarify the precise meaning of key words and phrases. **Also Foundational Skills 4.b., Speaking/Listening 4., 5., Language 4.**

Let's Learn It!

READING STREET ONLINE
ONLINE STUDENT EDITION
www.ReadingStreet.com

Vocabulary

Unknown Words

Dictionary/Glossary If you can't determine the meaning of an unknown word from context clues, you can find it in a dictionary or glossary. A dictionary also gives other information about a word, such as pronunciation and syllabication.

Practice It! Choose three unknown words from *The Unsinkable Wreck of the R.M.S.* Titanic. Use a dictionary or a glossary to look up their meanings. Write each word and its definition, syllabication, and part of speech. What other information does a dictionary give?

Fluency

Expression

Partner Reading As you read, you can use your voice to express emotions, such as excitement or suspense. Adjust the tone of your voice to match what's happening in the story.

Practice It! With a partner, take turns reading a page from *The Unsinkable Wreck of the R.M.S.* Titanic. Change the expression of your voice to fit the mood of the story. Give each other feedback to improve your reading.

226

Media Literacy

When speaking, use and understand descriptive adjectives (e.g., French, American).

Newscast

A newscast is a TV or radio broadcast devoted to current events, with the purpose of informing an audience about events.

**Practice It!** Imagine that the *Titanic* sunk today. With a partner, prepare a newscast about the *Titanic*. Use drawings or pictures to help you relate the news. Present the newscast to the class, and then discuss how newscasts present news differently from Internet news and newspapers.

Tips

Listening . . .

- Listen to the speaker's message.

- Ask questions to understand the speaker's purpose and main ideas.

Speaking . . .

- Enunciate while speaking.

- Speak at a natural rate.

Teamwork . . .

- Ask your partner for comments on your report.

- Consider suggestions from your partner.

Common Core State Standards

Language 6. Acquire and use accurately grade-appropriate general academic and domain-specific words and phrases, including those that signal contrast, addition, and other logical relationships (e.g., *however, although, nevertheless, similarly, moreover, in addition*).

Also Speaking/Listening 1.d.

Oral Vocabulary

Let's Talk About

Adventurers in Space

- Express opinions about space and adventure.

- Listen to a classmate's opinions about space and adventure.

- Determine classmates' main and supporting ideas about space.

READING STREET ONLINE
CONCEPT TALK VIDEO
www.ReadingStreet.com

Envision It! | Skill Strategy

Skill

Strategy

Comprehension Skill

Author's Purpose

- The author's purpose is the main reason an author writes. An author may write to persuade, to inform, to entertain, or to express ideas.

- You can use details from a text to determine an author's purpose.

- After reading a text, it is important to evaluate how well an author achieved his or her purpose.

- Use a graphic organizer like the one below to record the details about the author's purpose in "The United States in Space." Then, ask yourself if you think the author achieved his or her purpose.

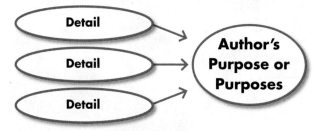

Comprehension Strategy

Monitor and Clarify

When you read nonfiction, you should always check your understanding of the text. One way to monitor understanding is to use your own knowledge about a topic. Another way is to make a list of important ideas in the text.

The United States in Space

The space program in the United States, known to most people as NASA (the National Aeronautics and Space Administration), began in 1958. NASA was formed because the United States wanted to beat the Soviet Union in the "space race."

At first, the Soviet Union was ahead in the space race. The Soviets sent the first satellite into space in 1957. The United States did not send a satellite into space until 1958. The Soviet Union also sent the first person to orbit Earth in 1961. The United States did not send a person into orbit until 1962. That person was John Glenn. He orbited Earth three times.

Over time, the United States moved ahead in the space race. President John F. Kennedy gave NASA the goal of putting a person on the moon by the end of the 1960s. NASA was able to meet that goal. In 1969, Neil Armstrong was the first person to take a step on the moon. This feat helped the United States win the space race.

Skill After reading the first sentence, what do you think is the author's purpose for writing? What clue does the sentence provide?

Strategy How does using your own knowledge help you clarify this paragraph?

Skill What is the author's purpose in this text? Did the author achieve his or her purpose? Why or why not?

APOLLO 11

Your Turn!

Need a Review? See the *Envision It! Handbook* for additional help with author's purpose and monitoring and clarifying.

Ready to Try It? Use what you have learned about author's purpose as you read *Talk with an Astronaut.*

231

Common Core State Standards
Language 4.a. Use context (e.g., cause/effect relationships and comparisons in text) as a clue to the meaning of a word or phrase. **Also Language 4.**

Envision It! | Words to Know

accomplishments

gravity

monitors

focus

role

specific

Vocabulary Strategy for

Multiple-Meaning Words

Context Clues Some words have more than one meaning. You can find context clues in nearby words to determine and clarify which meaning the author is using. Follow these steps.

1. Think about the different meanings the word can have.

2. Reread the sentence in which the word appears. Did you find any context clues? Which meaning fits in the sentence?

3. If you can't tell, look for more clues in nearby sentences.

4. Put the clues together and decide which meaning works best.

Read "To Be an Astronaut" on page 233. Use the context to decide which meaning a multiple-meaning word has in the article. For example, does the word *role* mean "a character in a play" or "a socially expected behavior"?

Words to Write Reread "To Be an Astronaut." Write a paragraph about what you think space travel will be like in the future. Be sure to use the correct meanings of each of the words from the *Words to Know* list in your paragraph.

To Be an Astronaut

Astronauts have a special place in our history. They are people of special character too. Like all explorers, astronauts must be curious and brave. As scientists, they must be well trained in physics and math with a focus on astronomy. They are also skilled pilots.

To live in space, astronauts must be in top shape. Because there is no gravity in space, they must get used to being weightless. Each flight brings different jobs with specific assignments. One time, astronauts may build part of a space station. Another time, they may carry out dozens of tests. They may have to use a robot arm and watch what the arm is doing on monitors. The computer screens let them adjust the arm's movements. These are only a few of the many tasks astronauts must accomplish in space.

Astronauts have many accomplishments, but none are more important than serving as positive role models for young people. These space explorers' courage, learning, and devotion to duty make them shining examples. They show us that people may reach for the stars.

Your Turn!

⏸ **Need a Review?**
For additional help with multiple-meaning words, see *Words!*

▶ **Ready to Try It?**
Read *Talk with an Astronaut* on pp. 234–245.

An **expository text** can tell about real people and events. In this interview, notice how the subject gives thoughtful answers about what it's like to be an astronaut.

TALK
WITH AN
ASTRONAUT

· ·

 Question of the Week
What is life like for an astronaut?

Ellen Ochoa is the first Hispanic American woman to fly in space. She is also an inventor of optical and robotic devices. She was interviewed by fifth-grade students.

Q. What are your Hispanic roots? Did you speak Spanish at home when you were growing up?

A. My Hispanic roots come from my father's side. His parents were Mexican, but my father was born in this country. He was one of 12 children. My father grew up speaking both Spanish and English, but unfortunately he didn't speak Spanish with us at home. When I was growing up, my father believed, as many people did at the time, that there was a prejudice against people speaking their native language. It's really too bad, and I'm glad that things have changed in recent years.

Q. Does your being Hispanic American make you feel more pressure and more pride about your accomplishments? Do you have that in mind when you think of how well you've done in life?

A. I don't believe that being Hispanic American puts any additional pressure on me. I seem to put enough pressure on myself as it is. As for my accomplishments, being an astronaut has given me the opportunity to speak to children all over, including children with the same background as myself. I think that it's important for children to have a role model to see what they can grow up to be. It's important they know that if they work hard, they can be and accomplish whatever they want. I am proud to be an example of that.

236

Q. Who do you think was the most influential person in your life?

A. My mother influenced me the most. When I was a year old, she started college. She had to raise five children primarily on her own, and so she couldn't take more than one class each semester. She didn't graduate until 22 years later, but she did finish. Her primary focus was the enjoyment of learning. That's what I got from her example.

Q. What were you interested in when you were in fifth grade?

A. When I was in the fifth grade, I think I wanted to be President. I got over that by the time I was in the sixth grade. I didn't think that I would be an astronaut. But you never know how your interests will change. That's why it's important never to shut down your options. In college, I changed my major five times. I started college interested in music and business and graduated with a degree in physics. I didn't actually pursue becoming an astronaut until graduate school, when I learned about the kinds of skills NASA was looking for in potential astronauts.

237

Q. Why did you want to go into space?

A. I can't imagine not wanting to go into space. But I never considered being an astronaut as an option because when I was growing up there were no female astronauts. It wasn't until the first six female astronauts were selected in 1978 that women could even think of it as a possible career path.

Q. What is it like to operate a robot arm in space?

A. I have worked the robot arm on all three of my space missions, and I really love it. It's challenging to do, but lots of fun. On my last mission to the space station I worked with the help of cameras and monitors because we were docked in a way that prevented me from seeing the robot arm. This made things more difficult, but then again, everything I've done on actual missions in space has always been easier than when I first tried it during training.

Q. What is NASA training like?

A. Everything is always harder to do in training. In training, we prepare for anything that could happen on a space mission—anything that could go wrong. In training, things keep breaking, problems have to be solved. Nothing has ever gone wrong on any of my missions, and our training helps us make sure that nothing will. Each mission has its own specific purpose. For my last mission, we trained for nine months before the actual flight. I started my formal NASA training in 1990. During that period I spent about half of the time in training; the other half I spent performing other duties. I was in training for three years before my first mission, which isn't that long of a wait. Some astronauts have waited 10, even 16 years before they finally go into space!

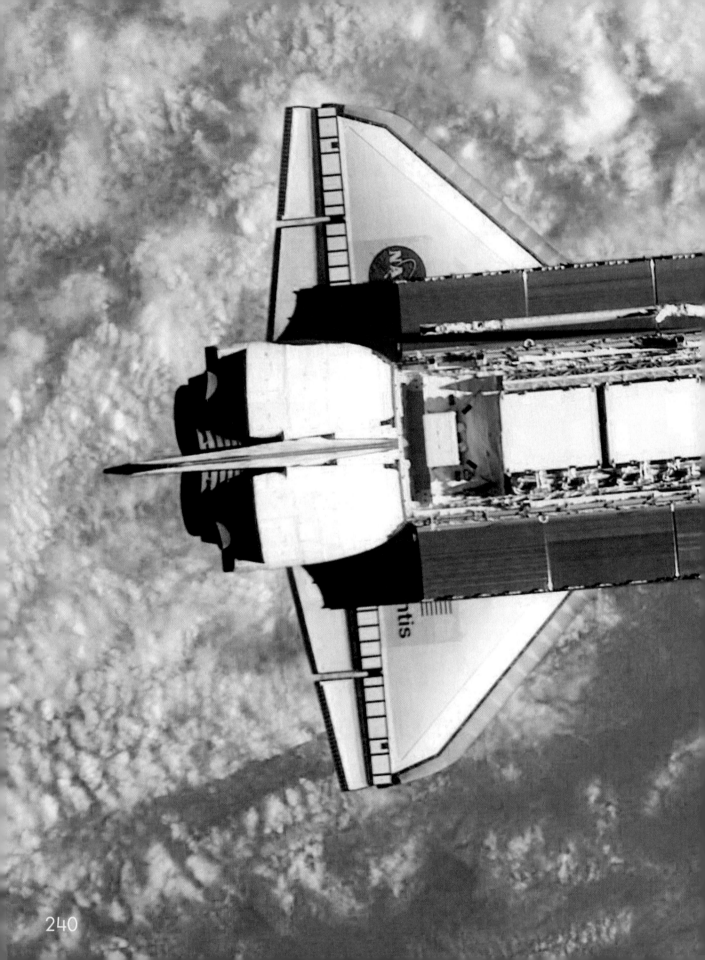

Q. What is it like to float in zero gravity?

A. Weightlessness is the fun part of the mission. There is really nothing to compare it to on Earth. I guess the closest thing would be swimming or scuba diving. It's a similar freedom of movement. What is odd is that weightlessness seems more natural. You don't have the same kinds of sensations in space as you do in the water.

Q. How do you sleep on the space shuttle? Does everyone sleep at the same time, or do you take turns? Do you have weird dreams because you're sleeping in space?

A. On my first two missions we slept in two shifts. We had sleeping compartments that looked like coffins. On my last mission we slept in a single shift. Instead of the sleeping compartments, we slept in what can best be described as a sleeping bag with hooks. You would find a place to hook on to and float in. As for my dreaming, it isn't that different in space. I tend to dream a lot, whether I'm in space or at home on Earth. I have floating dreams on Earth and non-floating dreams on a mission in space.

Q. What does Earth look like from space?

A. That's a really hard question. You have to remember that the shuttle is moving at five miles a second, so the Earth looks very different depending on where you are in space in relation to the position above Earth and what time of day it is. I have to say, though, Earth looks very much like I expected it to look. The *Imax* films are pretty close to what Earth really looks like from space. The main difference is that the colors are much more vivid when you're in space.

Q. How do you eat in space? Do you have to eat food out of a toothpaste tube? Does the food taste good?

A. Astronauts haven't eaten food out of tubes for over twenty years. Most of the food now is freeze-dried. All we do is add hot water. We eat a variety of foods, including nuts, granola, cookies, dried fruit, tortillas. We have drinks that we add water to as well.

242

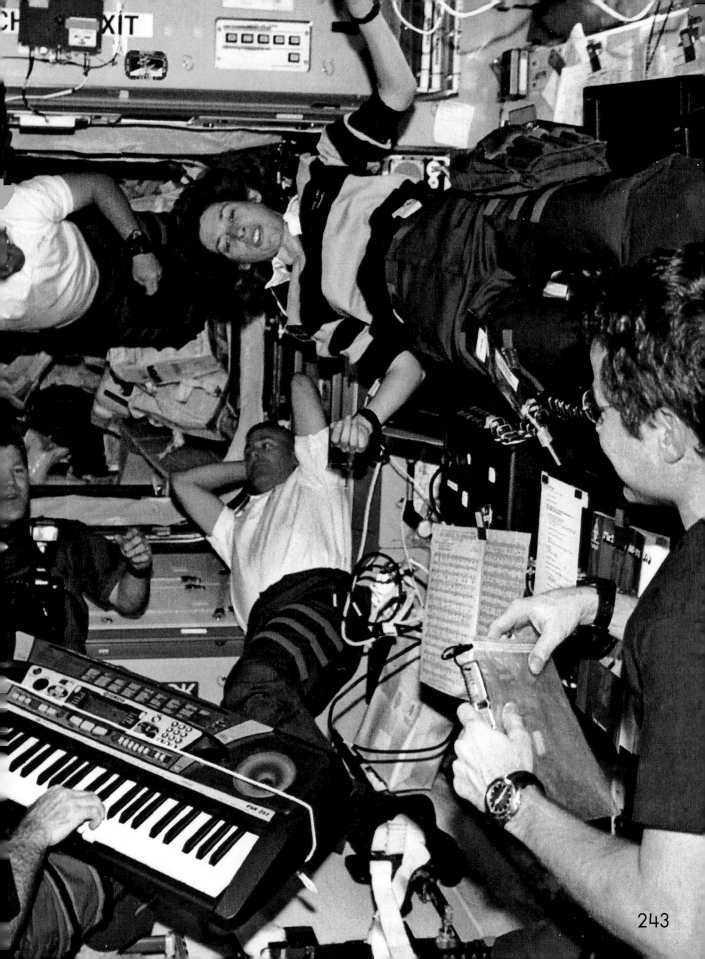

Q. Is it hard being an astronaut and a mother? Do you worry about going into space now that you're a mother? How does your son feel about your going into space?

A. I think it's hard being anything and a mother. Both are full-time jobs, and you have to work very hard at both to do a good job. Personally, I find both jobs wonderful. It is hard to be separated from my husband and son when I go on a mission, and I miss them a great deal. But lots of people have to be away from their families because of their jobs. Right now my son is only eighteen months old, so the last time I went into space, he didn't really know what was going on. I think it will be much harder the next time, since he will understand more.

Q. Can you talk to your family from space?

A. Yes, thanks to e-mail, when I am in space my husband and I are able to communicate every day—which is very nice. And on missions lasting more than ten days, we are allowed to visit with each other by having a video conference from space.

Q. What is the scariest thing that ever happened to you in space?

A. There's never really been anything for me to be scared of because nothing has ever gone wrong on any of my missions. For me, going into space is very exciting, not scary. The riskiest part of the flight is the launch because it's the phase of the flight when things are most likely to go wrong. But like I said, there have never been problems on my missions, and besides, we are trained to handle any problems that might come along.

Q. Do you think communication with extraterrestrials is possible? Do you think there are other life-forms out there?

A. I'm not really sure if communication is possible right now, with the technology we have today. Given the number of stars that have been discovered in the last couple of years, it isn't inconceivable that life exists on other planets. Though it is important to differentiate between life that is single-celled and life-forms that are intelligent and capable of communication.

Q. I love math and I want to become an astronaut. What can I start to do to prepare myself?

A. It's good that you love math, because in order to be an astronaut, a college degree in math or a technical science is very important to have. Being an astronaut isn't just the science, though. An astronaut must be both a team player and a leader as well. You should get involved in activities where you work closely with other people—because working closely with other people is an essential part of being an astronaut!

Common Core State Standards
Informational Text 1. Quote accurately from a text when explaining what the text says explicitly and when drawing inferences from the text. **Also Informational Text 8., Writing 8., 9.**

Envision It! | Retell

Think Critically

1. Ellen Ochoa tells how role models, interests, options, and teamwork apply to her life. How might they apply to your life? Text to Self

2. Suppose you were going to interview a famous adventurer. How might the questions in "Talk with an Astronaut" help you think up good questions for the interview?
Think Like an Author

3. One purpose of an interview is to gather facts about someone. Another purpose is to gather opinions. What are some of Ellen Ochoa's opinions? Use examples from the interview to explain your answer.
Author's Purpose

4. How is weightlessness like swimming? How is it different? Use quotes from the interview and your own knowledge to explain your answer. Monitor and Clarify

5. Look Back and Write Go back to page 238. Why is training harder than the actual space mission? Provide evidence to support your answer.
Key Ideas and Details • Text Evidence

Ellen Ochoa

Ellen Ochoa grew up in La Mesa, California. She received a degree in physics from San Diego State University and a Ph.D. from Stanford University. Some of her professors discouraged women from going into math and science, but she knew she could succeed.

At Stanford, Dr. Ochoa focused on the area where she would make her name: optical information systems. She developed ways for computers to "see" objects and analyze them. In 1987 she applied to the NASA astronaut program but was rejected. Rather than letting this get her down, Dr. Ochoa got her pilot's license! In 1990 NASA accepted her application.

In 1993 Dr. Ochoa became the first Hispanic woman to enter outer space. In four missions in space, she has researched issues such as the effect of the sun on Earth's atmosphere and has visited the International Space Station.

Dr. Ochoa lives with her husband and their two children. In her spare time she flies planes, plays volleyball, and goes bicycling. An accomplished flutist, she has even played her flute in space!

Here are other books about exploring space.

Space Station Science: Life in Free Fall by Marianne J. Dyson

To Space & Back by Sally Ride

Use the *Reader's and Writer's Notebook* to record your independent reading.

Common Core State Standards
Writing 2. Write informative/explanatory texts to examine a topic and convey ideas and information clearly. **Also Writing 2.b., Language 1.**

Biographical Sketch

A **biographical sketch** captures a moment in the life of a real person. It tells about one incident in a person's life, rather than the person's entire life. The student model on the next page is an example of a biographical sketch.

Writing Prompt Think about someone you know or someone you would want to know more about. Now write a biographical sketch about that person.

Let's Write It!

Key Features of a Biographical Sketch

- tells about a real person's life
- uses precise language and sensory details
- can show the subject's personality

READING STREET ONLINE
GRAMMAR JAMMER
www.ReadingStreet.com

Writer's Checklist

Remember, you should . . .

✓ tell about an event in the person's life.

✓ organize information in a logical way.

✓ use quotations to bring the person's thoughts to life.

✓ include specific facts, details, and examples.

My Cousin Ian

My cousin Ian loves animals. One day, he said to his parents, "Can I raise a helper dog? I think I would do a good job." Helper dogs are pets that are raised by families for a few years. Those dogs then go into training to become guide dogs or other dogs that help people.

His parents told Ian that it was a lot of work to raise this kind of a dog. Ian was determined. He said, "I will bring that dog with me everywhere I go. This way, the dog can become used to people, crowds, and loud noises."

Since he was willing to put in the work, Ian's parents got him a fuzzy yellow puppy-in-training. Ian named her Tonia. He took that dog with him everywhere: noisy soccer meets, festivals, and even the school picnic. (Ian had school permission, of course!)

After two years, Ian had to return Tonia to the training center. There she was reunited with her brother and sister; all of these dogs were to be trained as helper dogs. Ian felt sad, but knew he was doing the right thing.

Genre
Biographical sketches tell about an incident in a person's life.

Writing Trait Sentences
Quotations help show the subject's personality.

This, that, these, and those are used correctly.

Conventions

This, That, These, and *Those*

Remember *This, that, these,* and *those* are adjectives that tell which one or which ones. They make nouns and pronouns more specific. (For example, *Which dog is your favorite?* **That** *dog is my favorite.*)

Common Core State Standards

Informational Text 7. Draw on information from multiple print or digital sources, demonstrating the ability to locate an answer to a question quickly or to solve a problem efficiently.

Also Informational Text 10.

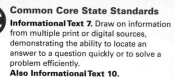

21st Century Skills
INTERNET GUY

Directories have large amounts of information. They organize things for you. Look for the link to the category you need. Then follow the links. Bookmark useful directories.

- Online directories list links to many Web sites that can help you learn about a topic.

- You can search for topics by keywords. Type a keyword into the search box and click on the search button.

- The search will list links to Web sites. Web sites can be written in a businesslike, or formal, way. They can also be written in informal language.

- Read "Women Astronauts." Think about if the language used is formal or informal.

Women Astronauts

Let's say you want to find out more about women astronauts. You go to an online directory on the Internet. Here are some of the topics you find listed there.

250

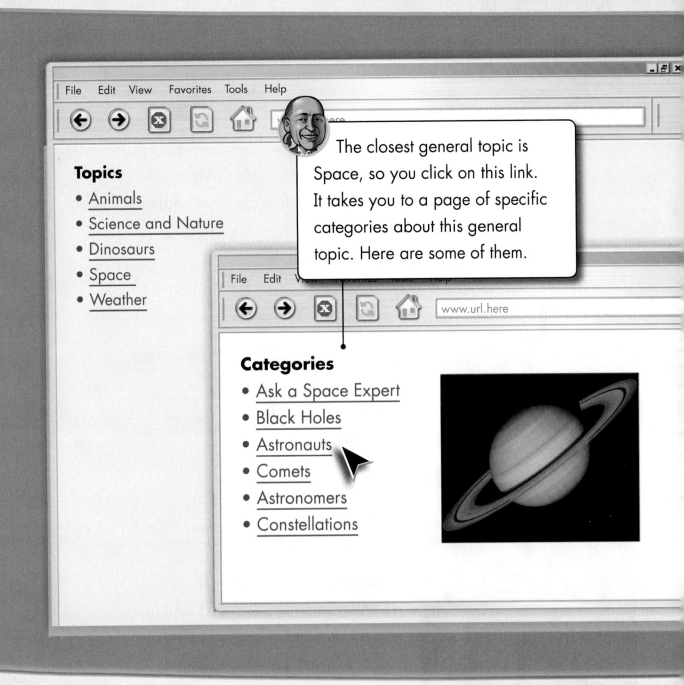

Topics
- Animals
- Science and Nature
- Dinosaurs
- Space
- Weather

The closest general topic is Space, so you click on this link. It takes you to a page of specific categories about this general topic. Here are some of them.

Categories
- Ask a Space Expert
- Black Holes
- Astronauts
- Comets
- Astronomers
- Constellations

When you click on <u>Astronauts</u>, you get a list of Web sites. You decide to click on this one:

Jemison, Mae

Sites

1. **Astronaut Bio: Mae Jemison**—Facts of her life, education, experience, from the National Science Foundation.

2. **NASA: Dr. Mae Jemison**—Read about the first woman of color to go into space, from NASA Quest.

3. **Women of The Hall—Mae Jemison**—Read about this medical doctor, engineer, and astronaut.

Here is what you get:

Mae Jemison

Hometown:
Chicago, Illinois

Greatest Achievement:
Mae Jemison is the first African American woman chosen by NASA to be a Space Shuttle astronaut.

How She Did It:
From her earliest years, Mae planned to be a scientist. Her parents

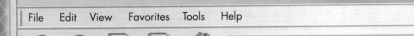
encouraged her to do her best, and she knew she had the ability to do just about anything she wanted. She earned a degree in engineering and then in medicine. Before she became an astronaut, Mae worked as a doctor in West Africa. Mae Jemison is a strong, determined person who used school to help her become a doctor, an engineer, and an astronaut—a real science star!

What She Says:

"Don't let anyone rob you of your imagination, your creativity, or your curiosity. It's your place in the world; it's your life. Go on and do all you can with it, and make it the life you want to live."

Common Core State Standards

Language 4. Determine or clarify the meaning of unknown and multiple-meaning words and phrases based on grade 5 reading and content, choosing flexibly from a range of strategies. **Also Foundational Skills 4.b., Speaking/Listening 6., Language 4.a.**

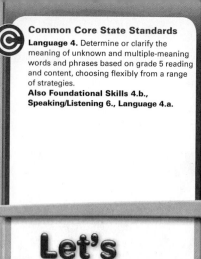

Let's Learn It!

READING STREET ONLINE
ONLINE STUDENT EDITION
www.ReadingStreet.com

Vocabulary

Multiple-Meaning Words

Context Clues Some words have more than one meaning. You can use context clues to help you determine which meaning is used. Think of all the meanings of the word. Then decide which meaning makes the most sense in the sentence.

Practice It! Reread *Talk with an Astronaut*. Find as many words as you can that have more than one meaning, and then determine their meanings. Copy a sentence from the story that has a multiple-meaning word in it. Then write a sentence of your own that uses another meaning of the word.

Fluency

Accuracy

Partner Reading You can increase your reading accuracy by previewing a story. Look at the story to identify unfamiliar words. Look up their meanings and pronunciations in a dictionary. Then practice saying each word aloud two or three times so that you can read it accurately in the story.

Practice It! With a partner, practice reading aloud *Talk with an Astronaut*. Preview the words on the page to make sure you understand all the words and know how to pronounce them. If you need help, use a dictionary. Have one partner read a question while the other partner reads the answer. Then switch roles.

254

Listening and Speaking

Get Ready For Middle School

When you tell a story, vary your speaking rate and the volume of your voice.

Storytelling

A tall tale is a humorous and exaggerated version of a heroic story, sometimes based on real characters and facts. The purpose of a tall tale is to entertain the reader or listener.

Practice It! With a partner, create a tall tale about an imaginary adventure in outer space. Fill your tall tale with exaggerations and surprising details. Describe the main character and the action of the story using vivid language. Use gestures and facial expressions to make your story funny and interesting. With your partner, tell the story to the class.

Tips

Listening . . .

• Listen to the speaker's message.

• Watch the speaker's face and hand gestures to interpret what's happening in the story.

• Ask questions to understand the character's point of view.

Speaking . . .

• Use enunciation and gestures to communicate effectively.

• Speed up and slow down your speaking rate to match what's happening in the story.

• Speak loudly to communicate adventure and excitement in the story.

Teamwork . . .

• Participate in discussions by eliciting suggestions from your partner.

• Identify points of agreement and disagreement in your discussion.

Common Core State Standards

Language 6. Acquire and use accurately grade-appropriate general academic and domain-specific words and phrases, including those that signal contrast, addition, and other logical relationships (e.g., *however, although, nevertheless, similarly, moreover, in addition*).

Also Speaking/Listening 1.d.

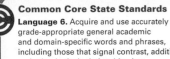

Oral Vocabulary

Let's Talk About

Adventures Underground

- Describe ideas about underground adventures.

- Listen to and ask questions about a classmate's ideas of underground adventures.

- Determine classmates' main and supporting ideas about underground adventures.

READING STREET ONLINE
CONCEPT TALK VIDEO
www.ReadingStreet.com

Common Core State Standards

Informational Text 3. Explain the relationships or interactions between two or more individuals, events, ideas, or concepts in a historical, scientific, or technical text based on specific information in the text. **Also Informational Text 1., 2.**

Envision It! | Skill Strategy

Skill

Strategy

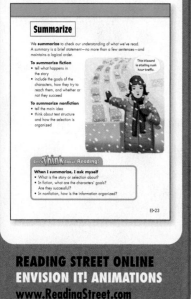

READING STREET ONLINE
ENVISION IT! ANIMATIONS
www.ReadingStreet.com

Comprehension Skill

Cause and Effect

- A cause (why something happens) may have several effects. An effect (what happens as a result of the cause) may have several causes.

- A text may be organized by cause-and-effect relationships among ideas.

- Sometimes clue words such as *since, as a result, caused, thus,* and *therefore* are used to show cause-and-effect relationships.

- Use a graphic organizer like the one below to help you record causes and effects. Then analyze how the cause-and-effect pattern in "Earth" influences the relationships among ideas in the text.

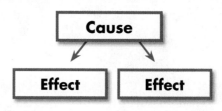

Comprehension Strategy

Summarize

Summarizing—telling what a story or article is about—helps you understand and remember what you read. It also helps you figure out main ideas and find important supporting details. As you summarize "Earth," it is important to maintain the meaning and logical order in the text.

EARTH

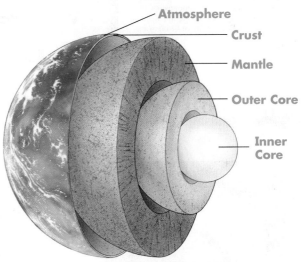

Atmosphere
Crust
Mantle
Outer Core
Inner Core

Until about sixty years ago, we didn't know much about the inside of the Earth. Then we invented drills called seismographs to measure movements below the surface. As scientists used these instruments to study what lies below ground, they learned more about what is inside the Earth.

The Earth is made of three layers. The outer layer is the *crust*, the middle layer is the *mantle*, and the center layer is the *core*.

The crust is the thinnest layer. It is hard and can break. The crust is also the coolest layer.

The mantle is hotter and thicker than the crust. Even though the mantle does not get hot enough to melt, it does get hot enough for rocks to move. This movement causes volcanoes and earthquakes.

The core has two sections. The outer core is a liquid. The liquid spins as the Earth spins, causing the Earth's magnetic field. The inner core is hard rock. The core is the hottest layer of the Earth.

Skill How does the cause-and-effect pattern in this paragraph show the relationship among ideas?

Skill What causes earthquakes and volcanoes? What clue word is used?

Strategy Summarize the text while maintaining its meaning and order.

Your Turn!

Need a Review? See the *Envision It! Handbook* for additional help with cause and effect and how to summarize.

Ready to Try It? Use what you have learned about cause and effect and how to summarize as you read *Journey to the Center of the Earth.*

Common Core State Standards
Language 4.a. Use context (e.g., cause/effect relationships and comparisons in text) as a clue to the meaning of a word or phrase. **Also Foundational Skills 4.c., Language 4.**

Envision It! | Words to Know

armor

plunged

serpent

encases

extinct

hideous

Vocabulary Strategy for

🎯 Unfamiliar Words

Context Clues As you read, you may come to a word you do not know. Look for clues in the context—the words and sentences around the word—to help you determine the meaning of the unfamiliar word.

1. Reread the sentence in which the unfamiliar word appears. Does the author include a synonym, an antonym, or other clue to the word's meaning?

2. If you need more help, read the sentences around the unfamiliar word.

3. Put the clues together and think of a logical meaning for the word. Does this meaning make sense in the sentence?

Read "The Land of Imagination" on page 261. Use context clues to help you determine and clarify the meaning of any unfamiliar words.

Words to Write Reread "The Land of Imagination." Write a description of the dinosaur you know the most about. Use words from the *Words to Know* list in your description.

The Land of Imagination

Dinosaurs are extinct creatures that used to roam the Earth. We can only imagine how the Earth quaked beneath the weight of these vanished creatures. Still, we have no trouble imagining them eating, drinking, or fighting with one another.

A beast like a serpent with legs, only many times larger, stands in the shallows of a warm ocean eating immense, strange water plants. On the shore, a hideous lizard with teeth like deadly knives stands on its powerful haunches. It roars as it charges the plant-eater. Soon both are plunged beneath the water, locked in a giant struggle. When they surface, the dying plant-eater's tormented cries echo through the trees.

Another dinosaur draws near. A thick, hornlike armor encases its thick body and long tail. These plates cover every square inch that the terrible lizard might attack. Angry-looking spikes bristle from its back as well. It waits to see if any dinner will be left for it. Did it really happen like this? We will never know for sure, but in the land of our imagination, it did.

Your Turn!

❚❚ Need a Review?
For additional help with context clues, see *Words!*

▶ Ready to Try It?
Read *Journey to the Center of the Earth* on pp. 262–273.

JOURNEY TO THE CENTER OF THE EARTH

by Jules Verne   illustrated by Marc Sasso

Question of the Week

How do we explore places underground?

Genre

A **novel** is an extended work of fiction that contains story elements such as plot and setting. As you read this excerpt, note how the author creates the setting using sensory language.

In 1864, when this story was written, people did not know what the center of the Earth was made of. One science fiction writer, Jules Verne, imagined what it might be like. In Verne's story, Professor von Hardwigg discovers a crater in Finland that leads to the very center of the Earth and sets out with his nephew, Harry, and a guide, Hans, to explore it. They descend many miles downward. Finally, they reach a deep ocean and decide to explore it on a raft. Young Harry keeps a diary of their adventures.

Tuesday, August 20.

At last it is evening—the time of day when we feel a great need to sleep. Of course, in this continuing light, there is no night, but we are very tired. Hans remains at the rudder, his eyes never closed. I don't know when he sleeps: but I find I am dozing, myself.

And then . . . an awful shock! The raft seems to have struck some hidden rock. It is lifted right out of the water and even seems to be thrown some distance. "Eh!" cries my uncle. "What's happening?" And Hans raises his hand and points to where, about two hundred yards away, a great black mass is heaving. Then I know my worst fears have been realized.

"It's some . . . monster!" I cry.

"Yes," cries the Professor, "and over there is a huge sea lizard!"

"And beyond it . . . a crocodile! But who ever saw such a crocodile! Such hideous jaws! Such terrible teeth!"

"And a whale!" the Professor shouts. "See those enormous fins! And see how it blows air and water!"

And indeed two columns of water rise from the surface of the sea as he speaks, reaching an immense height before they fall back into the sea with an enormous crash. The whole cave in which this great sea is set, its walls and roof invisible to us, echoes with the sound of it. We are at the center of the most tremendous uproar! And then we see—and how tiny we feel! —

that we are in the middle of a great circle of these creatures. Here, a turtle, forty feet wide: here, a serpent even longer, its ghastly head peering out of the water. Wherever we look, there are more of them: great teeth, frightful eyes, great coiling bodies! They are everywhere! I snatch up my rifle and think at once how useless it is. What effect would a bullet have on the armor that encases the bodies of these monsters?

There seems no hope for us. Though, suddenly, most of the creatures have plunged under the surface and are no longer to be seen, they leave behind a mighty crocodile and a prodigious sea serpent: and they are making toward us, and the end seems near. I think that, useless though it is, I will fire a shot. But Hans makes a sign for me to wait. For these monsters, having come so close to the raft, suddenly turn and make a rush at each other. In their fury they appear not to have seen us. And at that moment we realize how very small we are. To their great eyes, we must seem nothing bigger than an inch or so of floating scrap.

And so, in a thunder of broken water, the battle begins. At first I think all the other creatures have come to the surface and are taking part. *There* is a whale!—*there* a lizard!—a turtle!—and other monsters for which I can find no name. I point them out to Hans. But he shakes his head.

"*Tva!*" he cries.

"*Tva?* Two? Why does he say two? There are more than two!" I cry.

"No, Hans is right," says my uncle. "One of those monsters has the snout of a porpoise, the head of a lizard, the teeth of a crocodile . . . It is the ichthyosaurus, or great fish lizard."

"And the other?"

"The other is a serpent, but it has a turtle's shell. It is the plesiosaurus, or sea crocodile."

He is right! There seem to be half a dozen monsters, or more, but the truth is there are only two!

269

And ours are the first human eyes ever to look at these great primitive reptiles! I am amazed by the flaming red eyes of the ichthyosaurus, each bigger than a man's head. Those eyes, I know, are of enormous strength, since they have to resist the pressure of water at the very bottom of the ocean. The creature is a hundred feet long, at least, and when I see his tail rise out of the water, angrily flicked like the hugest whip you could imagine, I can guess at his width. His jaw is larger than I'd ever dreamed a jaw could be, and I remembered that naturalists have said the jaw of the ichthyosaurus must have contained at least one hundred and eighty-two teeth. They were making their calculations, of course, from the fossilized bones of creatures they imagined had been extinct for millions of years. Now I, and Hans, and the Professor, are gazing, from our tiny raft, at a living ichthyosaurus, rising from an ocean deep inside the Earth!

The other creature is the mighty plesiosaurus, a serpent with a trunk like an immensely long cylinder, and a short thick tail and fins like the banks of oars in a Roman galley. Its body is enclosed in a shell, and its neck, flexible as a swan's, rises thirty feet above the surface of the sea.

No other human being has ever seen such a combat! They raise mountains of water, and time and again the raft seems about to be upset. Time and again we imagine we are drowned. The creatures hiss at each other—and the hissing is worse than the sound of the wildest winds you can imagine, all blowing together. Then they seize each other in a terrible grip, giant wrestlers: and then, break away again. And again comes the great hissing, the furious disturbance of the water!

And in the middle of it all, how tiny we are! We crouch on the raft, expecting that any moment it will be overturned and we shall drown in that wildly disturbed sea, hundreds of miles below the surface of the Earth: far, far from the sky, trees, the blessed fresh air!

And then, suddenly, ichthyosaurus and plesiosaurus disappear together under the waves. Their going down, in one enormous plunge, draws the sea down with them, as if a great hole had been made in the water, and we are nearly dragged down with them. For a while there is silence. The water grows calmer. And then, not far from the raft, an enormous shape appears. It is the head of the plesiosaurus.

The monster is mortally wounded. All we can make out is its neck, a serpent's. It is twisted and coiled in the agonies of death. With it the creature strikes the water as if with some great whip. Then it wriggles, as some vast worm might do, cut in two. Every dreadful movement stirs the sea violently, and we are nearly blinded as the tormented water sweeps over the raft. But bit by bit the great writhings die down, and at last the plesiosaurus lies dead on the surface.

As for the ichthyosaurus, he was surely recovering from the struggle in some deep cave. He could not have been unhurt. He must need to lick his wounds.

Or was he on his way to the surface again, to destroy us?

Common Core State Standards
Literature 1. Quote accurately from a text when explaining what the text says explicitly and when drawing inferences from the text. **Also Literature 2., Writing 8., 9.**

Envision It! | Retell

READING STREET ONLINE
STORY SORT
www.ReadingStreet.com

Think Critically

1. The story you just read is a very dramatic and exciting adventure. Compare this story to *The Skunk Ladder*. How are the two adventures the same? What makes them different? You can compare and contrast different qualities, such as the stories' pictures, their characters, or how the stories were written. **Text to Text**

2. Jules Verne wrote *Journey to the Center of the Earth* more than a century ago, yet his science fiction stories are still popular. What elements in his writing make people still want to read his stories today? **Think Like an Author**

3. Why does Harry think there are more than half a dozen monsters when there are only two? **Cause and Effect**

4. Summarize the big battle at sea in your own words. Begin by telling who the fighters are and where the battle takes place. **Summarize**

5. **Look Back and Write** Look back at the battle scene on pages 269–273. The two monsters are made of different parts. List each of the monsters' parts. Provide evidence to support your answer.

Key Ideas and Details • Text Evidence

274

Meet the Author

JULES VERNE

Jules Verne was born in France in 1828. He studied to become a lawyer, but from the beginning he knew he would be a better writer than lawyer. He is one of the most translated authors of all time, and his books are read throughout the world.

Journey to the Center of the Earth is just one of his stories about extraordinary voyages. The source of the story probably was the "hollow Earth" theory that was being talked about in France at the time. There was growing interest in geology and in the seismograph, a machine invented in 1855 to measure earthquakes.

Once, when he was asked about his work habits, Jules Verne answered that he got up at five and worked for three hours before breakfast. Although he would work another couple of hours later in the day, he said his stories had "nearly all been written when most folks are sleeping."

Mr. Verne's books are a mix of fact and fantasy. They combine science with action and adventure. He created what he called a "novel of science," or "scientific novel." Today we call the genre science fiction. In modern times, many of his books, including *Journey to the Center of the Earth*, have been made into movies.

Here are other science fiction books you might enjoy.

A Wrinkle in Time by Madeleine L'Engle

20,000 Leagues Under the Sea by Jules Verne

Use the *Reader's and Writer's Notebook* to record your independent reading.

275

Common Core State Standards
Writing 1. Write opinion pieces on topics or texts, supporting a point of view with reasons and information.
Also Writing 1.a., 1.b., 4., Language 1.

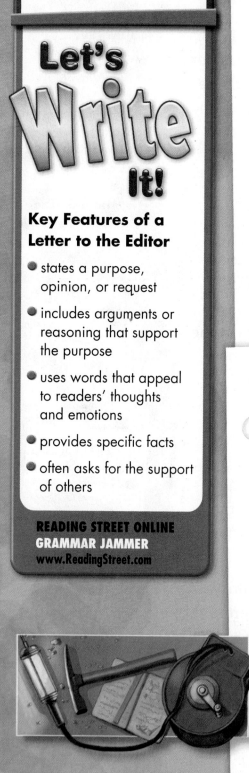

Let's Write It!

Key Features of a Letter to the Editor

- states a purpose, opinion, or request

- includes arguments or reasoning that support the purpose

- uses words that appeal to readers' thoughts and emotions

- provides specific facts

- often asks for the support of others

READING STREET ONLINE
GRAMMAR JAMMER
www.ReadingStreet.com

Letter to the Editor

A **letter to the editor** is a persuasive text written to a newspaper editor. The purpose of the letter is to convince others to support an idea. The student model on the next page is an example of a letter to the editor.

Writing Prompt Think about something that you want a parent or another adult to agree with. Now write a letter to the editor of a newspaper about it, using facts and details.

Writer's Checklist

Remember, you should . . .

☑ establish a position.

☑ include sound reasoning.

☑ support your position with evidence.

☑ include consideration of alternatives.

☑ use comparative and superlative adjectives to strengthen your argument.

276

To the Editor:

Our school can and should do more to help our Earth and save resources. Helping the planet also saves money.

First, I think everyone in the school should try harder to turn off lights when leaving a room. The last one out should shut off the lights to save on electricity costs. I am willing to create signs to place above each light switch.

Second, if people in charge turned down the heat just one degree, the school would save on heating costs. Although students and teachers might argue that they will be colder, we can make sure to close doors and keep out drafts. Also, we can bring sweaters to school to stay warm.

If we make just these small changes, we can make a big difference for our planet. We will also feel better about ourselves because we will all work together to help make our school greener. Maybe we can have the greenest school around if we try hard enough!

Alex Chadwick

Maple Tree Elementary

Writing Trait Voice This letter is written for a specific audience and purpose.

Genre A letter to the editor supports a position with logical arguments.

Comparative and superlative adjectives are used correctly.

Conventions

Comparative and Superlative Adjectives

Remember Comparative adjectives compare two things (*cleaner, better, worse*). **Superlative adjectives** compare three or more things (*cleanest, best, worst*).

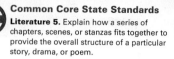

Science in Reading

Genre
Drama

- A drama is a story that is written to be acted in front of an audience. It includes dialogue, or lines that the characters speak to one another.

- A drama will also include descriptions of scenes or settings. This will let you know where and when the play takes place.

- Read "The Sea Battle." As you read, think about ways it is similar to and different from Jules Verne's *Journey to the Center of the Earth.*

The Sea Battle

from *Journey to the Center of the Earth* by Jules Verne

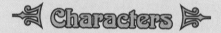 **Characters**

Professor von Hardwigg, a scientist
Harry, his nephew
Hans, their guide

Harry, Professor von Hardwigg, and Hans are on a small raft, adrift on an ocean. Hans is working the rudder. Von Hardwigg is curled up, asleep. Harry is dozing sitting up.

HARRY: *(jerking awake)* What? Where am I? Oh, the raft. I must have dozed off.

HANS: Yes. It was a hard day, Harry. But with the continuous light at this latitude, you can't tell when it is night.

HARRY: But you, Hans. You never seem to sleep. How do you do it?

HANS: *(with a shrug)* I am more used to these northern seasons, perhaps.

HARRY: Where are we? Can you tell anything?

HANS: Look. It is all water, water, water.

(There is a shock. All the men are jolted in their places.)

VON HARDWIGG: *(waking, sitting up)* Eh! What was that? What's happening?

HANS: Look, Professor! Over there!

HARRY: It's some . . . monster! Uncle, I was afraid something like this . . .

VON HARDWIGG: Yes, and over there is a huge sea lizard!

HARRY: And beyond it . . . a crocodile. But those jaws! Those teeth! Who ever saw such a . . .?

VON HARDWIGG: And a whale! See those enormous fins! How it blows air and water!

HARRY: We're surrounded by them! There are monsters all around us!

VON HARDWIGG: And the noise! Such an uproar they make!

HANS: I think . . . it's the cave we're in.

HARRY: But . . . we can't even see the walls or roof.

HANS: Even so, I think we're hearing echoes from the cries of these beasts.

VON HARDWIGG: Hans, what are we to do?

HANS: There is nothing . . .

HARRY: Where's my rifle?

Let's **Think** About...

How is the structure of this play different from the original text? **Drama**

Let's **Think** About...

Is this drama or the original text more exciting to you? Why? **Drama**

HANS: What good would that do? Look at the armor on their bodies.

HARRY: But I can try . . .

VON HARDWIGG: No, there they go . . . beneath the surface of the water.

HANS: But the waves they make! I can't control this raft at all. We're spinning around!

HARRY: I never thought before, Uncle . . . how small, how tiny we are . . . compared to those creatures!

VON HARDWIGG: And just think . . . ours are the first human eyes ever to look on them.

HANS: Here they come again!

HARRY: They're all back! The whale. The lizard. The turtle. The others . . . I have no name for them.

HANS: No . . . two.

HARRY: Two? What do you mean? There are more.

VON HARDWIGG: No, Hans is right. That one has a porpoise's snout, the head of a lizard, the teeth of a crocodile. It is the ichthyosaurus, or great fish lizard.

HARRY: Those flaming red eyes . . . they're bigger than my whole head!

HANS: And that tail is like a huge whip. If he hits us with it, this flimsy raft . . . we haven't a chance.

HARRY: And what's the other one, Uncle?

VON HARDWIGG: It's a serpent, but it has a turtle's shell. It's the plesiosaurus, or sea crocodile.

HARRY: Uncle, I think you're right.

VON HARDWIGG: We have thought these reptiles long extinct. A thrill for me, a scientist . . .

HANS: Well, whatever they're called, they're coming back, and they're headed our way.

VON HARDWIGG: We shall die . . . without a chance to tell the world . . . !

HARRY: No, wait . . . they're stopping.

HANS: They're looking at each other.

VON HARDWIGG: I think they're going to fight.

HANS: *(with a laugh)* They aren't after us at all. We must seem like nothing to them. . . .

VON HARDWIGG: There they go!

HARRY: They're attacking each other!

HANS: Hang on to whatever you can! We're in for some rough water!

(They all shout as the lights black out.)

Let's **Think** About...

Reading Across Texts *The Sea Battle* is an adaptation of Jules Verne's story. Think about all the similarities and differences between the two texts.

Writing Across Texts Write a paragraph comparing and contrasting the two selections. Use textual evidence.

Common Core State Standards

Language 4.a. Use context (e.g., cause/effect relationships and comparisons in text) as a clue to the meaning of a word or phrase. **Also Foundational Skills 4., Speaking/Listening 1.a., 4., Language 4.**

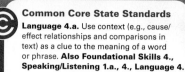

Let's Learn It!

READING STREET ONLINE
ONLINE STUDENT EDITION
www.ReadingStreet.com

Vocabulary

Unfamiliar Words

Context Clues Remember that you can use context clues to determine or clarify the meaning of an unfamiliar word by reading the words and sentences around it. Look for words or phrases that help you understand the meaning of the unfamiliar word.

Practice It! Find three or four unfamiliar words in *Journey to the Center of the Earth*. Look for context clues that give you ideas about each word's meaning. Based on these clues, write each word and what you think it means. Check your definitions in a dictionary.

Fluency

Appropriate Phrasing/ Punctuation Clues

Partner Reading Reading with appropriate phrasing means grouping words together to make sense of what you read. Use punctuation as a guide to help you with phrasing. When you read, group together words that are set off with commas. Remember to stop after a period at the end of a sentence. Appropriate phrasing can help you read aloud with comprehension.

Practice It! With your partner, practice reading aloud *Journey to the Center of the Earth*. As you read, identify the punctuation on the page. Pause for commas and stop at periods. Give your partner feedback to help improve phrasing and comprehension of the story and its plot.

Listening and Speaking

Interpret Fiction

When you interpret fiction, you look at the features and elements of a story. Science fiction stories involve new scientific ideas, along with traditional literary features, such as plot, characters, setting, and figurative language. The purpose of science fiction is to show a different point of view about the world.

Practice It! With a partner, prepare a presentation about *Journey to the Center of the Earth*. Evaluate the impact of Verne's use of figurative language. Then describe the characters, plot, and setting of the story. Include details in your description. Finally, share your presentation with the class.

Tips

Listening . . .

- Listen to and interpret the speaker's message about the story.

- Determine the main ideas and supporting ideas in the speaker's message.

Speaking . . .

- To make a comparison as you speak, use comparative and superlative adjectives (*good; better; best*).

- Enunciate clearly and speak at a natural rate.

Teamwork . . .

- Ask your partner for suggestions with interpreting fiction.

- Consider suggestions from your partner.

- Identify points of agreement and disagreement about science fiction and literary features.

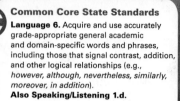

Common Core State Standards

Language 6. Acquire and use accurately grade-appropriate general academic and domain-specific words and phrases, including those that signal contrast, addition, and other logical relationships (e.g., *however, although, nevertheless, similarly, moreover, in addition*).

Also Speaking/Listening 1.d.

Oral Vocabulary

Let's Talk About

the California Gold Rush

- Share what you know about the California Gold Rush.

- Listen to a classmate discuss the Gold Rush.

- Determine main and supporting ideas in your classmates' messages about the Gold Rush.

READING STREET ONLINE
CONCEPT TALK VIDEO
www.ReadingStreet.com

Common Core State Standards

Informational Text 1. Quote accurately from a text when explaining what the text says explicitly and when drawing inferences from the text. **Also Informational Text 8.**

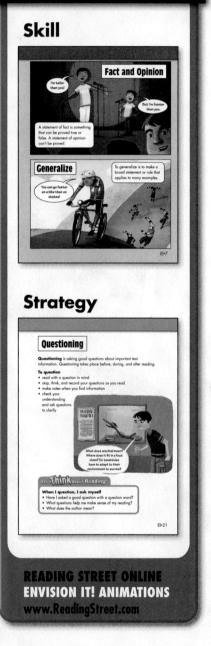

Comprehension Skill

Generalize

- To generalize means to make an inference that applies to several examples.

- Sometimes authors make generalizations in their writing. Clue words such as *all, many,* and *most* can signal generalizations.

- *Valid generalizations* are supported by the text or logic. *Faulty generalizations* are not supported by the text or logic.

- Use a graphic organizer like the one below to determine if the generalization in the final paragraph in "The Gold Rush" is *valid* or *faulty.*

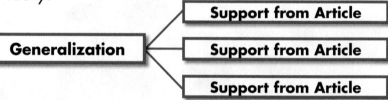

Comprehension Strategy

Questioning

As you read, it is important to ask different types of questions. When you ask an evaluative question, you make a judgment about what you read. Begin reading by asking a question about the author's purpose. Ask yourself why an author chose to write something.

THE GOLD RUSH

Abraham Lincoln described the western United States in the mid-1800s as the "treasure house of the nation." Why? People had found large, abundant amounts of gold, silver, and other precious metals there.

The first large amount, or lode, of gold was found near the Sacramento River in California in 1848 by John Sutter and James Marshall. They tried to hide their discovery, but soon people found out. By 1849, about eighty thousand people were in the area searching for gold. Many Americans had caught gold fever!

A lode of silver was found in 1859 in Nevada. Discovered on a property owned by Henry Comstock, it became known as the Comstock Lode. Many people got rich from the Comstock Lode. Grubby miners turned into instant millionaires. George Hearst and a group of friends made ninety thousand dollars in two months. One deposit, known as The Big Bonanza, produced more than one million dollars worth of gold and silver.

Many towns were built and destroyed by the Gold Rush. Towns such as Virginia City, Nevada, and Cripple Creek, Colorado, sprang up almost overnight. While the gold or silver lasted, the towns were successful. When the gold or silver was used up, however, many towns became deserted.

Skill Notice the three examples in the last sentence. From them, what generalization did Abraham Lincoln make about the West in the mid-1800s?

Strategy Evaluate what you have learned about the Gold Rush. Do you have any other questions? Will your questions help you recall what you've read?

Skill What generalization is made in this paragraph? Is this generalization valid or faulty? How can you tell?

Your Turn!

Need a Review? See the *Envision It! Handbook* for additional help with generalizations and questioning.

Ready to Try It? Use what you have learned about generalizations and questioning as you read *Ghost Towns of the American West*.

Envision It! | Words to Know

economic

independence

vacant

overrun

scrawled

Vocabulary Strategy for

Prefixes *over-, in-*

Word Structure Recognizing a prefix's meaning can help you determine the word's meaning. One of the meanings for the Old English prefix *over-* is "too much." A room that's *overcrowded* is "too crowded." The Latin prefix *in-* can mean "not." People who are *insensitive* are "not sensitive." Choose one of the *Words to Know*, and then follow these steps.

1. Look for a base word you know.

2. Check to see if a prefix has been added.

3. Ask yourself how the prefix changes the meaning of the base word.

4. Try the meaning in the sentence. Does it make sense?

Read "The Sky's the Limit" on page 289. Look for words with *in-* and *over-*. Use the prefixes to determine the meanings of the words.

Words to Write Reread "The Sky's the Limit." Imagine you are a reporter in the 1800s. Write an article describing why people are moving West, and how that is leading to the creation of boom towns. Use words from the *Words to Know* list.

The Sky's the Limit

Independence has always been an important value to people who live in the United States. It has been a cornerstone of American life ever since the Founding Fathers scrawled their signatures at the bottom of the Declaration of Independence.

Independence refers to people's freedoms, of course. But it also refers to their headlong way of pursuing prosperity. From all over the world, people have flocked to America in search of freedom. But many also have hoped to become rich. The building of America has been based on economic success and muscle as much as it has been based on armies and government.

This will to "make a better life" was behind the wagon trains that ventured into the West during the nineteenth century. It drove the settling of boom towns—towns that were overrun by miners. These towns grew quickly, died quickly, and soon became nothing but vacant buildings and empty streets. Every miner believed that he or she could strike it rich. The spread of railroads, then highways, recalled this theme. Every freight train chugged a message: "The sky's the limit!"

Your Turn!

❚❚ Need a Review?
For additional help with prefixes, see *Words!*

▶ Ready to Try It?
Read *Ghost Towns of the American West* on pp. 290–301.

GHOST TOWNS OF THE AMERICAN WEST

Question of the Week

What adventures helped drive westward expansion?

Genre

Expository texts explain a person, a thing, or an idea. Notice how the author maintains logical order to explain how ghost towns came to be.

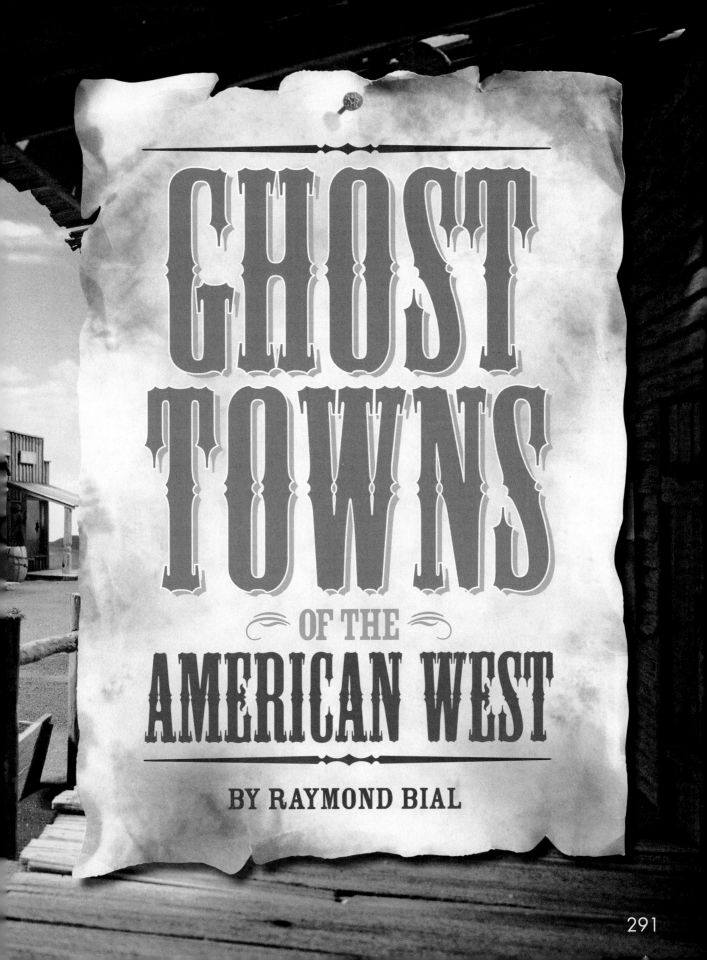

GHOST TOWNS
OF THE
AMERICAN WEST

BY RAYMOND BIAL

While its neighbor, Phoenix, flourished, Goldfield, a turn-of-the-century ghost town in Arizona, did so only briefly, and then declined as a mining town. However, the collection of buildings has since been given new life—as a ghost town.

An air of mystery swirls around the ghost towns of the American West. What sad and joyous events happened within the tumbledown walls and on the wind-blown streets? Why did people settle in these lonesome places? Why did they pull up stakes and move away? What went wrong in these towns? Virtually every ghost town has untold stories of people who longed for a chance at a better life. Relics of the past, the towns now stand as evidence of high adventure, hopes of striking it rich, and the sudden loss of fortune—or life.

Although ghost towns can be found throughout the world, in the United States they are most often thought of as the mining camps, cowboy towns, and other settlements of the sprawling western frontier.

Most ghost towns were originally mining camps where men sought gold, silver, copper, and other precious minerals.

Most were once mining camps where adventurous men came to seek their fortunes. These communities boomed as miners sought gold, silver, copper, or other precious minerals but died out when all of the ore was panned from streams or blasted from rocky tunnels. In cowboy towns, cattle were driven to other towns, and then shipped to markets in the East. Many lumber camps in deep forests and farming communities on the broad prairies also enjoyed brief prosperity before they were abandoned. Along with the miners, cowboys, and farmers, merchants and bankers, as well as doctors and schoolteachers, also went west. They laid out streets and put up buildings in hopes of growth and prosperity. As one newspaper editor declared, most folks wished "to get rich if we can."

In 1848, James W. Marshall discovered gold at Sutter's Mill when he shut down the water on the millrace and glanced into the ditch. "I reached my hand down and picked it up; it made my heart thump for I felt certain it was gold," he recalled. Soon the word was out. "Gold! Gold! Gold from the American River!" shouted Sam Brannon, waving a bottle of gold dust as he strode through the San Francisco streets. Seeking pay dirt, "forty-niners" (as the prospectors came to be known) streamed into California in the first of the great American gold rushes. Yet, over time, people came to refer to the sawmill as "Sutter's Folly" as the land of John Sutter was overrun with prospectors. Everywhere, men claimed "squatter's rights," in which they settled on land without paying for it.

Towns sprang up overnight. Charles B. Gillespie, a miner who worked near Coloma, California, described the typical main streets of these towns as "alive with crowds." To him, the miners were ragged, dirty men who were otherwise good-natured. They were a mix of Americans and immigrants—Germans, French, and other Europeans,

After several hard hours of travel, these trail-weary settlers paused in the foothills of the Rocky Mountains. Unhitching their wagon, they watered their livestock, ate a noonday meal, and briefly rested.

Loading all of their possessions in Conestoga wagons with billowing canvas tops, settlers seeking independence moved westward to homestead farms, staked a mining claim, or set up storekeeping in a new town.

and gold seekers from China and Chile, along with British convicts from Australia. Mark Twain declared, "It was a driving, vigorous, restless population in those days . . . two hundred thousand *young* men—not simpering, dainty, kid-gloved weaklings, but stalwart, muscular, dauntless young braves, brimful of push and energy."

In 1851, when a Scottish artist named J. D. Borthwick arrived to try his luck as a prospector, he wrote that the main street of Hangtown, later renamed Pacerville, "was in many places knee-deep in mud, and was plentifully strewn with old boots, hats, and shirts, old sardine-boxes, empty tins of preserved oysters, empty bottles, worn-out pots and kettles, old ham-bones, broken picks and shovels, and other rubbish." Borthwick described the town as "one long straggling street of clapboard houses and log cabins, built in a hollow at the side of a creek, and surrounded by high and steep hills." Along the creek, he said, "there was continual noise and clatter, as mud, dirt, stones, and water were thrown about in all directions, and the men, dressed in ragged clothes and big boots, wielding picks and shovels . . . were all working as if for their lives."

In the typical western town, the buildings were often skirted with a sidewalk of wooden planks, along with hitching posts and water troughs for horses. There might be a bank made of solid brick to assure depositors that their hard cash or gold dust was safe from robbers. There might also be a mercantile store, an early version of the department store, as well as a general store. The town certainly had to have a blacksmith shop and livery stable, as well as corrals for horses and cattle. Some towns had a telegraph office and their very own newspaper. The town might be lucky enough to be on a stagecoach route, a Pony Express station, or, better yet, a railroad stop.

"The Americans have a perfect passion for railroads," wrote Michel Chevalier, a French economist, in the 1830s. If the railroad bypassed the village, it quickly became a ghost town. Helen Hunt Jackson described Garland City, Colorado, where she lived: "Twelve days ago there was not a house here. Today, there are one hundred and five, and in a week there will be two hundred." However, the town lasted only a few months, at least at that site. When the railroad passed thirty miles to the west, folks moved the entire town—walls and windows, as well as sidewalks, furnishings, and goods—to the railroad tracks. Railroads laid down thousands of miles of gleaming tracks across the grasslands, with a transcontinental link completed in 1869.

None of these towns would have prospered, even briefly, and the frontier would never have become settled, without women and children. Storekeepers and farmers occasionally brought their wives and children with them, but men still outnumbered women nine to one. Most towns actively sought women. In 1860, a letter to the editor of the *Rocky Mountain News* from the new settlement of Breckenridge, Colorado, read: "A few very respectable looking women have ventured over to see us. Send us a few more." Another Colorado writer asked, "We have one lady living in Breckenridge and one on Gold Run; we would be glad to welcome many arrivals of the 'gentler' portion of the gold-seeking humanity, and can offer a pleasant country, good locations, and peaceable neighbors . . . except for an occasional lawsuit."

The waves of western migration reached a peak between 1860 and 1880. Over time, some towns grew into large cities, such as Denver and Phoenix, while many others were abandoned and forgotten in the desert sands or mountain snows. Most went bust because of economic failure—all the gold or silver was mined or the cattle were driven to another market town. A few people got rich, but others suffered heartbreak, hunger, and plain bad luck, and then abandoned the town. Perched on mountain cliffs, tucked into a wooded valley, or baking in the desert sun, these ghost towns are so remote that they are almost impossible to find. People often have to travel to them by four-wheel-drive vehicles and then hike several miles up rocky slopes or over cactus-studded deserts. Finding the ghost towns may be as difficult as the search for gold that led to the founding of the towns.

John Steele described Washington, California, in the 1840s, just six months after it had been founded: "With a large number of vacant cabins it contained several empty buildings and quite a large hotel, closed and silent." Once ringing with the voices of cheerful people, the towns have now fallen silent. They have become little more than empty shells of their former selves. There may be a handful of old false-front buildings, weathered to a haunting gray, with open doorways and broken windows. But little else remains; few people even remember the place. Even the memories, along with the hopes and dreams of the inhabitants, have blown away, like so much dust in the wind.

ABOVE: Cabezon, New Mexico, ghost town. In ghost town cemeteries, names of the dead were sometimes scrawled on rough boards.

RIGHT: Here, a group of men have set up a mining camp at a place known as Gregory's Diggings during the early days of the gold rush in Colorado.

Common Core State Standards

Informational Text 1. Quote accurately from a text when explaining what the text says explicitly and when drawing inferences from the text. **Also Writing 8., 9.**

Envision It! | Retell

Think Critically

1. The people who moved out West in the nineteenth century had very good reasons for doing so. What were some of those reasons? Do you think those reasons still relate to our world today? Why or why not? Text to World

2. Authors of nonfiction often do more than report the facts. They may also state their feelings about those facts. Find parts of this selection that reveal the author's feelings about ghost towns. Why do you think the author includes those feelings?

   Think Like an Author

3. Make a generalization about ghost towns. Use details and your own background knowledge to support it. Generalize

4. What questions do you have about ghost towns that were not answered by the selection? How might you go about finding the answers? Questioning

5. **Look Back and Write** Reread pages 297–298. What business buildings would you find on the streets of a town when it was thriving, before it became a ghost town? Sketch and label a typical ghost town's business area. Provide evidence to support your answer.

   Key Ideas and Details • Text Evidence

Meet the Author

RAYMOND BIAL

Raymond Bial says about *Ghost Towns of the American West*, "I actually stayed in a ghost town with my wife, Linda, and two of my children to make photographs for this book." A photographer who works in both color and black and white, he has published more than thirty books for children and adults.

Ghost Towns of the American West is a blend of photographs and text called a photo essay. Mr. Bial says, "Whenever I ask groups of schoolchildren why photo essays should be written as stories, they always answer correctly, 'So they won't be boring.'"

Mr. Bial says his work as a writer and photographer grew out of his experiences growing up. "Having spent a good portion of my childhood in a small town in southern Indiana, I have vivid memories of those joyous years of bicycling around the neighborhood, swimming at the municipal pool, stopping for ice cream at the local hot spot, and frequently visiting our Carnegie public library."

Today he lives in an old house in Urbana, Illinois, creating nonfiction photo essays. "I now draw upon my experiences with my family," he says, "as well as memories of my childhood."

Here are other books by Raymond Bial.

Tenement: Immigrant Life on the Lower East Side

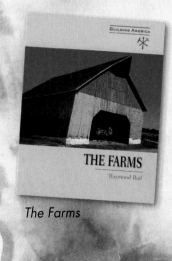

The Farms

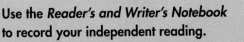
Use the *Reader's and Writer's Notebook* to record your independent reading.

303

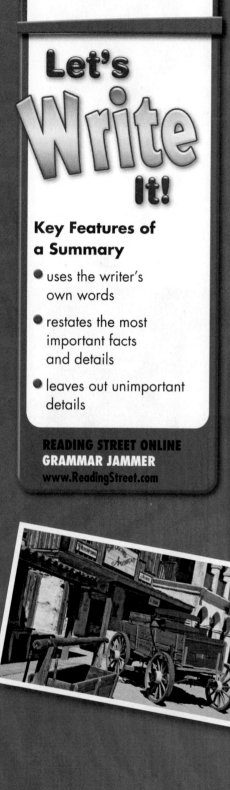

Common Core State Standards

Informational Text 2. Determine two or more main ideas of a text and explain how they are supported by key details; summarize the text. **Also Writing 2.a., Language 1.**

Let's Write It!

Key Features of a Summary

- uses the writer's own words
- restates the most important facts and details
- leaves out unimportant details

READING STREET ONLINE
GRAMMAR JAMMER
www.ReadingStreet.com

Expository

Summary

Writing a **summary** will help you figure out the main ideas of a text. A summary is written in your own words and contains only the most important details. The student model on the next page is an example of a summary.

Writing Prompt *Ghost Towns of the American West* describes old towns that have now become tourist attractions. Summarize the selection. Focus on only the most important facts and details.

Writer's Checklist

Remember, you should . . .

- ☑ ask yourself what is most important in each paragraph.
- ☑ list only the most important points.
- ☑ keep your summary short.
- ☑ avoid repeating details.
- ☑ use and understand adverbs.
- ☑ use and understand transitional words.

Ghost Towns

Ghost towns are abandoned towns that were once **very** busy. But what happened to them? Why did they become abandoned?

Many ghost towns in this country were once mining towns. When the gold or silver or other precious metal was gone, people left the town. It **usually** became a ghost town.

Towns were abandoned **sometimes** when a new railroad passed far away from a town. People wanted to be near the railroad, so they rebuilt their homes near the railroad. Some towns were abandoned **almost** overnight when railroads came through a few miles away.

Also, towns were **sometimes** abandoned when cattle were driven to other markets. Other towns were settlements on the western frontier that were abandoned when pioneer families no longer traveled through the town.

Today many ghost towns are **very** hard to get to. There are not many clues left behind, therefore a lot remains a mystery about the people who lived there.

Writing Trait Focus/Ideas Paragraphs focus on the most important information.

Adverbs are used correctly.

Genre Summaries restate only the most important ideas of a selection.

Conventions

Using Adverbs

Remember **Adverbs** tell more about verbs. They explain how, when, or where actions happen. Some adverbs show intensity *(almost, a lot)*. Other adverbs show frequency, or how often something happens *(usually, sometimes)*.

Common Core State Standards
Literature 6. Describe how a narrator's or speaker's point of view influences how events are described. **Also Literature 2., 10.**

Genre
Historical Fiction

- Historical fiction is a story set in a particular historical period. The background of the story is based on fact, but the story itself is fiction.

- Historical fiction often uses omniscient third-person point of view. *Omniscient* means "all knowing." In this point of view, authors use words such as *he, she,* and *they*.

- Read "Gold Dreams." As you read, think about which historical event or movement is involved in the theme of the story, and look for examples of third-person points of view in the story.

GOLD DREAMS
by Heather Miller

William Leyden wiped the dust from his eyes. The covered wagon groaned and lurched. The exhausted horses began to slow down.

"We'll stop here for the night," Papa said. "There's a town here. Name of Goldfield. We can rest up. We'll start again tomorrow."

William and his older brother, John, jumped out. So this was Arizona. The air was dry and hot. The mesa was breathtaking.

It was 1893, and the family had been traveling for months. Like many others before them, they had decided to move out west. They were looking for a better life.

Papa helped Mama out of the wagon. "I miss New York," Mama said wearily.

"In New York, we were seven people living in two rooms," Papa reminded her. "In California, we'll have a farm and fresh air. It will be worth it. You'll see," Papa promised.

They unhitched their wagon. John and William led the horses to a watering hole. As the horses drank, the brothers overheard some travelers talking. One man said to another, "I was headed to Wyoming. But now I'm going to make a fortune right here."

"How do you intend to do that?" the other asked.

"There's gold in this ground," the first traveler said. "Anybody who stays to mine it is going to get rich."

William and John exchanged glances. John whispered, "No wonder they call this town Goldfield!"

When the boys returned to the wagon, John said, "Papa, let's become miners. We'll be rich."

Papa shook his head. "No, son. Back in the old country, our family farmed. We can make a go of a farm and sell our crops. We're going on to California where we can get land with good soil and lots of it."

The next day, John walked around Goldfield. It was a busy, noisy place full of boarding houses and stores. John's mind was made up.

Let's **Think** About...

Why did William's family, and so many other people, move west in the late 1800s? **Historical Fiction**

Let's **Think** About...

What historical event or movement is referred to in the story, and how does it affect the story? **Historical Fiction**

"Papa, I'm 18 years old," John said. "I'm a man and I know my own mind. You go on without me to California. I'll seek my fortune here in Goldfield."

Papa was too proud to argue with his son. Mama cried so hard she couldn't speak. Papa hitched the wagon and everyone got in. Except John.

"So long, William," John said proudly. "When you see me next, I'll be rich. You can count on that!"

The family settled in California. After years of hard work, the farm was a success. The family started a dry-goods store, and built a large farmhouse near a beautiful orchard. They were comfortable, and they lived a peaceful and rewarding life.

One day, as William took a walk on the family's land, he saw a man approaching, looking worn and tired. William recognized him immediately. It was his brother, John.

"John!" William cried.

"William! I heard that the Leydens lived up here," John said. "Thought maybe it was my family!"

Let's **Think** About...

Why do you think John wanted to stay in Goldfield? Are these reasons a result of the historical movement or period the story is based on?
Historical Fiction

"I'm so glad you found us," William said. We tried sending letters, but they were all returned."

John smiled sadly. "Goldfield's post office closed down years ago. The place is a ghost town now. Guess there wasn't much gold there after all."

"What have you been doing all these years, John?"

"Living off the land. It gets mighty lonely though. I've missed you, William."

"We've missed you too," William said. "Mama and Papa will be so glad to see you!"

"You're looking like you've done well. I hope that family that owns that house is good to you," John said.

"Oh, John," laughed William. "We own that house up on that hill. This entire farm is ours."

John was stunned silent. Then he said, "All this time, I've looked for the easy way to riches. Looks like I should've stayed with my family."

William put his arm around his brother and led him to the house. John was happy to be home again.

Let's **Think** About...

An omniscient narrator tells this story. How might the plot, or story, have changed if the narrator had focused on John's decision to stay in Arizona?
Historical Fiction

Let's **Think** About...

Reading Across Texts Look back at *Ghost Towns* and "Gold Dreams." What did you learn about American history in each of them?

Writing Across Texts Using details from both stories, write a journal entry for John as he describes how Goldfield became a ghost town.

Common Core State Standards

Language 4.b. Use common, grade-appropriate Greek and Latin affixes and roots as clues to the meaning of a word (e.g., *photograph, photosynthesis*). **Also Foundational Skills 3.a., 4.b., Speaking/Listening 1.b., Language 6.**

Let's **Learn** It!

Vocabulary

Prefixes *over-, in-*

Word Structure Prefixes are word parts added to the beginning of words that change a word's meaning. The Old English prefix *over-* means "too much." The Latin prefix *in-* often means "not."

Practice It! Work with a partner to create a list of words from stories you've read this year that begin with *over-* or *in-*. Use what you know about the meanings of the prefixes to determine definitions for each word. Then use a dictionary or glossary to check your definitions.

Fluency

Rate

Partner Reading Adjusting your reading rate helps you better understand an article or story. Slow your reading when you read sentences and paragraphs with many facts and a lot of information.

Practice It! With your partner, practice reading aloud a page from *Ghost Towns*. Take turns reading aloud  each paragraph. First read quickly and then slowly. Decide which rate helps you better comprehend the article.

Listening and Speaking

Get Ready For Middle School

Use adverbs as you speak to show frequency and intensity (usually, a lot, sometimes, almost).

Debate

In a debate, two sides present arguments for and against an issue. The purpose of a debate is to inform listeners about issues and to try to convince people to agree with an opinion.

Practice It! Work with a partner to debate whether ghost towns should be torn down. Assign each partner one side: in favor of or opposed to tearing down ghost towns. Use details from *Ghost Towns* as support. Prepare your arguments and hold a debate.

Tips

Listening . . .

- Listen to your partner's message.
- Ask questions to clarify the main idea and supporting details.

Speaking . . .

- Make eye contact.
- Adjust your volume as you speak.
- Use transitional words, such as *therefore* and *also*.

Teamwork . . .

- Identify how you agree with your partner.
- When you disagree, support your opinions with evidence.

Common Core State Standards

Language 5. Demonstrate understanding of figurative language, word relationships, and nuances in word meanings. **Also Literature 5., 10.**

Poetry

- Some poets use sound effects, such as alliteration and onomatopoeia, to reinforce meaning in their poems.

- Alliteration is the repetition of consonant sounds at the beginning of words. As you read, think about the words poets choose for alliteration.

- Onomatopoeia is a word that is also the sound that it makes, such as *buzz* or *boom*. Poets use onomatopoeia to draw your attention to important words or ideas in poems.

Let's Think About...

Why do you think Georgia Douglas Johnson chose the words she did for alliteration?

Your World

by Georgia Douglas Johnson

Your world is as big as you make it.
I know, for I used to abide
In the narrowest nest in a corner,
My wings pressing close to my side.

But I sighted the distant horizon
Where the sky line encircled the sea
And I throbbed with a burning desire
To travel this immensity.

I battered the cordons around me
And I cradled my wings on the breeze
Then soared to the uttermost reaches
With rapture, with power, with ease!

Share the Adventure

by **Patricia and
Fredrick McKissack**

Pages and pages
A seesaw of ideas—
Share the adventure

Fiction, nonfiction:
Door to our past and future
Swinging back and forth

WHAM! The book slams shut,
But we read it together
With our minds open

Let's **Think** About...

How does the onomatopoeia in "Share the Adventure" help you understand the poem?

313

A Path to the Moon

by bp Nichol

From my front door there's a path to the moon
that nobody seems to see
tho it's marked with stones & grass & trees
there's nobody sees it but me.

You walk straight ahead for ten trees or so
turn left at the robin's song
follow the sound of the west wind down
past where the deer drink from the pond.

You take a right turn as the river bends
then where the clouds touch the earth
close your left eye & count up to ten
while twirling for all that you're worth.

And if you keep walking right straight ahead
clambering over the clouds
saying your mother's & father's names
over & over out loud

you'll come to the place where moonlight's born
the place where the moonbeams hide
and visit all the crater sites
on the dark moon's secret side.

From my front door there's a path to the moon
that nobody seems to see
tho it's marked with stones & grass & trees
no one sees it but you & me.

The Unexpected

What can we learn from encounters with the unexpected?

Common Core State Standards

Language 6. Acquire and use accurately grade-appropriate general academic and domain-specific words and phrases, including those that signal contrast, addition, and other logical relationships (e.g., *however, although, nevertheless, similarly, moreover, in addition*).
Also Speaking/Listening 1.c.

Oral Vocabulary

Let's Talk About

Unplanned Situations, Positive Outcomes

- Describe ways unplanned situations can have positive outcomes.

- Listen to and interpret messages other students have about unplanned situations.

- Ask questions to clarify classmates' messages.

READING STREET ONLINE
CONCEPT TALK VIDEO
www.ReadingStreet.com

Common Core State Standards
Informational Text 2. Determine two
or more main ideas of a text and explain
how they are supported by key details;
summarize the text.
Also Informational Text 1.

Envision It! | Skill Strategy

Skill

Strategy

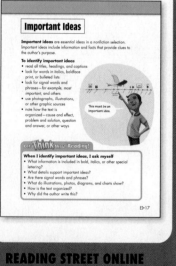

Comprehension Skill

↻ Draw Conclusions

- Active readers make decisions based on evidence in the text or on their own background knowledge.

- When you form an idea or opinion about a text, you are drawing a conclusion.

- Examine your own conclusions as you read. Ask yourself if you can support them with facts from the text or facts you already know.

- Use a graphic organizer like the one below to draw conclusions about "The Mystery of the Monarchs."

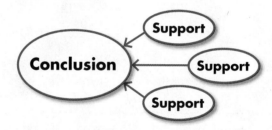

Comprehension Strategy

↻ Important Ideas

Good readers pay close attention to the important ideas in a piece of writing. Important ideas are the details and essential information that help you understand what an author is writing about.

The Mystery of the Monarchs

Have you ever seen the orange-and-black butterflies known as monarchs? If you have, it was probably autumn. The butterflies were migrating through your area on their way to Mexico.

All monarch butterflies spend the winter months in forests in Mexico, where it is warm. They fly there in large groups. In the spring these monarchs repeat the same flight in the other direction. They fly back to the North as far as Canada and lay eggs along the way. Then they die.

But when those eggs hatch, a new generation of butterflies is born. When another autumn comes, they take off for Mexico. They repeat the flight path of the original butterflies, and, amazingly, they fly to the same forests and sometimes the exact same trees where their parents came from previously. Think about it: they fly to the same forests and trees and they've never been there before!

Scientists think the butterflies begin their journey because of the position of the sun in the sky as the seasons change. But for now, though, no one can explain how the butterflies know where to go. That remains the "mystery of the monarchs."

Skill Draw a conclusion about why butterflies migrate to Mexico.

Strategy What information does this paragraph tell you? Is it important to understand these ideas to know what the author is writing about?

Skill What conclusion can you draw about ongoing study of the monarch butterflies?

Your Turn!

⏸ **Need a Review?** See the *Envision It! Handbook* for additional help with drawing conclusions and important ideas.

Let's Think About...

▶ **Ready to Try It?** Talk about what you've learned about drawing conclusions and important ideas as you read *Austin's Amazing Bats*.

The Truth About
Austin's Amazing Bats

Common Core State Standards

Language 4.c. Consult reference materials (e.g., dictionaries, glossaries, thesauruses), both print and digital, to find the pronunciation and determine or clarify the precise meaning of key words and phrases. **Also Language 4.**

Envision It! | Words to Know

bizarre

headline

Monday July 21 1969
59: Man makes his first sp
On the moon
fter perfect
ouchdown

roost

breathtaking

high-pitched

vital

Vocabulary Strategy for

🔊 Unknown Words

Dictionary/Glossary Sometimes a writer doesn't include context clues in the sentences surrounding an unknown word. In this case, you have to look up the word in a dictionary or glossary to find its meaning, pronunciation, part of speech, and syllabication. Choose one of the *Words to Know,* and then follow these steps.

1. Check the back of the book for a glossary, or use a dictionary.

2. Find the word entry. If the pronunciation and syllabication are given, read the word aloud. You may recognize the word when you hear yourself say it.

3. Look at all the meanings and parts of speech listed in the entry. Try each meaning in the sentence that contains the unknown word.

4. Choose the meaning that makes sense in your sentence.

Read "Ears for Eyes" on page 323. Use a dictionary or a glossary to determine the meanings of words you cannot figure out from the text.

Words to Write Reread "Ears for Eyes." Think of other mammals that hunt at night and write an article about them. Use words from the *Words to Know* list in your article.

Ears for Eyes

What do bats and dolphins have in common? It's certainly not where they live! It's echolocation, the process of using sound to "see" in the dark. Instead of relying on eyesight, these mammals locate prey with high-pitched sounds, creating for each other a breathtaking symphony.

Echolocation is bizarre, and you won't read explanations of it in newspaper headlines. Here's how it works. Mammals that use echolocation listen to the differences in sound between their right and left ears to locate objects. As sounds emitted by the mammals bounce off an object and come back, the mammals keep track of the time it takes for the sound to reflect off the object. In this way, they are able to calculate where their prey is—all in a matter of seconds!

It might seem strange that mammals use their ears instead of their eyes to locate prey. Why do they? For one, echolocation provides them an ecological advantage. For example, if bats can roost during the day and hunt at night, they can take advantage of prey when it is vulnerable. Also, bats can hunt while their predators are sleeping. Indeed, echolocation is vital to these mammals' survival.

Your Turn!

Need a Review?
For additional help with using a dictionary or glossary, see *Words!*

Ready to Try It?
Read *The Truth About Austin's Amazing Bats* on pp. 324–335.

The Truth About Austin's Amazing Bats

By Ron Fridell

Question of the Week

How can unplanned situations have positive outcomes?

Expository texts tell about what certain things are and how they came to be. As you read, notice how the author explains how bats came to live in Austin, Texas.

Let's **Think** About **Reading!**

Let's **Think** About...

How does visualizing the sky as the bats emerge help you understand the article? **Visualize**

Let's **Think** About...

What details tell you that the bats are welcomed and admired by the citizens of Austin? **Important Ideas**

Where can you see a summer sky filled with 1.5 million bats? Austin, Texas, is the place. They fly out from under the Ann W. Richards Congress Avenue Bridge around sunset. Just a few at first, like scouts sent ahead to see if the coast is clear. Then dozens more emerge, then hundreds, then thousands. The bats keep pouring out until more than a million swirl above the bridge like a bat tornado. Finally, they zoom off in all directions, while the spectators below reverberate with wonder.

The bats attract an estimated 100,000 tourists to Austin each summer, bringing in close to $10 million to Austin's tourism industry. Every night crowds gather on or near the bridge for the event. An imposing sculpture, in the shape of a bat, called *Nightwing* stands at the foot of the bridge, welcoming visitors to the sight. Even Austin's former professional hockey team, the Ice Bats, embraced the creatures. The team's mascot was a fierce-looking cartoon bat gripping a hockey stick. Austin loves its bats so much that it holds a two-day summer Bat Festival to honor the flying mammals.

Spectators watch the nightly display from all sorts of places, high and low. Some watch from up on the Congress Avenue Bridge. Others watch from the lake below. The bridge spans Town Lake on the Colorado River, where people watch the bats from rowboats, canoes, and kayaks. There is even a riverboat that gives special bat cruises. Some people spread blankets on the lake's grassy shores to watch. Nearby downtown restaurants have tables set up on patios for viewing. When the bats come out, the guests put down their knives and forks to watch a breathtaking display of nature in the city.

But once upon a time, Austin's bats were neither loved nor admired, and were breathtaking for a different reason. To a great many Austin residents the bats were a bizarre and frightening sight. The bats were also a health hazard, they insisted. After some debate, a decision was made. The bats must be removed from the bridge or destroyed.

Let's Think About...

What clues in the text tell you that the events in the article are written in sequential order? **Text Structure**

327

How were Austin's bats saved? The story begins in 1980. That's when workers began reconstructing the Congress Avenue Bridge. The bridge is a landmark in the heart of downtown, just ten blocks from the Texas state capitol. The engineers in charge of the project didn't know that their work would create an ideal habitat for bats. Otherwise they would not have left so many openings on the bridge's concrete underside.

The long, narrow, dark crevices became instantly popular with migrating bats, because bats prefer to make cozy spots to roost and raise their young. Most of the bats are pregnant females. In March they fly north from Mexico to give birth and raise their young, called pups. That's why in August the bridge's bat population of 1.5 million is double what it was in March. Austin's human population is about 740,000. That means that in summer, Austin has twice as many bats as people!

Let's **Think** About...

What can you do to better understand why Austin's bat population doubles in size during August? **Monitor and Clarify**

Why were so many people so scared of the bats beneath the bridge? The reasons are based on fear and misinformation. Fear of the dark is one reason. Many children—and even some adults—are afraid of the dark, and bats are creatures of the night. During the day they inhabit dark spaces such as caves and tunnels. At night they come out to hunt. Bats' anatomy and appearance scares some people too, with their pointed ears and noses and sharply curved wings. And when people think of bats, they often think of vampires, mythical creatures that drink blood. Or they picture a great big bat flying blindly at them and getting all tangled in their hair, or biting them and giving them rabies.

Let's **Think** About...

Why does the author ask a question and then follow it with the answer?

Important Ideas

329

Austin resident Mari Murphy remembers how fearful Austin residents used to be. "For years, local newspapers had carried headlines like 'Bat colonies sink teeth into city' and 'Mass fear in the air as bats invade Austin,'" she writes. "Misinformation abounded, and the bats that made Austin, Texas, their summer home were regarded as something to be eliminated, not as something wonderful to see."

Ms. Murphy belongs to Bat Conservation International (BCI). BCI's mission is to teach people the truth about bats and to protect and conserve bats' habitats. BCI moved their headquarters to Austin in 1986. One of their goals was to protect the bats that spent summers under the Congress Avenue Bridge.

Let's Think About...

What essential information does the author give to help you understand the BCI's mission?

Important Ideas

The Daily Journal

MASS FEAR IN THE A
AS BATS INVADE AUST

Facts on the Fly!

BAT CONSERVATION INTERNATIONAL
www.batcon.org

THINGS YOU CAN DO TO PROMOTE BAT CONSERVATION

You do not need to travel far or have a degree in biology to help bats. You can make a big difference for bat conservation by working on local projects. Each community has unique needs. The following suggestions may apply to your bats locally.

Things that EVERYONE can do for bats:
Due to myths and misunderstandings, bats have acquired a poor public image. You can counter these myths by raising public awareness about bats in your community. Because bats are mammals, they are susceptible to the rabies virus, making sick bats a possible risk to people who know little about them. Although the risk is greatly exaggerated, many bats are [...] from needless [...]

• **Educating** local pest control operators about humane exclusion techniques. Exclusion is the only effective way to remove a nuisance colony of bats from buildings. Poisons, naphthalene flakes and harmless repellant devices do not deter bats and may actually harm humans. For more information, visit _www.batcon.org_ and click on 'Bats in Buildings' under 'Conservation Programs' or call (512) 327-9721.

[...] bats and rabies facts to local health [...] and personal [...] about bats

BAT CONSERVATION INTERN
BAT HOUSE PROJEC

Bat Houses? Here's H

Thank you for your interest in bat houses. Many people are discovering the bene[...] homes for these fascinating mammals. We have learned much about the roostin[...] share the latest information through BCI's website, free electronic newsletter, an[...] Homeowners, farmers, organic gardeners, foresters and recreation managers ar[...] education and pest reduction. Please join us by providing an acceptable home f[...] the design, location and use of bat houses. Thanks again for your interest.

Answers to Frequently Asked Bat Hous

[Wi]ll attracting bats to bat houses in my yard increase the likelihood that t[...]
If bats liked your attic or wall spaces, they probably would already be living[...]

[Ho]w many bats can potentially occupy my bat house?
[Sin]gle-chamber house can shelter 50 bats, while a larger multi-chamber des[...]

[How] can I determine the likelihood of attracting bats?
[Throug]hout most of the United States and much of Canada there are occupie[...]
[America]'s many crevice-dwelling bat species. Wherever bats live, they must f[...]
[prefere]nce for roosting near aquatic habitats. The closer you live to cave or m[...]
[presen]ce of bat colonies in nearby buildings and bridges also increases your[...]

[Mi]ght bats not be attracted to my bat house?
[The cause] of failure is inappropriate exposure to solar heating [...]

There's a saying that goes "The more you know about bugs, the less they will bug you." The same can be said of bats. That's why BCI members told Austin residents all about the bats under the bridge. Their plan: Bring all the fears and misinformation about bats out into the open, and then show Austin's residents what bats are really like. Then they will learn to like, and even love, the bats. With this plan in mind, BCI members set to work spreading the truth about bats.

Yes, they told Austin residents, there are such things as vampire bats. They drink the blood of birds, goats, and cattle. First they lick the animal's skin in a spot where the blood vessels are close to the surface. Then they bite the skin and drink. A vampire bat will drink about four teaspoons of blood per day. But no, they do not prey on humans, and there are no vampire bats in Austin.

Let's **Think** About...

No vampire bats prey on humans. On what animals do they prey?
Questioning

Facts on the Fly!

DEALING WITH UNWANTED GUESTS

BAT CONSERVATION
INTERNATIONAL
www.batcon.org

ONAL'S

...wonder of bats by providing new ...and preferences of bats, and we ...at House Builder's Handbook. ...e world are installing bat houses for ...eneficial bats and helping us improve ...s.

...uestions

...move into my attic or wall spaces?

...attract colonies of 200 or more bats.

...uses being used by one of North ...gh insects to eat, largely explaining their ...rnating sites the better, and the ...s.

...tively, bats may not be able to live in your ...nd mines within 50 to 100 miles (80 to

...e detailed info on exclusion techniques you can do yourself (includ... ...g page on the BCI web site: http://www.batcon.org/home/index.asp?id...

...u encountered a stray bat flying around in your house? Bats that ...ost youngsters whose primary goal is a safe escape. They often v... ...he outside is opened while others leading to the rest of the hous... ..., but may bite if grabbed. As with any wild animal, bats should ... ...astened by catching the bat in flight with a hand net (swung fr... ...it with a coffee can and slipping a piece of cardboard over the ... ...Or you may also catch it by hand, using leather work gloves t...

...g a Colony from Your House ...can be excluded from living quarters by ...chimneys and vents with half-inch ...e cloth screens, by installing draft guards ...doors, and by sealing any other possible ...utes, especially around screen doors, ...and plumbing. Bats potentially can enter ...mall as 3/4" in diameter or 3/8" by 7/8", ...not chew insulation or otherwise make new ...eir entries can be plugged with silicone ...steel wool, or temporarily even with tape. ...bat colony must be evicted from a wall or

netting"...
preferr...
of near **Bat Conservation International** is a
hours nonprofit organization supported by 15,000
tape c members in 65 countries. We work around
wide the world to teach people the value of bats,
hole protect and conserve critical bat habitats,
the and advance scientific knowledge through
research.

We believe that real conservation be...
the field rather...

BAT CONSERVA
INTERNATION
www.batcon.org

Welcome to the Amazing W

Why are b...
More...
for almost a...
yet they rece...
research and...
More t...
species are in...
as endan...

Let's **Think** About...

How is the description of bats flying at night important to the article? **Visualize**

No, they told residents, a bat will not fly into your hair. Bats are not blind. They can see just as well as opossums, raccoons, and other animals that come out at night. Plus, bats use sound as well as sight to get around. They send out squawks and squeals through their noses and mouths. The sounds are so high-pitched that humans can't hear them. When the sound waves hit something, they echo back to the bat. Bats' ears are set wide apart to help pick up the echoes.

This special skill is known as echolocation. Ecologist Paul Garret writes, "I observed this amazing ability in the attic of a historic church in Pennsylvania, where I stood among a colony of ten thousand little brown bats. I watched them fly around the small space, and they never collided with one another, the walls or columns, or my hair."

Yes, BCI members said, bats can carry rabies, a serious disease. But so can dogs, cats, raccoons, and foxes. Raccoons are to blame for half of the rabies cases in the United States. Bats, on the other hand, hardly ever carry the disease. And bats do not want to bite you or get tangled in your hair. Bats are shy and gentle creatures. People who come out to watch them on summer nights have nothing to fear.

The Austin bats are a species called Mexican Free-tailed bats. Free-tails are medium-sized bats, with bodies that are around 3.5 inches (9 centimeters) long, and they weigh about half an ounce—1/32 of a pound. The Free-tails migrate each spring from central Mexico to roosting spots all over the southwestern United States. Bats live in big groups called colonies. The 1.5 million Austin bats make up the largest urban bat colony in North America.

But overall, Free-tail populations in America are in trouble. Each year more of them are killed. Some die from the poisonous pesticides farmers spray on their crops. Others die or become homeless when people destroy the caves, old buildings, and bridges where they roost. Austin's love for the bats is vitally important because it results in an undisturbed Free-tail colony.

Let's Think About...

What can you do to better understand what echolocation is? **Monitor and Clarify**

333

Let's **Think** About...

What important details help you understand how Free-tailed bats benefit Austin?
🎯 **Important Ideas**

Let's **Think** About...

What essential information explains how Free-tails help farmers of Austin?
🎯 **Important Ideas**

Having so many bats in Austin has many benefits, and BCI members educated the public about these benefits. Like honeybees, bats help plants grow by pollinating flowers and scattering seeds. They also help control costly crop and yard pests. When Austin's bats go hunting at night, their prey is flying insects. Their echolocation skills make them expert bug hunters. The echoes from the noises the bats make bounce back and tell them exactly where the insect is, where it's headed, and how fast it's moving.

Farmers have a special reason to love the bats. Many of the insects they eat, such as cutworms and corn-borer moths, are serious crop pests. Without the bats out there gobbling them up, these pests would be munching on cotton, corn, and other crops in the countryside outside Austin.

The 1.5 million hungry Free-tails cover more than a thousand square miles of countryside each night, and they fly as high as 10,000 feet (3,048 meters) to catch their prey. During these nightly flights each bat eats close to its own body weight in insects. In total, Austin's hungry Free-tailed bats can consume up to thirty thousand pounds of insects each night.

The people who live in the city have their own special reasons for loving the Free-tails. For one thing, Austin's bats eat loads of mosquitoes. If not for the bats, Austin's residents would have tons more mosquitoes biting their skin and sucking their blood on summer evenings.

August is the best month for bat-watching. That's when most of the young pups are ready to leave the roost and join their mothers to hunt. The bats usually start coming out from under the bridge between 8:00 and 8:30 P.M. People can call the special Bat Hotline for updates on the most likely time that night, and BCI members are at the bridge each night to hand out information and answer questions. They want to make sure that everyone knows the truth about Austin's amazing bats.

What is it about the bats—besides the benefits to farming and tourism—that captivates visitors and residents of Austin? City dwellers often forget about the natural world beyond their streets and skyscrapers, but when they watch the bats soar, they rediscover the joy and mystery of nature. Some believe that observing the bats links spectators to nature, and that the resulting thrill is unforgettable. Photographer Tim Flach writes, "I've been fortunate enough to see a number of natural wonders, but the bats will stay in mind for the rest of my life."

Let's **Think** About...

What clues make you think the author wants people to care for the natural world?
Inferring

Common Core State Standards

Informational Text 1. Quote accurately from a text when explaining what the text says explicitly and when drawing inferences from the text. **Also Informational Text 2., Writing 8., 9.**

Envision It! Retell

Think Critically

1. Many tourists travel to Austin to see the amazing bats. What tourist attractions are in your area? Do you know of any tourist attractions that involve interesting animals? **Text to World**

2. On pages 334–335, the author goes into great detail about how Austin's bats help people who live in the city and the surrounding countryside. Why do you think the author decided to include this information in the article? **Think Like an Author**

3. At first, many of Austin's citizens had a very negative attitude toward the bats living under the Congress Avenue Bridge. Why did this attitude change? **Draw Conclusions**

4. Think about the title of the article. Then skim through the article and list several essential ideas about bats the author provides to readers. **Important Ideas**

5. **Look Back and Write** Reread the saying on page 331: "The more you know about bugs, the less they will bug you." What does this saying mean? Do you agree with this saying when it's applied to bats? Provide evidence from the article to support your answer.

Key Ideas and Details • Text Evidence

Ron Fridell

Ron Fridell is an author and an editor of children's books and books for young adults. Mr. Fridell often undertakes serious topics in his writing. War and politics are the topics of many of his books, such as *Prisoner of War, Dictatorship, Military Technology,* and *Spy Technology.*

Mr. Fridell was a member of the Peace Corps in Bangkok, Thailand, where he taught English as a second language. He earned a Master's degree in radio, television, and film from Northwestern University. He lives in Tucson, Arizona.

Here is another book by Ron Fridell.

Spy Technology

Use the *Reader's and Writer's Notebook* to record your independent reading.

Common Core State Standards

Writing 3. Write narratives to develop real or imagined experiences or events using effective technique, descriptive details, and clear event sequences.
Also Writing 3.a., 3.d., Language 1.

Let's Write It!

Key Features of a Journal Entry

- usually records the date

- expresses personal ideas and experiences

- often intended only for the writer to read

- may be experimental and informal

READING STREET ONLINE
GRAMMAR JAMMER
www.ReadingStreet.com

Narrative

Journal Entry

A **journal entry** is usually a personal message you write to yourself. The student model on the next page is an example of a journal entry.

Writing Prompt Think about a time you felt misunderstood. Write a journal entry about that experience.

Writer's Checklist

Remember, you should ...

☑ share thoughts and feelings about an experience.

☑ use descriptive details to recall the experience.

☑ include the date.

Monday, May 25

Dear Journal,

Boy, did my best friend Izzie make me furious today! When I got on the bus, I saw that she hadn't saved me a seat. Then, when I talked to her across the aisle, she pretended not to hear me, but I knew she did. Later, at lunch, I saved her a seat at my table, but she ignored me!

After lunch, I caught up with her and asked her what was going on. Well, I couldn't believe it: she tells me that I'm a lousy friend! Then she says that she saw me at the mall Saturday afternoon, with our other friends, and I never invited her!

"Well," I said, "of course I never called you because you told me Friday morning that you had to visit some relatives over the weekend with your family!" Izzie's face turned red, and she said she was sorry—she must have mixed up the dates! Next weekend is when she has to go with her family. I'm just relieved she is not mad at me anymore!

Ana Luz

Genre A **journal entry** expresses thoughts about an idea, event, or experience.

Writing Trait Voice can be revealed through the writer's emotions and opinions.

Modifiers are used correctly.

Conventions

Modifiers

Remember A **modifier** is an adjective, adverb, or prepositional phrase that adds meaning to other words in a sentence. For example, the phrase *with green stripes* in the sentence *The towel with green stripes is mine* gives you more information about the towel.

339

Genre
Autobiography

- An autobiography is the story of a person's life written by the person who lived it.

- Autobiographies are written in the first person, using *I, me,* and *my.*

- The events in an autobiography are actual events and experiences in a person's life.

- Read "The Animals in My Life." Look for elements that make this story an autobiography. What language does the author use when he discusses major events in his life?

THE
ANIMALS
IN MY LIFE
By Ron Fridell

I have been writing nonfiction for my entire adult life. I've written on many science topics, from the life cycle of the pumpkin to fingerprinting, from water pollution to space travel. But my favorite topic is animals.

The very first animal I wrote about was my collie dog, Ranger. I wrote action-packed tales of our fictional adventures together. We would battle everything from dinosaurs to pirates. Whenever I was in trouble, my brave and clever Ranger was always there to rescue me. I was in the third grade at the time.

Since then I've written about many animals, small and big. Ants, spiders, frogs, turtles, vultures, camels, elephants—and now bats.

Why the Austin bats? I saw them fly out from under the Congress Avenue Bridge once, in the 1980s. I'd forgotten all about them until the summer of 2008. That's when I learned that Mexican Long-tongued bats were visiting my hummingbird feeder.

I live in southern Arizona, out on the desert. The feeder is right outside the kitchen window. I wait until dark. Then I shine a flashlight through the window. And there they are with their big eyes and long, long tongues.

The Long-tongued bats reminded me of the Austin bats, so I did some Internet research. To my surprise, I read that the Austin bats are now a huge tourist attraction, thanks to the good people at Bat Conservation International. I also talked with a scientist at BCI by e-mail. I loved what I discovered in my research. I don't like to see anyone misunderstood, whether it's a person or an animal. And I love happy endings. That's why I had to write about the Austin bats. I hope their story makes my readers feel happy too.

Let's **Think** About...

How does the point of view tell you this is an autobiography? **Autobiography**

Let's **Think** About...

Reading Across Texts After reading about Austin's bats and about the author, what conclusions can you draw about the author?

Writing Across Texts Imagine that you are a member of BCI. Write a journal entry about your life helping Austin's bats.

Common Core State Standards
Language 4.c. Consult reference materials (e.g., dictionaries, glossaries, thesauruses), both print and digital, to find the pronunciation and determine or clarify the precise meaning of key words and phrases. **Also Foundational Skills 4.b., Speaking/Listening 1.d., Language 4.**

Let's
Learn
It!

Vocabulary

Unknown Words

Dictionary/Glossary If you can't determine a word's meaning from the context, look it up in a dictionary or glossary. A dictionary also gives other information, including the right way to pronounce the word.

Practice It! Choose three unknown words from *The Truth About Austin's Amazing Bats* or from another text. Use a dictionary or glossary to look up their meanings. What other information does a dictionary give you about each word?

Fluency

Accuracy

Accuracy is being able to read without having to stop often to figure out words. One way to build accuracy is by rereading.

Practice It! With a partner, practice reading a page from *The Truth About Austin's Amazing Bats*. Read the paragraphs aloud three times. Take turns reading and giving each other feedback.

Listening and Speaking

In a debate, listen for the main ideas in each speaker's arguments.

Debate

In a debate, people take opposing sides of an issue. A person from each side takes turns making his or her arguments and then rebuts, or disagrees with, the other side.

Practice It! Work with your partner to debate one side of the following issue: *The bridge bats should be forced to move elsewhere.* Decide which side to take. Then prepare your arguments and hold a debate.

Tips

Listening . . .

- Listen to each speaker's messages.
- Identify the main ideas and supporting ideas in each speaker's message.

Speaking . . .

- When you speak, use eye contact to communicate your ideas.
- Raise and lower the volume of your voice to present your opinions effectively.

Teamwork . . .

- Identify points of agreement and disagreement.
- Elicit suggestions from group members.

343

Let's Talk About

Humans' Effects on Nature

- Share what you know about humans' effects on nature.

- Listen to a classmate's messages about humans and nature.

- Ask questions to clarify classmates' messages.

READING STREET ONLINE
CONCEPT TALK VIDEO
www.ReadingStreet.com

Año Nuevo Island

CLOSED TO PUBLIC USE TO PROTECT THE NATURAL WILDLIFE HABITAT

Common Core State Standards

Informational Text 2. Determine two or more main ideas of a text and explain how they are supported by key details; summarize the text. **Also Informational Text 1., 5.**

Envision It! | Skill Strategy

Skill

Strategy

Comprehension Skill

Main Idea and Details

- The main idea of a selection is the most important idea about the selection's topic.

- The author may state the main idea in a single sentence. Sometimes the reader must figure it out on his or her own.

- Use a graphic organizer like the one below to summarize the main idea and details in "Works of Art or Works of Aliens?" Be sure to summarize while maintaining meaning, and organize your summary in logical order.

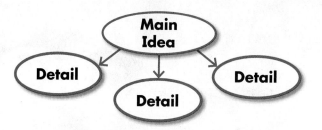

Comprehension Strategy

Text Structure

Text structure is the organizational pattern of a text. The piece may show relationships among ideas in sequence, in cause-and-effect patterns, or in a series of comparisons and contrasts. Active readers analyze how text structure influences relationships among ideas.

READING STREET ONLINE
ENVISION IT! ANIMATIONS
www.ReadingStreet.com

Works of *ART* or Works of *ALIENS?*

In the farm fields of Southern England during the 1970s, simple designs, called crop circles, were formed from flattened stalks of grain. Some were only a few feet in diameter. Others were as big as 1,500 feet across. How did they get there?

Some scientists claimed these mysterious designs were caused by the weather. Other people believed they were caused by aliens or by humans here on Earth. No one knew for sure. More designs appeared in fields each year.

In 1991, two men calling themselves crop artists admitted they were responsible for some of the crop circles. Crop artists think of their designs as art. Each one takes up to two weeks to finish, but crop artists hardly ever take credit for their designs. They believe that the mystery is part of their art.

The relationship between crop artists and farmers sometimes benefits both parties. While farmers provide the "canvas," the artists bring in the tourists. Farmers often charge tourists a small fee to see the circles. Are farmers concerned about the origin of the crop circles? Many feel that as long as they are well made, people can believe whatever they want to believe.

Strategy After reading the first paragraph, can you tell how ideas will be organized in this text?

Skill Summarize the main ideas and details in what you've read so far.

Skill What is the main idea of this selection?
a) causes of crop circles
b) aliens from outer space
c) tourism in England

Your Turn!

Need a Review?
See the *Envision It! Handbook* for help with main idea and text structure.

Ready to Try It?
Use what you have learned about main idea and text structure as you read *The Mystery of Saint Matthew Island.*

347

Common Core State Standards
Foundational Skills 3.a. Use combined knowledge of all letter-sound correspondences, syllabication patterns, and morphology (e.g., roots and affixes) to read accurately unfamiliar multisyllabic words in context and out of context. **Also Language 4.**

Envision It! Words to Know

decay

parasites

tundra

bleached

carcasses

scrawny

starvation

suspicions

Vocabulary Strategy for

Endings -s, -es

Word Structure An ending is a letter or letters added to the end of a base word that changes how the word is used. For example, the endings -s and -es from Old English make singular nouns plural. Recognizing an ending may help you determine the meaning of a word.

1. Look at the unknown word to see if it has a base word you know.

2. Check to see if the ending -s or -es has been added.

3. Ask yourself how the ending changes the meaning of the base word.

4. See if the meaning makes sense in the sentence.

Read "Cleanup by Mother Nature." Look for words ending in -s or -es. Use the endings to determine the meanings of the words.

Words to Write Reread "Cleanup by Mother Nature." Imagine you are a scientist talking about the life cycle of animals. Write a speech that explains the ideas from the selection. Use words from the *Words to Know* list in your speech.

CLEANUP BY MOTHER NATURE

All living things die. This is not a pleasant fact. Most people do not think about it very often. Seeing the carcasses of animals that have been hit on the road can be a startling reminder.

Some animals die to provide food for other animals. Perhaps you have seen a scrawny wild animal. This arouses suspicions in your mind that the animal is unhealthy. It may die from starvation, sickness, or parasites, such as worms, that live off its tissues. Many house pets pass through their entire life cycle and die of old age. What happens to the bodies of animals when they die?

In nature, nothing is wasted. Whether in the frozen tundra or the steamy jungles, bodies of dead animals are broken down. Through the process of decay, their tissues are changed into simpler chemicals. These chemicals go into the soil, and plants use them. Soon all that can be seen of a dead animal are bleached bones. In time, these break down and disappear as well.

Your Turn!

⏸ Need a Review?
For additional help with endings, see *Words!*

▶ Ready to Try It?
Read *The Mystery of Saint Matthew Island* on pp. 350–359.

The Mystery of Saint Matthew Island

by SUSAN E. QUINLAN

351

Map Labels

River

Wrangel
Island

*Chukchi
Sea*

BROOKS RANGE

CANADA

RUSSIA

Chukchi
Peninsula

Kolyma

KOLYMA RANGE

Bering Strait

Seward
Peninsula

Yukon River

• Fairbanks

Alaska

ALASKA RANGE

Ugol'nyye
Kopi

*Gulf of
Anadyr*

Nome • 64°N

Anchorage •

• Seward

St. Lawrence
Island

*Kenai
Peninsula*

Gulf of Alaska

St. Matthew
Island

Nunivak
Island

• Kodiak

Bering Sea

*Kodiak
Island*

ALEUTIAN RANGE

56°N

N

Aleutian Islands

miles
0   250   500

0   250   500
kilometers

168°W   160°W   152°W

W hen twenty-nine reindeer were released on Saint Matthew Island in 1944, the future of the herd seemed bright. This island in the midst of the Bering Sea offered plenty of plants and lichens for the reindeer to eat. No wolves, bears, or other large predators lived on the island.

Biologists expected the herd to grow quickly, and it did. By 1963, just nineteen years later, the herd numbered more than six thousand animals.

Then something went terribly wrong. Sailors who visited Saint Matthew to hunt reindeer in 1965 found the island littered with reindeer skeletons. They saw only a few live reindeer.

When the sailors' disturbing report reached Dr. David Klein, a scientist who had studied the herd, he immediately made picked up within two weeks, the investigators were left on the lonely shore.

The first step of their investigation was to determine if the disaster report was true. On his two previous visits to Saint Matthew years before, Klein had seen small groups of reindeer everywhere. But now the island was strangely still. The bleached skeletons of reindeer lay scattered across the tundra. Klein had a few suspicions about the disaster based on his earlier trips to the island. But to solve the mystery, he needed to conduct a thorough investigation.

As a first step, the researchers explored the mountainous island. After several days of difficult hiking, they found that only forty-two live animals remained on the entire island. All of these were adult females, except one scrawny adult male. There were no calves. The absence of calves meant that the lone male was unable to sire young. So the herd was doomed to disappear

plans to investigate. Arranging transportation to the remote island was difficult. Located halfway between Alaska and Siberia, this American island is so far from anywhere that it is nearly impossible to reach. No one lives there, so the island has no airports, and it is too far offshore for small planes to venture. For most of the year, it is surrounded by polar sea ice and thus unreachable even by boat. So it was over a year before Klein and two co-workers were able to reach the island by Coast Guard ship. With camping gear, food, and a promise that they would be completely someday. When and how had the other six thousand animals perished? And why had such a disaster happened to this once healthy herd?

Perhaps there was a clue in the reindeer skeletons. Klein noticed that nearly all of the

skeletons were in the same state of decay. That meant the entire herd had died at about the same time. Based on the moss growing on the bones and their bleached condition, Klein estimated that the carcasses had lain around for at least three years. Klein had counted six thousand animals when he visited the island in summer 1963, so he concluded that the reindeer had died sometime between that summer and the summer of 1964.

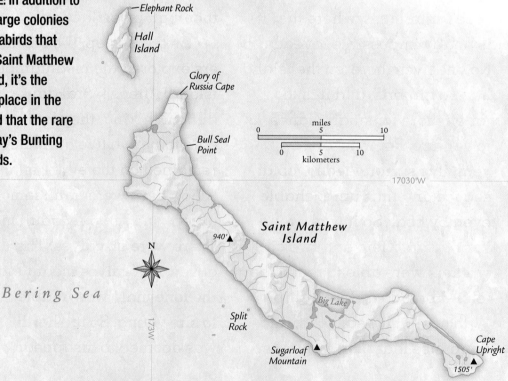

ABOVE: In addition to the large colonies of seabirds that use Saint Matthew Island, it's the only place in the world that the rare McKay's Bunting breeds.

— Elephant Rock

Hall Island

Glory of Russia Cape

Bull Seal Point

miles
0   5   10

kilometers
0   5   10

17030'W

Saint Matthew Island

940'▲

N

Bering Sea

173W

Split Rock

Big Lake

Sugarloaf Mountain ▲

Cape Upright

1505' ▲

Klein examined the skeletons more carefully, hoping to find more clues about the date of the die-off. He soon found the tiny, newly formed bones of baby reindeer that had died while still inside their mothers. These tiny bones told Klein that the female reindeer had died in late winter when their calves were still developing.

With the time of death narrowed down to late winter 1963–1964, Klein searched for clues about the cause of death. No predators lived on the island, and people rarely visit it. So neither of these potential killers were suspects in the case.

During the winter, the reindeer fed off vegetation such as lichen (TOP LEFT), sedge (TOP RIGHT), and willow (RIGHT), which grew on the windswept areas of the island where the snow is often blown free.

Klein ruled out diseases and parasites because he had found almost no signs of disease or parasites on his earlier visits to Saint Matthew. And it was not possible that an infected animal from somewhere else had brought in any disease or parasite. Saint Matthew Island is too remote.

Klein found skeletons from animals of all ages. Therefore old age was not the cause of the die-off either. That left weather and starvation as possible causes.

Weather seemed likely to be involved. The 1963–64 winter included some of the deepest snows and the coldest temperatures ever recorded in the Bering Sea area. But Klein thought a severe winter alone should not have caused such a massive die-off. Reindeer are arctic animals. As long as they have enough food, most healthy reindeer should be able to survive, even in a severe winter.

Thus Klein suspected that the Saint Matthew Island reindeer had been unhealthy or had run out of food during the winter of 1963–64. With this marrow cavity

compact bone

spongy bone

shrunken marrow of
a starving animal

thought in mind, Klein looked for evidence of starvation in the skeletons. An important clue lay hidden inside the bones. A well-fed animal has fat in its bone marrow. This fatty marrow remains in the bones for five years or more after an animal dies. Knowing this, Klein cracked open the leg bones of the skeletons to examine the marrow. Bone after bone, skeleton after skeleton, the marrow was completely gone. None of the animals had fat in their bone marrow when they died. This was clear evidence that the herd had starved to death.

When Klein visited the island three years earlier, he had noticed that some important winter food plants of the reindeer looked overgrazed. When he looked around this time, he noticed more severe damage. Many of the small plants looked as if they had been clipped back. And lichens, mosslike organisms that once carpeted the island, were now absent from many areas. Klein observed that the most serious damage was on hilltops and ridges, where winds keep the ground snow-free in winter. Such places would have been used heavily by reindeer during winter.

The damaged plant life led Klein to suspect that the reindeer had run out of nutritious food. Knowing that a lack of healthy food would show up in the weights of the reindeer, Klein reviewed the records from his earlier visits to Saint Matthew. The animals he had examined in 1957 weighed 199 to 404 pounds—more than most reindeer elsewhere. Clearly, the animals had plenty of food then. In contrast, the reindeer Klein had weighed in 1963 averaged 50 to 120 pounds less in weight. These lower weights showed that when the herd had numbered six thousand animals, many of the reindeer were not getting enough to eat. Klein next weighed a few of the live reindeer that remained on the island. These animals still weighed less than normal. They were not getting enough good food. That clinched the case. Klein was now certain what had happened.

Without predators or disease to limit its numbers, the small reindeer herd had grown quickly. Many young were born, and all the animals had plenty to eat. But after a few years, there were too many animals. The reindeer ate and trampled the tundra plants and lichens faster than these could grow. Crowded onto the windswept

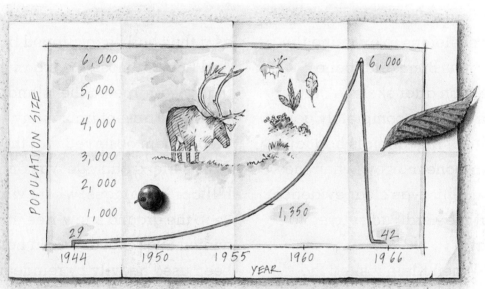

Assumed population of the Saint Matthew Island reindeer herd.
Actual counts are indicated on the population curve.

ridges in winter, the large herd destroyed the lush lichen carpet. When the most nutritious plants and lichens became scarce, the reindeer began to lose weight. In poor condition, and with little food to sustain them, disaster was inevitable. The harsh winter of 1963–64 spelled the end for the once healthy herd. The Saint Matthew Island reindeer had literally eaten themselves out of house and home. By their numbers alone, they had destroyed their island home and their future.

When Klein and his co-workers left Saint Matthew Island, they brought with them an important understanding of the connections between animals and their environment. Populations of all living things can skyrocket in numbers, like the reindeer herd. Usually, however, animal numbers are kept in check by predators, parasites and diseases, or other factors. The mystery of the Saint Matthew Island reindeer showed that in the absence of these natural checks, a growing population eventually destroys its own environment. And disaster strikes.

Common Core State Standards
Informational Text 1. Quote accurately from a text when explaining what the text says explicitly and when drawing inferences from the text.
Also Informational Text 2., 5., Writing 8., 9.

Envision It! | Retell

Think Critically

1. Think of other mysteries you have read. How would you compare "The Mystery of Saint Matthew Island" to another mystery you have read? How are the mysteries similar? How are they different? **Text to Text**

2. Dr. David Klein did not guess at answers. He searched for them and found them. How does the author portray Dr. Klein as a scientist rather than a guesser?
   Think Like an Author

3. Think of the main idea of the selection as a piece of advice for both animals and humans. What would the advice be? Use details from the selection to support your answer. **Main Idea and Details**

4. The selection can be seen as a series of clues that add up to a solution. Identify and list the major clues, from start to finish. Then discuss how they add up to the solution.
   Text Structure

5. **Look Back and Write** Reread the end of the selection on page 359. The author's last line in the selection talks about disaster striking. Why did disaster strike for the reindeer? Write an explanation to this question. Provide evidence to support your answer.
   Key Ideas and Details • Text Evidence

Meet the Author

Susan E. Quinlan

Susan E. Quinlan loves wildlife. She says, "It's hard to draw a line between what I do for a living and what I do for hobbies." As a biologist and naturalist guide, she has explored environments in many parts of the world. "The Mystery of Saint Matthew Island" is one of fourteen accounts in *The Case of the Mummified Pigs and Other Mysteries in Nature*. To write the book, she followed up on "wisps of knowledge" she had collected from her experiences in the field and from interviewing scientists.

Ms. Quinlan says, "My primary career interest is to share my fascination with nature and science with other people. Through my years of education and work as a wildlife biologist, I gradually realized that people who are trained as biologists look at nature differently from other people. This different way of looking at things results from acquired nature observation skills and from learning about the research of other scientists. One of my goals as a writer is to help others learn to look at nature in the ways that a biologist might. I also want to interpret the research work of scientists in ways that children and non-scientists can understand and enjoy."

Here are other books by Susan E. Quinlan.

The Case of the Monkeys That Fell from the Trees and Other Mysteries in Tropical Nature

The Case of the Mummified Pigs and Other Mysteries in Nature

Use the *Reader's and Writer's Notebook* to record your independent reading.

Reading Log

Common Core State Standards

Writing 3. Write narratives to develop real or imagined experiences or events using effective technique, descriptive details, and clear event sequences.
Also Writing 3.b., 3.d., Language 1.a.

Let's Write It!

Key Features of a Mystery

- a problem or mystery is presented early in the story

- facts and details are provided to help solve the mystery

- the mystery is resolved at the end

READING STREET ONLINE
GRAMMAR JAMMER
www.ReadingStreet.com

Mystery

A **mystery** is a story in which clues are presented in such a way that the readers have a chance to solve the problem. The student model on the next page is an example of a mystery.

Writing Prompt In *The Mystery of Saint Matthew Island*, scientists discover what was happening to reindeer on the island. Write your own mystery. Explain what the mystery is, and then use clues to reveal what happened, how it happened, and why.

Writer's Checklist

Remember, you should . . .

✓ guide the reader's understanding of key ideas and evidence.

✓ use organized paragraphs that include specific facts, details, and examples.

✓ provide details in ways that help readers solve the mystery.

✓ have a clearly defined focus and point of view.

The Mystery of the Missing Ping-Pong™ Balls

Last week, I went into the basement to play ping-pong, **because** it was too cold to play outside. I got out the ping-pong paddles **and** strung the net. Then I noticed the box of ping-pong balls was empty.

Where could the balls have gone? I looked all over the basement **but** could not find them.

Who would take ping-pong balls? Would the dog take them? I looked in the dog bed of Mustard, our yellow lab. There were some toys, **but** no ping-pong balls.

I asked my older sister, **but** she had not seen the balls either. That left my curious three-year-old brother. **While** he was sweet, he also often ran off with my playthings. **If** anyone knew where the ping-pong balls were, he would.

"Pop-pop balls?" he said. Then he pointed under his bed.

The balls were there, **although** most were as flat as postage stamps. He took one out **and** stomped on it. The flattened ball made a hollow crunching noise under his feet.

From now on, I am going to hide my ping-pong balls!

Genre
Mysteries
present a puzzle that readers try to solve as they read.

Writing Trait
Focus/Ideas
The writer uses facts and details to explain the mystery.

Conjunctions
are used correctly.

Conventions

Conjunctions

Remember Conjunctions are words such as *and, or,* and *but* that join words, phrases, or sentences. Subordinating conjunctions, such as *while, because, although,* and *if,* connect independent and dependent clauses.

363

Genre
Expository Text

- Expository texts contain facts and information about different subjects.

- Some authors of expository texts use sequential order to explain the relationships among ideas.

- Some authors of expository texts use graphics to explain information. These graphics can give you an overview of the contents.

- Read "City Hawks." Look for elements that make this article an expository text. How do the graphics help you understand the text?

The residents of one New York City apartment building were finding dead pigeons and other small animals near the entrance to their building. The sidewalk outside their home was dirty with bird droppings. The mess was coming from somewhere high on the side of the building, twelve stories up. That was where Pale Male and Lola, two red-tailed hawks, had built their nest.

Red-tailed hawks are not normally found in the middle of a busy city. They prefer wide-open country. They migrate as far north as Canada in the summer and live throughout North America and Mexico in the winter. But for whatever reason, the hawk that came to be known as Pale Male stopped migrating and made New York City his year-round home.

Let's **Think** About...

How do the photos and the text help you understand the contents of the article?
Expository Text

HAWKS

Pale Male builds a nest for himself and Lola.

Pale Male had picked a great place to live. Red-tailed hawks like to build their nests on cliffs, so the side of a concrete building must have seemed a lot like home to this red-tailed hawk. The apartment building was next to Central Park, which is so large that more than 280 different species of birds live there. The park is also a great habitat for small animals such as squirrels and chipmunks. These animals are exactly what hawks eat in the wild, and the large lake in the park was a plentiful source of water.

Pale Male had lived on the buildings around Central Park for years. He developed a large following of bird lovers who would sit in Central Park and watch him soar over the area. Pale Male found a mate, a bird the watchers called First Love. But First Love ate a pigeon that had been poisoned and she died. Pale Male had two more mates that also died. Then he found Lola. With his four female mates, Pale Male fathered more than two dozen city-raised hawks.

Let's **Think** About...

How does the time line help you understand the information in the article?
Expository Text

1993	1996	2004	2005
Pale Male builds first nest on NYC building.	Pale Male and Lola's first brood hatches.	Pale Male and Lola's nest is dismantled.	The hawks build a nest on their new perch.

Protesters push to have Pale Male's nest restored.   **Pale Male**

But in December 2004, the human residents of Pale Male and Lola's apartment building had had enough. They wanted a clean sidewalk and no more "surprises" from the pair of hawks. The building owner had an engineer remove the nest and the metal bars that held it up. Pale Male tried rebuilding the nest, but without the metal bars, the nest would not hold.

The removal of the nest made the news in New York. The story caught the attention of animal lovers around the world. People asked the building owner and city officials to put the nest back. Protesters set up on the street outside the building, demanding that the nest be restored.

The Audubon Society, an organization that protects birds and other wildlife, offered to help. They said they would work with the building owner to make the nesting place less of a nuisance to people in the building, while still allowing Pale Male and Lola to have their favorite perch.

With a new nesting site built specifically for them, Pale Male and Lola returned to their "apartment" on New York's Fifth Avenue. And the people looking out for Pale Male and Lola continue to make sure they stay safe from harm.

Let's Think About...

What happened after Pale Male's nest was removed? **Expository Text**

Let's Think About...

Reading Across Texts In *Saint Matthew* and "City Hawks," you read about problems in nature. Think about ways the problems are similar in each text, and in "Cleanup by Mother Nature" on page 349.

Writing Across Texts Write a paragraph explaining how the problems in each text are similar.

Pale Male's nest is replaced with new spikes and a nest cradle.

Common Core State Standards
Speaking/Listening 1.c. Pose and respond to specific questions by making comments that contribute to the discussion and elaborate on the remarks of others. **Also Foundational Skills 3.a., 4., 4.b.**

Vocabulary

Endings -s, -es

Word Structure The plurals of most English words are formed by adding -s to the singular form. If the noun ends in -ch, -sh, -s, -z, or -x, the plural is formed by adding -es to the singular form. For some nouns that end in -f, the plural is formed by changing the f to ve, and then adding -s.

Practice It! Read through *The Mystery of Saint Matthew Island*. Find and define at least two examples each of plural nouns ending in -s, -es, and -ves. For each one, write out both the singular and plural forms.

Fluency

Appropriate Phrasing

When you use appropriate phrasing, you group words together as you read, using the sentence's punctuation as a guide.

Practice It! With a partner, practice reading from *The Mystery of Saint Matthew Island*, page 356, paragraphs 1–3. Take turns reading aloud, pausing at punctuation. Offer each other feedback.

Listening and Speaking

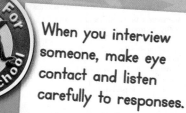

When you interview someone, make eye contact and listen carefully to responses.

Interview

In an interview, one person asks another person questions. The purpose of an interview is to find out what the person being interviewed knows about or has done.

Practice It! With a partner, conduct an interview in which one partner acts as Dr. Klein and the other partner acts as the interviewer. Work together to prepare questions for Dr. Klein. Then present your interview to the class.

Tips

Listening . . .

- Listen to the interviewer's messages.

- Ask questions to clarify the speaker's perspective.

Speaking . . .

- Speak loudly and enunciate clearly to communicate your ideas.

- Use and understand subordinating conjunctions, such as *while, because, although,* and *if.*

Teamwork . . .

- Ask for and listen to suggestions from other group members.

369

Common Core State Standards

Language 6. Acquire and use accurately grade-appropriate general academic and domain-specific words and phrases, including those that signal contrast, addition, and other logical relationships (e.g., *however, although, nevertheless, similarly, moreover, in addition*).

Also Speaking/Listening 1.d.

Oral Vocabulary

Let's Talk About

Unexpected Results of Our Actions

- Describe actions resulting in the unexpected.

- Listen to a classmate's messages about unexpected results.

- Determine classmates' main and supporting ideas about the unexpected.

READING STREET ONLINE
CONCEPT TALK VIDEO
www.ReadingStreet.com

Envision It! | Skill Strategy

Skill

Strategy

Comprehension Skill

Compare and Contrast

- When writers compare and contrast things, they tell how those things are alike or different. Words such as *same*, *also*, *before*, *although*, and *however* are clues that things are being compared and contrasted.

- You can compare and contrast different things you read about with one another.

- Use the organizer to record comparisons and contrasts that you find in "Andrew's Wish."

Beginning	End

Comprehension Strategy

Story Structure

Active readers notice story structure, including the problems characters face and the rising action, climax, and outcome. Authors use story incidents to advance plots and give rise to future events. After reading "Andrew's Wish," describe the incidents that advanced the story or foreshadowed the events at the end.

Andrew's Wish

Andrew had always dreamed of his very own mountain bike. Like his friends, Andrew loved riding on the trails. However, sometimes he chose not to ride because he hated having to borrow one of his friends' bikes.

As Andrew walked home from school one day, he noticed a frog following him. When he asked what the frog wanted, the frog said, "I want to grant you a wish because you did not step on me." Andrew immediately asked for a bike. The frog said he could give Andrew a magic bicycle that only Andrew could see. Whenever someone else got close, the bike would disappear. Andrew agreed to this because he wanted a bike so much.

Later, Andrew rode his bike alone. He had a lot of fun, but he missed his friends. The next day, Andrew rode his magic bike to meet his friends. When he met them, the bike disappeared. Andrew realized that having a bike was not as important as having friends, so he returned the magic bike to the frog. The next day, Andrew happily borrowed a bike and went riding with his friends.

Skill What comparisons and contrasts can you find in this paragraph?

Skill Compare Andrew's feelings about borrowing a bike at the beginning of the story to those he had at the end of the story.

Strategy Identify and explain the events in the story that gave rise to the story's ending.

Your Turn!

Need a Review? See the *Envision It! Handbook* for additional help with comparing, contrasting, and identifying story structure.

Ready to Try It? Use what you have learned about comparing and contrasting and story structure as you read *King Midas and the Golden Touch*.

Common Core State Standards
Language 4.b. Use common, grade-appropriate Greek and Latin affixes and roots as clues to the meaning of a word (e.g., *photograph, photosynthesis*).

Envision It! | Words to Know

adorn

cleanse

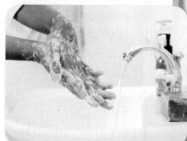

spoonful

lifeless

precious

realm

Vocabulary Strategy for

Suffixes *-less, -ful*

Word Structure A suffix is an affix added to the end of a base word that changes the base word's meaning. Sometimes the spelling of the base word changes when a suffix is added. Knowing the meaning of the suffix can help you determine the meaning of the word.

1. Look at an unfamiliar word to see if it has a base word you know.

2. Check for the suffix *-less* or *-ful*.

3. Decide how it changes the base word's meaning. The suffix *-less* can mean "without," as in *harmless*. The suffix *-ful* can mean "the amount that will fill," as in *handful*.

4. Try this meaning in the sentence to see if it makes sense.

As you read "Hospital for Wild Animals," look for words with the suffix *-less* or *-ful*. Use the suffixes to determine the meanings of the words.

Words to Write Reread "Hospital for Wild Animals." Imagine you are the narrator. Write a short note to a friend explaining the most meaningful part of your experience. Use words from the *Words to Know* list in your note.

Hospital for
WILD ANIMALS

There are places around us where magic happens. I learned about one such place when I found an injured owl in my backyard. It had been shot in one wing. My heart sank as I bent over the apparently lifeless form. Then it moved! What could I do to save the owl?

My mom told me to call the local wildlife rehabilitation center. They told us how to carefully wrap and carry the owl to them. The worker on duty was careful to cleanse the wound. She said the owl was weak, but it might live. Over the next few weeks, I visited this magic realm every day and saw kind people helping foxes, raccoons, and birds of all kinds. Soon the helpless owl was ravenous and ate its first spoonful of meat. I saw the complex patterns of color that adorn owls' feathers.

There was a special kind of enchantment about the place. I felt lucky to see these wild creatures up close and to be able to help them get well. It is good to know there are people who realize that the lives of wild things are precious.

Your Turn!

Need a Review? For additional help with suffixes, see *Words!*

Ready to Try It? Read *King Midas and the Golden Touch* on pp. 376–393.

Question of the Week

How can we learn from the results of our actions?

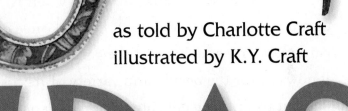

KING

as told by Charlotte Craft
illustrated by K.Y. Craft

MIDAS

and the
GOLDEN TOUCH

Genre

Myths are tales handed down by word of mouth for generations. They tell about nature and human behavior. As you read, notice that the author points out how the king's behavior leads to tragedy.

There once lived a very rich king called Midas who believed that nothing was more precious than gold. He loved its soft yellow hue and comforting weight in the palm of his hand. The chink of gold coins dropped into a leather purse sounded sweeter to him than the songs of his finest musicians. There was only one thing that Midas loved more, and that was his daughter, Aurelia.

"Aurelia," he often told her as she played by the throne, "someday I shall bequeath to you the greatest treasury of gold in all the world."

There had been a time, however, when King Midas loved roses as much as he now loved gold. He had once called together the best gardeners in his realm, and the garden they created for him became renowned for the beauty and variety of its roses.

But in time the delicate fragrances and exquisite colors meant nothing to Midas. Only Aurelia still loved the garden. Every day she would pick a bouquet of the most perfect roses to adorn the king's breakfast table. But when Midas saw the flowers, he would think, *Their beauty lasts but a day. If they were gold, it would last forever!*

One day the king's guards found an old man asleep under the rosebushes and brought him before King Midas.

"Unbind him," Midas ordered. "Without my gold, I would be as poor as he. Tonight he shall dine with me!"

So that night the old man sat at the king's table, where he was well fed and entertained by the king himself. And after a good night's sleep, the old man went on his way.

That morning, as he often did, Midas went down into his dungeon. With a large brass key, he unlocked the door to the secret chamber where he kept his gold. After carefully locking the door behind him, he sat down to admire his precious wealth.

"Ah, I do love it so," he sighed, gazing at his riches. "No matter how hard I work, no matter how long I live, I will never have enough."

He was lost in these thoughts when the chamber suddenly filled with light. King Midas looked up and was amazed to behold the glowing figure of a young man. Since there was no way into the room but through the locked door, Midas knew that he was in the presence of magic.

"Do you not recognize me, friend?"

Midas shook his head. The mysterious stranger smiled at him, and it seemed that all the gold in the dungeon glittered even brighter.

"I am the old man from the rose garden. Instead of punishing me for trespassing, you entertained me at your table. I had thought to reward you for your kindness, but with so much gold, you must surely want for nothing."

"That's not true," cried Midas. "A man can never have enough gold."

The stranger's smile broadened. "Well, then, what would make you a happier man?"

Midas thought for only a moment. "Perhaps if everything I touched would turn to gold," he said.

That is your wish?"

"Yes, for then it would always be at my fingertips," Midas assured him.

"Think carefully, my friend," cautioned the visitor.

"Yes," replied Midas. "The golden touch would bring me all the happiness I need."

"And so it shall be yours."

With that, the mysterious figure became brighter and brighter, until the light became so intense that Midas had to close his eyes. When he opened them, he was alone once again.

Had the enchantment worked?

Midas eagerly rubbed the great brass door key but was greatly disappointed. There was no gold in his hands. Bewildered, he looked around the dim room and wondered if perhaps he had been dreaming.

But when King Midas awoke the next day, he found his bedchamber bathed in golden light. Glistening in the morning sun, the plain linen bedcovers had been transformed into finely spun gold!

Jumping out of bed, he gasped with astonishment. The bedpost turned to gold as soon as he touched it. "It's true," he cried. "I have the golden touch!"

Midas pulled on his clothes. He was thrilled to find himself wearing a handsome suit of gold—never mind that it was a bit heavy. He slid his spectacles onto his nose. To his delight, they too turned to gold—never mind that he couldn't see through them. With a gift as great as this, he thought, no inconvenience could be too great.

Without wasting another moment, Midas rushed out of

the room, through the palace, and into the garden.

The roses glistened with the morning dew, and their scent gently perfumed the air. Midas went from bush to bush, touching each of the blossoms.

"How happy Aurelia will be when she sees these roses of gold!" he exclaimed. He never noticed how the perfect golden blossoms drooped and pulled down the bushes with their weight.

Soon it was time for breakfast. Midas sat down just as Aurelia entered the room, clutching a golden rose, her face wet with tears.

"Father, Father, a horrible thing has happened," she said, sobbing. "I went to the garden to pick you a flower, but all of the roses have become hard and yellow."

"They are golden roses now, my love, and will never fade."

"But I miss their scent, Father," cried Aurelia.

"I am sorry, my dear. I thought only to please you. Now we can buy all the roses you could ever wish for." Midas smiled at his daughter to comfort her. "Please wipe your eyes, and we'll have our breakfast together."

Midas lifted a spoonful of porridge to his mouth, but as soon as the porridge touched his lips it turned into a hard golden lump.

Perhaps if I eat quickly, he thought, puzzled, and snatched
a fig from a bowl of fruit. It turned to solid gold before he could
take a bite. He reached out for some bread, but his fingertips had
no sooner brushed against the loaf than it, too, turned to gold.
He tried cheese and even a spoonful of jam, but all to no avail.
"How am I to eat?" he grumbled.

"What's wrong, Father?" asked Aurelia.

"Nothing," he answered, wishing not to worry her. "Nothing
at all, my child."

But Midas began to wring his hands. If he was hungry now,
he imagined how much more hungry he would be by dinner.
And then he began to wonder: Will I ever eat again?

Aurelia, who had been anxiously watching her father all this
time, slipped out of her chair and went to comfort him. "Please
don't cry," she said. Midas smiled and took her hand in his. But
suddenly he recoiled in horror.

His daughter stood before him, an expression of concern
frozen on her face, a teardrop clinging to her golden cheek.
His cursed touch had turned Aurelia into a lifeless statue.

Midas howled in anguish and tore at his hair. He couldn't bear
to look at the statue, but neither could he bear to leave her side.

"Well, King Midas, are you not the happiest of men?" Midas
wiped his eyes and saw the mysterious stranger standing before
him once again.

"Oh, no, I am the most miserable of men!" he cried.

"What? Did I not grant your wish for the golden touch?"

"Yes, but it is a curse to me now." Midas wept. "All that I truly loved is now lost to me."

"Do you mean to say," asked the young man, "that you would prefer a crust of bread or a cup of water to the gift of the golden touch?"

"Oh, yes!" Midas exclaimed. "I would give up all the gold in the world if only my daughter were restored to me."

"Then make your way to the river that flows past the borders of your kingdom. Follow the river upstream until you reach its source. As you cleanse yourself in the foaming spring, the golden touch will be washed away. Take with you a vase so that you may sprinkle water over any object you wish to change back to its original form." With those words, the young man vanished.

As soon as Midas reached the spring, he plunged in without removing even his shoes. As the water washed the gold from his clothes, he noticed a pretty little violet growing wild along the banks and gently brushed his finger against it. When he saw that the delicate purple flower continued to bend with the breeze, he was overjoyed.

Midas made his way back to the palace, where the first thing he did was to sprinkle the water over his beloved Aurelia. No sooner did the water touch her cheek than she was restored, laughing at her father's game and remembering not a moment of being a golden statue.

Together, the two went out to the rose garden. Midas sprinkled each frozen rose with a little river water, and Aurelia clapped her hands when she saw them cured of their golden blight.

Joyfully, then, Midas restored all else he had transformed—except for a single rose, kept forever as a reminder of the golden touch.

Common Core State Standards

Literature 1. Quote accurately from a text when explaining what the text says explicitly and when drawing inferences from the text. **Also Literature 2., 3., Writing 9.**

Envision It! | Retell

Think Critically

1. The story of King Midas warns us against something. Compare and contrast the theme or moral lesson from this story with another story you know such as "Little Red Riding Hood" or "The Tortoise and the Hare."

Text to Text

2. What words, details, and phrases does the author use to let the readers know when this story takes place? Make a list of your answers. **Think Like an Author**

3. The King is restless at the start of the story and content at the end. What brought about this transformation? Use details from the story to explain the change.

Compare and Contrast

4. What do you think of the character of Midas? How do his traits and actions affect the story's conflict and outcome?

Story Structure

5. Look Back and Write The "Midas touch" is a saying some people use. Reread pages 384–387. What do you think the "Midas touch" means? Write a possible definition of the saying. Provide evidence to support your answer.

Key Ideas and Details • Text Evidence

Meet the Author and Illustrator
Charlotte Craft
and Kinuko Craft

Kinuko Craft, illustrator of *King Midas and the Golden Touch*, says, "I feel that, throughout time, each generation has a person with a 'golden touch' who learns the same lesson Midas did." In her paintings for some of the scenes in the book, she used geometric patterns. These come from the designs on small objects found at a burial site believed to be that of the real King Midas. Archaeologists found the objects during a dig at the site in Turkey.

Kinuko Craft is one of the most widely respected illustrators of fantasy in the United States today. In an interview, she said, "From grade school through my high school days, my effort was to imitate nature—anything natural." Later, she worked in the world of commercial art, where she used a large variety of styles and mediums. About ten years ago, she began creating paintings for picture books using oil over watercolor.

Charlotte Craft is the daughter of illustrator Kinuko Craft. She lives in Scotland with her family.

Here are other books illustrated by Kinuko Craft.

Use the *Reader's and Writer's Notebook* to record your independent reading.

Let's Write It!

Key Features of a Parody

- imitates a familiar story's plot, style, and language

- changes details of the original story for comic effect

- may include action that rises to a climax

READING STREET ONLINE
GRAMMAR JAMMER
www.ReadingStreet.com

Narrative

Parody

A **parody** retells a familiar story in a new and comical way. Readers should be able to recognize the story on which the parody is based. The student model on the next page is an example of a parody.

Writing Prompt In *King Midas and the Golden Touch*, a greedy king wishes that everything he touches would turn into gold. Imagine if the king's touch had turned things into something other than gold. What would it be? Write a parody, telling this story.

Writer's Checklist

Remember, you should ...

☑ retell the story in a new and funny way.

☑ keep some of the story's original details.

☑ have a clearly defined focus, plot, and point of view.

☑ use sensory details to create the setting.

396

King Impulsive

King Impulsive was known as a pet-lover who had no pets. So one day, without any thought, he cried, "I wish that every animal I touched would become my pet."

The next day, King Impulsive went outside and saw a scrawny dog. The king patted the dog's head, and at once the dog stopped slinking and trotted confidently into the palace kitchen, where it found a royal meal.

Minutes later, a mouse scampered across King Impulsive's foot. As soon as it touched him, the mouse stopped. It looked at the King and then headed for the palace. King Impulsive followed the mouse. There, he saw mice running and dogs barking—everywhere!

"I can't take this!" King Impulsive screamed, and he wished for the magic touch to be removed.

Now, it would be nice to tell you that King Impulsive was less impulsive after his pet experience. However, the next day he impulsively changed his name to King Midas, and you've heard all about him!

Writing Trait
Voice The story uses the third person point of view, and has an informal tone.

Commas are used correctly.

Genre
A **parody** is a comical imitation of a familiar story.

Conventions

Commas

Remember Commas can clarify meaning and tell readers when to pause. Place a comma before a conjunction in a compound sentence. (For example: *"I can't take this!" King Impulsive screamed, and he wished for the magic touch to be removed.*)

Common Core State Standards
Literature 9. Compare and contrast
stories in the same genre (e.g., mysteries
and adventure stories) on their approaches
to similar themes and topics.
Also Literature 10.

Social Studies in Reading

Genre
Myth

- A myth is an ancient story that is handed down by word of mouth for generations, often using vivid sensory language.

- Some myths are known as origin myths because they describe how natural phenomena, or things that happen in nature, came to be.

- Origin myths can be found in various cultures.

- Read "Prometheus, the Fire-Bringer." As you read, think about why this is an origin myth.

PROMETHEUS
THE FIRE-BRINGER
An ancient Greek myth

The people of ancient Greece told many myths. This is a myth about the origin of fire.

Prometheus was a Titan, one of the many gods in Greek mythology. The goddess Athena taught him many things. One day, Athena told him, "Our studies have come to an end."

She asked Prometheus, "What will you do with all your knowledge?"

Prometheus answered, "I will teach humans. I will teach them everything I know."

And that is what he did. He taught people about math, medicine, and how to build houses. He even taught them about the stars.

The people were grateful for Prometheus. However, this made Zeus angry. Zeus was the greatest of all Greek gods. He did not want people to have knowledge, so he punished the people. He took fire away from them.

The people begged Zeus to let them keep fire. But Zeus showed them no mercy. "I am returning to my home on Mount Olympus," Zeus said, "and I am taking fire with me."

The people were very upset. They needed fire in order to stay warm. They asked, "How will we cook? How will we stay warm? How will we light the darkness at night?"

Prometheus returned to the people and said, "Do not worry. I will return fire to you."

That day, Prometheus climbed Mount Olympus. He made sure that nobody saw him. He picked up a stick and lit it with fire from the sun. Then he carried the torch back down the mountain.

The people could not believe their eyes. Prometheus was bringing fire back to them! "You kept your promise!" the people exclaimed.

"I am returning fire to you," Prometheus said, "and you will never lose it again."

The people were relieved and happy. They thanked Prometheus for what he had done.

Ever since that day, people have used fire to cook. They have used it to make light and to stay warm. Just as Prometheus promised, they never lost it again.

Let's **Think** About...

How does this myth differ from myths you've read from other cultures? **Myth**

Let's **Think** About...

What explanation does this myth give for how fire came to be? **Myth**

Let's **Think** About...

Reading Across Texts Compare and contrast King Midas and Prometheus. What kinds of characters are they?

Writing Across Texts Using sensory details and imagery, write a dialogue between Prometheus and King Midas in which Prometheus helps King Midas with his mistakes.

Common Core State Standards
Foundational Skills 4.b. Read on-level prose and poetry orally with accuracy, appropriate rate, and expression on successive readings.
Also Speaking/Listening 4., Language 4.b.

Let's Learn It!

READING STREET ONLINE
ONLINE STUDENT EDITION
www.ReadingStreet.com

Vocabulary

Suffixes -less, -ful

Word Structure You can use a word's structure to learn more about what the word means. The suffix *-less* means "without." The suffix *-ful* means "full of" or "characterized by."

Practice It! Work with a partner to create and define a list of words from stories you've read ending in the Old English suffixes *-less* and *-ful*. What is the root word in each one? Can the same root be used with both suffixes?

Fluency

Rate

You can use different rates to mimic the flow of everyday language. Slow down for emphasis, and speed up to express the energy in a text.

Practice It! With a partner, practice reading aloud three paragraphs from *King Midas and the Golden Touch*. Focus on reading at an appropriate rate. Take turns reading and offering each other feedback.

400

Listening and Speaking

When you speak, use gestures to make a point.

Storytelling

Storytelling is a way of sharing information orally. Stories have a beginning, a middle, and a satisfying end, and use vivid oral language.

Practice It! With a partner, prepare a myth, fable, or other kind of story to present to the class. Identify the main plot points. Rehearse the story so that you can tell it—not just read it—to an audience. Then present your story to the class.

Tips

Listening . . .

- Pay attention to what each speaker is saying.

- Listen for the main ideas and supporting ideas in the story.

Speaking . . .

- Make eye contact with your audience and use gestures to communicate.

- Keep your listeners interested by varying the volume of your voice as you speak.

Teamwork . . .

- Consider suggestions from your partner.

- Ask your partner questions.

Oral Vocabulary

Let's Talk About

Safe Travel

- Express your opinions about travel safety.

- Listen to and ask questions about a classmate's experiences with travel safety.

- Determine main and supporting ideas in your classmates' messages.

READING STREET ONLINE
CONCEPT TALK VIDEO
www.ReadingStreet.com

◄EXIT►

You've learned
2 8 0
Amazing Words
so far this year!

Common Core State Standards

Informational Text 1. Quote accurately from a text when explaining what the text says explicitly and when drawing inferences from the text. **Also Informational Text 2.**

Envision It! Skill Strategy

Skill

Strategy

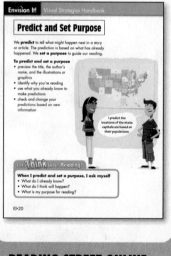

Comprehension Skill

Fact and Opinion

- Statements of fact can be proved true or false. You can verify facts through established methods, such as using prior knowledge, asking an expert, or checking a reference.

- Statements of opinion are personal judgments that cannot be proved true or false. Determine if opinions are either valid or faulty by using your prior knowledge.

- Use a graphic organizer like the one below to help you record opinions and determine and verify facts in "How Blimps Are Used."

Statement of Opinion	Support	Valid or Faulty?

Comprehension Strategy

Predict and Set Purpose

Active readers try to predict what they will learn when they read nonfiction. Predicting as you preview the article can also help you set a purpose for what you are reading. After you read, see whether your prediction was correct.

How Blimps Are Used

There is no better outdoor advertisement than the blimp. These flying billboards carry advertising messages hundreds and thousands of feet in the air, where they can be viewed by hundreds and thousands of people at once. These flying machines have appeared in the skies for more than eighty years.

In 1925, the American tire company Goodyear built its first blimp. It was a huge success. Goodyear built almost three hundred blimps, all promoting their products. They are often seen on TV sports programs. Cameras on board give viewers aerial shots of the action.

These blimps are faster than most ocean ships. In fact, the U.S. Navy used them during the Second World War. Large enough to carry equipment and stay in the air for days at a time, they are also used by law enforcement officers.

Because blimps have the best safety record of any flying vehicle today, they are used to cover many special events. Today, tourists also use them. There is no better way to see the African plains than by floating above them. A ride in a blimp is truly a unique adventure.

Strategy Preview the title. What do you think this article will be about? What purpose for reading will you be setting?

Skill Which statements in this paragraph are facts? How would you go about verifying them?

Skill Based on your own knowledge, is this statement of opinion valid or faulty? Why?

Your Turn!

Ⅱ Need a Review? See the *Envision It! Handbook* for additional help with facts and opinions and predicting and setting purpose.

▶ Ready to Try It? Use what you have learned about facts and opinions and predicting and setting purpose as you read *The* Hindenburg.

Common Core State Standards

Language 4.a. Use context (e.g., cause/effect relationships and comparisons in text) as a clue to the meaning of a word or phrase. **Also Language 4.**

cruised

explosion

hydrogen

criticizing

drenching

era

Vocabulary Strategy for

⊙ Unfamiliar Words

Context Clues As you read, you may see a word you do not know. Often the author will give clues to determine and clarify the meaning of an unfamiliar word. Check the words and sentences around the unfamiliar word for these clues.

1. Reread the sentence where the unfamiliar word appears.

2. Is there a specific clue to the word's meaning?

3. For more help, read the sentences around the sentence with the unfamiliar word.

4. Try the clue's meaning in the sentence with the unfamiliar word. Does it make sense?

Read "The Birth of the Automobile" on page 407. Use the context to help you determine and clarify the meanings of this week's *Words to Know*.

Words to Write Reread "The Birth of the Automobile." Imagine you live in that era. Write about the transportation you are using. Use words from the *Words to Know* list in your writing.

The Birth of the Automobile

The automobile may well have been the most important invention in transportation history. However, it took many people many years to come up with an engine that worked well. In 1771 a Frenchman invented a three-wheeled sort of tractor. It ran on steam power, and it cruised along at 2½ miles per hour. (Get a horse!) It crashed into a stone wall. Don't worry—all the riders survived! In 1807 a Swiss man invented an engine that used a mix of hydrogen and oxygen for fuel. (Can you imagine the explosion?) Neither of these succeeded.

Not until the 1880s did inventors come up with an engine that was practical. A gas engine was mounted on an open coach. (If it rained, the driver and guests got a drenching!) This four-wheeled vehicle had a top speed of 10 miles per hour.

Improvements happened fast after that. The era of the automobile had begun. This age has continued to the present time and shows no signs of stopping. Instead of criticizing the early cars, we should admire them for pointing the way.

Your Turn!

Need a Review?
For additional help with context clues, see *Words!*

Ready to Try It?
Read *The Hindenburg* on pp. 408–423.

Expository texts explain what certain things are and how and why they came to be. As you read, notice how the author explains the origins of the *Hindenburg*—and its disastrous end.

THE HINDENBURG

PATRICK O'BRIEN

Question of the Week

How can unexpected encounters reveal hidden dangers?

Hugo Eckener piloting the Graf Zeppelin

In Germany in 1900, the first dirigible was successfully flown. This mammoth airship consisted of several giant, gas-filled balloons inside a hard, hollow structure that was moved along by motors and steered by fins. In 1931 the most advanced dirigible yet, the *Graf Zeppelin,* began flying from Germany across the Atlantic and back, carrying twenty passengers in dreamy luxury. Meanwhile, its designer, Hugo Eckener, had even grander plans in mind.

The Graf Zeppelin over Tokyo

While the *Graf Zeppelin* was busy with these transatlantic flights, Eckener planned another airship that was soon taking shape at the Zeppelin Company in Germany. A bigger and better ship. The perfect airship. The *Hindenburg*.

The new zeppelin was to be so big that a giant new hangar had to be made to house it.

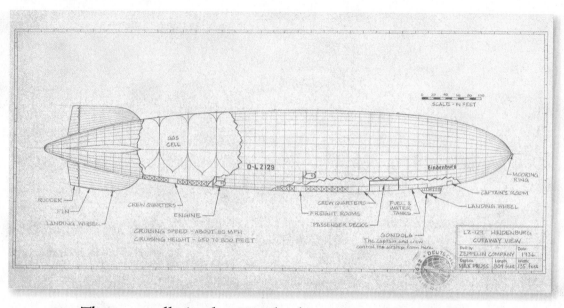

The gas cells in the *Hindenburg* were filled with hydrogen. Hydrogen can be extremely dangerous because it will explode if it comes into contact with a spark or a flame. All the German zeppelins ever made had been filled with hydrogen, but the zeppelin workers were very careful and they had an excellent safety record. In the early days there had been a few accidents in which crew members were killed, but no paying passenger had ever been hurt or killed in a German zeppelin accident.

The designers of the *Hindenburg* included all the latest safety measures in their new zeppelin. An American naval officer examined the ship and reported, "I consider all possibilities of danger in the new zeppelin eliminated."

In the 1930s, the Nazis came into power in Germany. Eckener did not like their brutal ways. He resisted their control whenever he could, and he made speeches criticizing the Nazi party. Eckener thought that transatlantic travel could help create better understanding between different countries. He said that he wanted "to be of service to mankind in the development of air travel." But the Nazis wanted zeppelins only to glorify Germany and to symbolize Nazi power.

The Nazis did not like Eckener, so they made him
a "nonperson." This meant that his name could not be
mentioned in newspapers, and no one was allowed to print
a picture of him. Eckener was forced to put the Nazi symbol,
the swastika, on the *Hindenburg*. His dream airship would
have to fly the Atlantic with the hated swastika displayed on
the tail fins.

The *Hindenburg* made its first flight to America in May of 1936. The takeoff was so smooth that passengers did not even know the ship was airborne unless they were looking out the windows. The ride was perfectly steady and quiet as the ship cruised at 80 miles per hour over the Atlantic Ocean.

Only the rich could afford to travel by airship. The tickets were $400, about the price of a small car in those days. The passengers had their own rooms with beds and sinks, and there was even a shower on board. The kitchen was well stocked with the finest foods. On Atlantic crossings, the chefs used 440 pounds of meat and poultry, 800 eggs, and 220 pounds of butter.

When the airship arrived in America, cruising low over New York City, thousands of people filled the rooftops, windowsills, and streets, cheering wildly as the huge zeppelin floated overhead. Eckener later tried to explain the strange appeal of his giant soaring ships. A zeppelin, he said, was "like a fabulous silvery fish, floating quietly in the ocean of air. . . . It seemed to be coming from another world and to be returning there like a dream."

The *Hindenburg* made nine more round-trip flights to the United States in 1936. The landing spot was in Lakehurst, New Jersey, about an hour south of New York City. During the winter of that year, the *Hindenburg* made seven trips down to Rio de Janeiro.

The first flying season was a huge success, and eighteen trips to the United States were scheduled for the next year. At the same time, the Zeppelin Company's other ship, the *Graf Zeppelin,* was still keeping a schedule of regular flights from Germany to Rio de Janeiro.

Because of the success of the *Hindenburg,* Hugo Eckener was able to make an agreement with an American company. The Americans would build two big airships, and the Zeppelin Company in Germany would build two more. There would be four new airships flying the Atlantic. Eckener's dream of regular transatlantic travel was beginning to come true.

On May 3, 1937, sixty-one crew members and thirty-six passengers boarded the *Hindenburg* for the flight to America. Fourteen-year-old Werner Franz was thrilled to be a cabin boy on the famous airship. He was the youngest member of the crew. Two of the passengers were even younger—Werner and Wallace Doehner, ages six and eight. Somewhere over the Atlantic, a steward politely took away Werner's toy truck. It made sparks when it rolled. In an airship filled with explosive hydrogen, sparks could mean disaster.

The *Hindenburg* cruised low over the icebergs of the North Atlantic, close to the spot where the *Titanic* had gone down twenty-five years before. At four o'clock on the afternoon of May 6, the *Hindenburg* arrived over the landing field in Lakehurst, New Jersey.

There were thunderstorms in the area, so it cruised south over the beaches of the Atlantic coast to wait out the storms.

Shortly after seven o'clock, the *Hindenburg* returned to the landing field and slowed to a stop about 250 feet above the ground. The crew dropped ropes from the ship's nose so the men below could help bring the ship in. Everything was done according to plan. It was a routine landing. There was no warning of what was about to happen.

In thirty-two seconds, the mighty airship *Hindenburg*
was a mass of flaming wreckage on the ground.

Amazingly, of the ninety-seven people on board, sixty-seven survived the explosion. One person on the ground was killed, and five survivors died later in the hospital.

One passenger who was an acrobat was able to hang on outside a window of the burning airship until it was low enough that he could drop off onto the sandy ground below. He stood up, brushed himself off, and limped away. One older couple walked down the steps of the slowly falling ship as if it was a normal landing. They escaped, injured but alive. The Doehner brothers survived when their mother threw them out of a window into the arms of the rescuers below.

Werner Franz, the fourteen-year-old cabin boy, rode the flaming airship almost all the way to the ground. A large water tank in the ship above his head burst, drenching him with water. He jumped to the ground as the flaming airship was falling around him and dashed out, soaking wet but unharmed.

The cause of the *Hindenburg* explosion is still a mystery. Hugo Eckener felt that there was static electricity in the air because of the thunderstorms in the area, and that this electricity might have ignited some hydrogen that was leaking near the back of the airship. Some people believe, however, that a bomb caused the explosion. There was no evidence of a bomb, but the swastikas on the tail of the ship might have made the *Hindenburg* a target for people who wanted to destroy a symbol of Nazi power.

Millions of people around the world watched newsreels of the *Hindenburg* explosion and heard reports about it on the radio. Zeppelins were now seen as death traps, and all interest in building more of them died with the *Hindenburg*. Eckener wrote that "it appeared to me the hopeless end of a great dream, a kind of end of the world."

Over the years, airplanes have been developed to be much faster and bigger than they were before. People now fly in airplanes instead of airships. Even Hugo Eckener had to admit that "a good thing has been replaced by a better." The mighty zeppelins no longer cruise through the ocean of air on grand voyages to distant lands. Like the *Hindenburg,* the era of the great airships is gone forever.

Did you know?

◀ The *Hindenburg* made the trip from Germany to America in two and a half days. The only other way to cross the Atlantic was by ship, and the fastest ships needed five days to make the trip.

On one return trip from Rio de Janeiro, someone sneaked five monkeys on board the *Graf Zeppelin*. They soon got loose and were seen swinging through the girders inside the airship. Pets were shipped on the *Hindenburg*—dogs, birds, fish, and even a deer. ▼

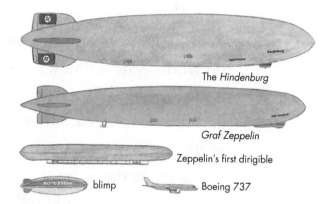

The *Hindenburg*

Graf Zeppelin

Zeppelin's first dirigible

blimp   Boeing 737

▲ The *Hindenburg* was the biggest thing that ever flew.

The *Hindenburg* was ▶ named for a former president of Germany, Paul von Hindenburg.

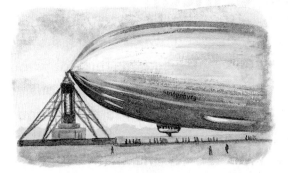

The tower on the top of the Empire State Building was built as a mooring mast. It was never used. ▼

▲ Airships docked at mooring masts. A ring on the front of an airship was attached to the top of the mast. This allowed the ship to swing with the wind while moored.

◄ Play stopped at a baseball game between the Brooklyn Dodgers and the Pittsburgh Pirates in Brooklyn when the *Hindenburg* flew over on its way to a landing. Everyone wanted to watch the airship.

Eckener went to a party in New York City to celebrate the *Hindenburg's* first flight. In the middle of the table was a mound of ice cream in the shape of a zeppelin. ▶

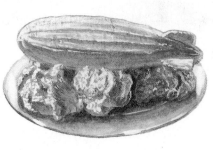

Common Core State Standards
Informational Text 1. Quote accurately from a text when explaining what the text says explicitly and when drawing inferences from the text. **Also Writing 9.**

Envision It! Retell

Think Critically

1. You have read about two disasters, the *Hindenburg* and the *Titanic*. Think of what you have learned about these two crafts, including the reasons they were built, and about the accidents that became part of history. What are the similarities? What are the differences? **Text to Text**

2. Nonfiction authors often include human-interest stories to help readers identify with historical people and situations. What is one human-interest story in *The* Hindenburg? **Think Like an Author**

3. One word on page 419 strongly signals an opinion. What is that word and the opinion it signals? Is this opinion valid or faulty? Use details from the page to support your answer. **Fact and Opinion**

4. What clues does the author provide in the selection to help you predict that something disastrous will happen to the *Hindenburg*? **Predict and Set Purpose**

5. Look Back and Write Reread the last sentence on page 421. Is it a statement of fact or of opinion? Do you agree or disagree with this statement? Write your answer. Provide evidence to support your answer.

Key Ideas and Details • **Text Evidence**

Patrick O'Brien

Patrick O'Brien has been working as an illustrator since the 1980s, specializing in animal and historical illustrations. He also does freelance art for advertising agencies, providing illustrations for video boxes, posters, stickers, and refrigerator magnets. In 1998 Mr. O'Brien began writing and illustrating children's books.

Mr. O'Brien says, "I began working on *The Hindenburg* after my editor asked me if I would be interested. I did a lot of research. I went up to Lakehurst, New Jersey, where the crash site is. I bought a plastic model of the *Hindenburg* and photographed that to get the different angles and do it accurately. I often use models if I can find them. I had to order it from Germany on the Internet. For the explosions, I watched historical films of the actual event and other movies with big explosions."

Mr. O'Brien says the main thing about writing the story was deciding which part to focus on. "I decided to use the most famous character in the story, Mr. Hugo Eckener, as the main character. He was involved in making airships since the beginning and was a strong anti-Nazi."

Here are other books by Patrick O'Brien.

The Great Ships

Duel of the Ironclads

Use the *Reader's and Writer's Notebook* to record your independent reading.

Reading Log

425

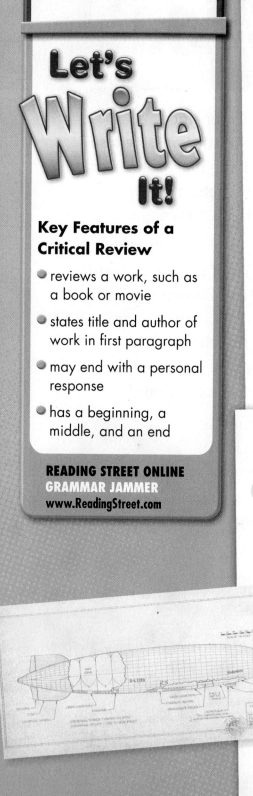

Common Core State Standards

Writing 1. Write opinion pieces on topics or texts, supporting a point of view with reasons and information. **Also Writing 1.a., 1.d., 9., Language 2.d.**

Let's Write It!

Key Features of a Critical Review

- reviews a work, such as a book or movie

- states title and author of work in first paragraph

- may end with a personal response

- has a beginning, a middle, and an end

READING STREET ONLINE
GRAMMAR JAMMER
www.ReadingStreet.com

Critical Review

A **critical review** examines something, such as a short story, novel, work of art, or movie, and offers the writer's opinion, or claim, about it. The student model on the next page is an example of a literary review.

Writing Prompt Think of a nonfiction book or story you've read recently. Did you like the way information was presented? Write a review of the book or story, using examples from the text and your own opinion. Make sure you develop an argument and support your claim with reasons and evidence from the book or story.

Writer's Checklist

Remember, you should . . .

☑ give details from the text to support your argument.

☑ include your opinion of the text.

☑ use proper punctuation and spacing for quotations.

Review of "True Tales of the American West"

I recently read the magazine article "True Tales of the American West" by Hale Chisholm. The article told about the lives of six American pioneers—a cowboy, a cowgirl, a gold seeker, a Pony Express rider, a farmer, and a rancher. Most of the people in the article lived in the 1800s.

This article really brought the period alive. I felt as if I knew what it was like to step into a stirrup, ride like the wind, herd cattle, and break wild mustangs.

Mr. Chisholm says, "These brave men and women from the early American West were truly pioneers. They needed nerves of steel and an optimistic outlook to overcome the challenges and obstacles of everyday life. Little came easy."

Before I read the article, my ideas about the American West came mostly from the movies, where life seemed full of adventure. Now I see that life was often difficult, dangerous, and full of disease.

Reading the article doesn't make me want to live in the Old West. Instead, I feel lucky to live in modern America.

Writing Trait
The **paragraph** includes details that introduce the topic.

Quotations and quotation marks are used correctly.

Genre
A **literary review** analyzes a text.

Conventions

Quotations and Quotation Marks

Remember Use **quotation marks** to set off a speaker's exact words. They show where exact words begin and end. Quotation marks are also used to enclose titles of short works, such as short stories, magazine articles, poems, or songs.

Common Core State Standards

Informational Text 7. Draw on information from multiple print or digital sources, demonstrating the ability to locate an answer to a question quickly or to solve a problem efficiently. **Also Informational Text 10.**

21st Century Skills
INTERNET GUY

What is the first thing to do at a new **Web site?** Find out who wrote the information. Use the "About this site" button. Can you believe them? How else can you evaluate information?

- Some Web sites are more reliable and useful than others.

- Addresses that end in *.gov* (government) and *.edu* (education) are often reliable. Sites that end in *.com* (commercial), *.net* (network), or *.org* (organization) may or may not be reliable. They usually present points of view instead of only facts.

- Read "The Mystery of the *Hindenburg* Disaster." Think about point of view on Web sites. Look at each site and ask yourself if they are all reliable.

The Mystery of the Hindenburg Disaster

Let's say you are using the Internet to find descriptions of the *Hindenburg* disaster by people who witnessed it first-hand. Which of these might prove useful for your report?

This is a *.org* Web site. The letters *org* are short for *organization*. A *.org* site is a nonprofit organization. It is probably reliable, but it may present points of view as well as facts. You decide it is not useful for your report.

File   Ed

← → ⊗ ↻ 🏠   http://www.url.here

Search
═══**Engine**   Hindenburg

Search

Paul von Hindenburg
Paul von Hindenburg (October 2, 1847–August 2, 1934) was a German field marshal and statesman.
www.website_here.org

Hindenburg Zeppelin
Buy a replica of the famous airship at the lowest price ever! **www.website_here.com**

Eyewitness Reports
Individuals describe their experiences during the *Hindenburg* disaster. **www.website_here.edu**

This is a *.com* Web site. The letters *com* are short for *commercial*. It may or may not be reliable. After you read the description, you decide it is not useful.

This is a *.edu* Web site. The letters *edu* are short for *education,* and the sites are usually sponsored by an educational institution. This site is probably reliable. After you read the description, you decide it is worth looking at. You click the link Eyewitness Reports. This Web site is from a state university. It is probably reliable.

View   Favorites   Tools   Help

http://www.url.here

HINDENBURG
FIRSTHAND REPORTS

HELMUT LAU was working in the tail of the airship. Within the airship there were 16 cells, or sections, that held bags of gas. In this case, the gas was hydrogen. A crewmember asked Lau to help with a tangled rope. Lau remembers that first he saw one cell of the ship burning. Quickly he saw three more cells catch fire.

"The fire proceeded farther down and then it got air. The flame became very bright and the fire rose up to the side, more to the starboard side, as I remember it, and I saw that with the flame aluminum parts and fabrics were thrown up. . . . At that time parts of girders, molten aluminum, and fabric parts started to tumble down from the top. The whole thing lasted a fraction of a second."

Helmut and the other men who were with him managed to climb out through a hatch when the back end of the ship had collapsed to the ground. All four men managed to escape with only minor injuries.

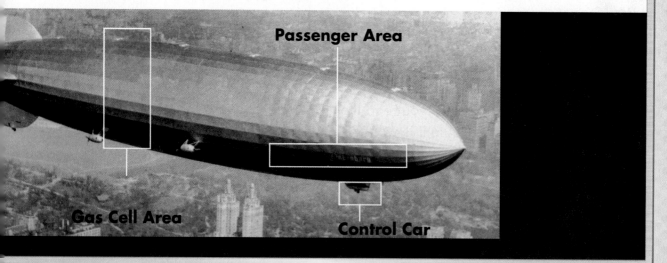

Passenger Area

Gas Cell Area

Control Car

File Edit View Favorites Tools Help

http://www.url.here

HINDENBURG
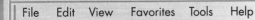

FIRSTHAND REPORTS

WERNER FRANZ was a cabin boy on the *Hindenburg*. This is how he remembered the disaster.

"The ship prepared for landing at a height of 80 meters. The mooring lines were dropped as usual. Shortly after the ropes hit the ground, there was a big shaking on the ship." Franz knew he was in trouble. "I sat down and stamped my feet through the gangway till I saw the ground coming up towards me through the hole. And I jumped out. In these moments, my life just rushed past me, like in a film. I was so agitated that I broke into hysteria and just ran away."

The *Hindenburg* in flames

You make notes on these sources and then continue looking for more firsthand accounts of the disaster.

Common Core State Standards

Language 4.a. Use context (e.g., cause/effect relationships and comparisons in text) as a clue to the meaning of a word or phrase.
Also Foundational Skills 4.b., Speaking/Listening 1.d., 4., Language 3., 4.

Let's
Learn
It!

READING STREET ONLINE
ONLINE STUDENT EDITION
www.ReadingStreet.com

Vocabulary

Unfamiliar Words

Context Clues One way to determine the meaning of a word is to look at context clues. Clues can include synonyms, antonyms, definitions, examples, or explanations of the word.

Practice It! Find three unfamiliar words in *The Hindenburg*. Look for clues in the text to figure out their meanings. Write down the words and what you think they mean. Then check your definitions against a dictionary or glossary.

Fluency

Appropriate Phrasing

When you use appropriate phrasing, you group words together as you read, using the sentence's punctuation as a guide.

Practice It! With your partner, practice reading page 414 of *The Hindenburg*. Pay attention to using appropriate phrasing and punctuation. Take turns reading and offering each other feedback.

432

Media Literacy

When you give a presentation, speak loudly and clearly.

Newscast

In a newscast, TV reporters tell news stories. The purpose of a televised newscast is to inform people about important events in ways that are easy to understand.

Practice It! With a partner, create a newscast about the *Hindenburg*. Keep the newscast brief, including only the most important details. Deliver your newscast to the class. Then discuss the ways newscasts present information differently from commercials or documentaries.

Tips

Listening . . .

- Listen to the speaker's messages.
- Identify the main ideas and supporting ideas in the speaker's messages.

Speaking . . .

- Use the conventions of language in your newscast.
- Make eye contact with your listeners during your newscast.

Teamwork . . .

- Elicit suggestions from group members.
- Identify points of agreement and disagreement.

Common Core State Standards

Language 6. Acquire and use accurately grade-appropriate general academic and domain-specific words and phrases, including those that signal contrast, addition, and other logical relationships (e.g., *however, although, nevertheless, similarly, moreover, in addition*).
Also Speaking/Listening 1.d.

Let's Talk About

Influences

- Describe people or things that influence you.

- Listen to a classmate and discuss his or her influences.

- Determine main and supporting ideas in your classmates' messages.

READING STREET ONLINE
CONCEPT TALK VIDEO
www.ReadingStreet.com

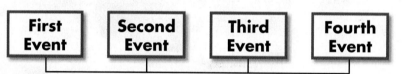

Common Core State Standards

Informational Text 2. Determine two or more main ideas of a text and explain how they are supported by key details; summarize the text. **Also Informational Text 1.**

Skill

Strategy

READING STREET ONLINE
ENVISION IT! ANIMATIONS
www.ReadingStreet.com

Comprehension Skill

Sequence

- Sequence is the order of events in a selection. Dates and times of day or clue words such as *first, next,* and *then* can help you summarize the sequence of events in a text or story.

- Clue words such as *meanwhile* or *during* signal events happening at the same time.

- Use a graphic organizer like the one below to summarize the sequence of events in "What Do You Know About Harlem?"

First Event	Second Event	Third Event	Fourth Event

Comprehension Strategy

Background Knowledge

Background knowledge is what you can find out or what you already know about a topic. Active readers connect their background knowledge to the text to help them understand it. They add to and revise their background knowledge as they read and think about the text.

WHAT DO YOU KNOW ABOUT HARLEM?

Harlem was founded in 1658 as a Dutch settlement, and through the 1700s it was a farming area. Later, high-class houses and apartments were built there, but the hard times of the panic of 1893 left many of these places empty. Many African Americans had moved to the north to find jobs. Some settled in Harlem. Before World War I, Harlem became the largest African American neighborhood in the United States.

Skill As you read, what clues help you summarize the sequence of events in the selection?

In the 1920s, music, literature, and arts began to blossom in a time known as the Harlem Renaissance. Harlem offered amazing music in the form of jazz, blues, and ragtime. Shows at the Apollo Theatre and the Cotton Club helped race relations in America.

Strategy How does your background knowledge about American history help you understand this paragraph?

The books, poems, and art showed a strong sense of pride. This was the first time that African American arts gained attention from the whole country. The Great Depression brought an end to the Harlem Renaissance, but not before America had been changed forever.

Skill Do you need the actual dates to summarize the text's sequence? Why or why not?

Your Turn!

⏸ **Need a Review?** See the *Envision It! Handbook* for additional help with sequence and background knowledge.

▶ **Ready to Try It?** Use what you have learned about sequence and background knowledge as you read *Sweet Music in Harlem*.

437

Common Core State Standards
Language 4.a. Use context (e.g., cause/effect relationships and comparisons in text) as a clue to the meaning of a word or phrase. **Also Language 5.**

clarinet

jammed

nighttime

bass
fidgety
forgetful
secondhand

Vocabulary Strategy for

🎯 Homographs

Context Clues Homographs are words that are spelled the same but have different meanings. Some homographs also have different pronunciations. For example, *minute* (MIN-it) means "sixty seconds," while *minute* (my-NOOT) means "tiny." Use the words and sentences around a homograph to determine and clarify which word (and meaning) is being used.

1. Read the words and sentences around the homograph.

2. Think about its possible meanings.

3. Reread the sentence and put in one of the meanings.

4. See if the meaning makes sense in the sentence. If not, try another meaning for the homograph.

Read "Jazz in Harlem" on page 439. Use the words and sentences around a homograph to determine and clarify which meaning the author is using.

Words to Write Reread "Jazz in Harlem." Imagine you can hear jazz music as you read. Write a description of the music. Use words from the *Words to Know* list in your description.

Jazz in Harlem

No history of black Harlem would be complete without talking about culture. In writing, art, and music, African American creators shone. In no area was that light brighter than in jazz. It grew out of the blues and ragtime. It was wild and free and toe-tapping. In the 1920s in Harlem, the nighttime was alive with this music.

Great musicians such as Louis Armstrong and Duke Ellington jammed far into the night. The sounds of trumpet, drums, clarinet, and bass spilled from the nightclubs. The jazz they played had big muscles and a big heart. It wanted to dance. Never mind that some of the instruments were secondhand, and the musicians didn't make as much money as they deserved.

Crowds listened with rapt attention. From the most forgetful old-timer to the most fidgety baby, people soaked up the music as if it were sunshine. Harlem in the 1920s was a place for African Americans to show their culture and their spirit.

Your Turn!

⏸ Need a Review?
For additional help with homographs, see *Words!*

▶ Ready to Try It?
Read *Sweet Music in Harlem* on pp. 440–457.

BY DEBBIE A. TAYLOR

ILLUSTRATED BY FRANK MORRISON

Sweet Music in Harlem

Genre

Realistic fiction has characters, settings, and plots that seem real, but the author has made them up. As you read, look for how characters play different roles in the plot.

"C. J., where can my hat be?" called Uncle Click from the bathroom. "That photographer from *Highnote* magazine will be out front in an hour, and I've got to look good. It's not every day a Harlem trumpet player gets his picture taken."

C. J. smiled at the old poster on the wall. A young Uncle Click with a snappy black beret blew a gleaming trumpet. C. J. looked at that poster every morning and dreamed of standing onstage, blowing his own sweet music for a roomful of admiring folks.

During the four years he had lived with Uncle Click, C. J. had learned to hold his clarinet just right, to practice every day, and to keep a penny in his shoe for good luck. When he blew out the candles on his birthday cake next week, he'd wish that one day his own picture would be on a poster too. But for now C. J. just tried to make his notes ring out clear and strong from his dented, secondhand clarinet.

Uncle Click chuckled as he walked into the room. "Those were the days," he said, nodding at the poster. "Back then I played the meanest trumpet in Harlem. Now all I do is lose things."

"Don't worry, Uncle Click. I'll find your hat," C. J. said. "Where could you have left it?"

"Well," said Uncle Click as he looked behind the couch. "Last night I stopped at the barbershop and the diner. Later on I jammed at the Midnight Melody Club . . ." Uncle Click's voice trailed off as he searched under the cushion of his favorite chair.

When music was on Uncle Click's mind, he forgot everything else. He could have left his hat anywhere, and there wasn't much time to find it.

443

C. J. ran down the street. The striped pole outside Garlic's Barbershop glistened like a candy cane. Inside, the place buzzed as everyone talked at once. At Garlic's, neighborhood news traveled faster than a subway train speeding downtown.

"Did you see that Kansas City drummer cut loose at the Midnight Melody last night?" one of the men shouted.

"Yeah, he was cool, but it sure was hot in there!" someone else replied.

Mr. Garlic talked louder than anyone. A toothpick jutting from the corner of his mouth bounced up and down as he scolded a fidgety customer.

445

"Mr. Garlic," C. J. called, but no one heard him.

"Mr. Garlic!" C. J. said again, louder.

The barber finally spotted C. J. and smiled. "Looky here, it's my favorite young jazzman. Mark my words, he'll be a headliner soon! What can I do for you, C. J.?"

"A photographer from *Highnote* magazine is coming soon,"
C. J. blurted out, "and Uncle Click lost his hat. Did he leave it here?"

"Your uncle didn't leave his hat, but he did leave this," said
Mr. Garlic, holding up a shiny watch. "When Click blows his
horn that barber pole spins, but he *is* a little forgetful."

C. J. thanked Mr. Garlic and slipped the watch into his pocket.

"You say some photographer is coming from *Highnote*?" Mr.
Garlic said. "Well, a photo without big Charlie Garlic wouldn't
be much of a picture, right folks?"

As C. J. hurried away, he could hear the people in the
barbershop buzzing about the photographer. "I've got to find
that hat," C. J. muttered to himself.

C. J. rushed around the corner and into the jam-packed Eat and
Run Diner. Just inside the door he jumped back as a waitress zipped
past, balancing plates of ham and eggs on one arm
and home fries and sausage on the other.

The waitress grinned at C. J., her apron still swaying from her dash across the room. "Hey, C. J.," she said.

"Hi, Mattie Dee," said C. J. "Did Uncle Click leave his hat here? A photographer from *Highnote* magazine is coming to take his picture in a few minutes, and Uncle Click needs his hat."

"Honey, Click didn't leave his hat, but he did leave this," said Mattie Dee. She pulled a handkerchief from her pocket and dropped it into C. J.'s hand.

"Your uncle leaves his things all over Harlem, but when he wails on his trumpet, the saltshakers bounce! And if you keep practicing, one day you'll make them bounce too."

"Thanks for the hankie, Mattie Dee," C. J. said.

"Did you say a photographer from *Highnote* is coming?" Mattie Dee asked. "I'd love to be in the picture—especially if I can stand right next to your handsome uncle."

As C. J. left the diner, he could hear Mattie Dee telling her customers about the photographer. "But I've still got to find Uncle Click's hat!" C. J. moaned.

C. J. raced down the block, then bounded down the stairs of the Midnight Melody Club. Even though the club was closed, eight musicians were crowded onto the small stage, playing as if it were still show time. The bass player's eyes glistened as he plucked his instrument. The vibraphone player tapped the keys with his eyes closed.

"C. J.!" the drummer shouted without losing the beat. "We're saving a spot for you here. I reckon you'll be joining us in a few years."

A woman strolled toward C. J. from the back of the club. She didn't seem to notice that it wasn't nighttime. She still wore a fancy dress, and rings glittered on her fingers.

"Miss Alma!" C. J. called. "A photographer from *Highnote* magazine is coming to take Uncle Click's picture, and he can't find his hat. Did he leave it onstage last night?"

Canary Alma shook her head. "Your uncle didn't leave his hat here, but he did leave this," she said, and plucked a bow tie from the piano bench. "He's forgetful, but when Click blows his trumpet the wallpaper curls."

C. J. thanked Canary Alma and slid the tie over his wrist.

"A photographer from *Highnote*!" Canary Alma exclaimed, smoothing her dress. "My face next to your uncle's will give that photo a touch of class."

C. J.'s shoulders drooped as he left the Midnight Melody Club. He didn't want to disappoint Uncle Click, but he just couldn't find that hat anywhere.

C. J. dragged his feet up the steps of the brownstone where his uncle waited. A lump like a sour ball wedged in C. J.'s throat.

"Uncle Click," C. J. said. "I didn't find your hat, but I did find these." He held out the watch, the handkerchief, and the bow tie.

Uncle Click looked at C. J., and a huge smile spread across his face. "Looks like you found something else too," he said, pointing behind C. J.

C. J. turned around. Big Charlie Garlic, Mattie Dee, and Canary Alma were walking down the street toward them. But they weren't alone! They were followed by men from the barbershop, people from the diner, and musicians from the Midnight Melody Club. There were also folks C. J. had never seen before and people he'd only seen on posters or record covers.

"Hey, Click," called Charlie Garlic. "You sure know how to gather a crowd."

"Wasn't me," said Uncle Click, winking at C. J.

C. J. could hardly believe his eyes. Here were some of the greatest musicians and singers in Harlem. It was like seeing the sun, the moon, and the stars all shining at once.

"Your nephew drew a crowd without even blowing a note!" said Charlie Garlic. "He won't have any trouble packing them in at the Apollo in a few years."

"I've never seen so many jazzy folks in one place, and right in front of my very own home!" said Uncle Click, a twinkle in his eyes. "This really is something special. Who needs a hat to appreciate that?"

"The photographer's here!" someone yelled.

Everyone scrambled to get a good spot on the steps. There were so many people, some ended up sitting on the curb and standing on the sidewalk.

The photographer laughed from behind his camera. "Guess I'd better use a wider lens!" he called.

As the photographer adjusted his camera, the crowd settled into position for the picture.

"Smile!" the photographer finally shouted, and then *POP!*, a bright light flashed.

Laughter and clapping filled the air.

That night as C. J. lay in bed, light from the hallway crept into his room. Uncle Click stood in the doorway with a large box wrapped in bright red paper.

"I know your birthday's not until next week," said Uncle Click, "but I wanted to give you this before all the magic of today wears off."

C. J. opened the box and lifted out a black case. His eyes widened as he raised the lid. Inside, nestled in velvet, was a brand-new clarinet.

"It's perfect!" C. J. said, cradling the horn gently in his hands.

C. J. hugged his uncle tightly. Then he noticed something else in the box. "Uncle Click, your hat!"

"Well, look at that!" said Uncle Click. "It must have fallen in there last night when I was wrapping your present."

"You know, a jazzman like you is going to need a good hat," said Uncle Click as he placed the beret neatly on C. J.'s head. "Besides, I'm getting used to not wearing one."

C. J. adjusted the hat and put the clarinet to his lips. He started to blow while his fingers danced over the keys. Uncle Click beamed and nodded to the beat as C. J.'s own sweet music rang out clear and strong for the most admiring audience in all of Harlem.

Common Core State Standards
Literature 1. Quote accurately from a text when explaining what the text says explicitly and when drawing inferences from the text. **Also Literature 2., Writing 8., 9.**

Think Critically

1. Mr. Garlic, Mattie Dee, and Miss Alma all want to be in Uncle Click's photograph. Why? Would you be excited to be in someone else's magazine article? Why or why not? Text to Self

2. With just a few words, the author makes you see a character: Charlie Garlic with his toothpick, Canary Alma's "touch of class." Find other examples that show how the author brings the story's characters to life. Think Like an Author

3. On page 444, the author gives readers an idea of where C. J. will be going for the rest of the story. Where is C. J. going and why? Make a flow chart of the places he visits. Sequence

4. Think about the way you feel about the music you like. How does it compare with the way C. J. and the other characters in the story feel about music? How are their feelings and yours alike and different? Background Knowledge

5. Look Back and Write Reread the last two pages of the story. Where was Uncle Click's hat? Do you think it got there by accident? Provide evidence to support your answer. Key Ideas and Details • Text Evidence

Meet the Illustrator

Frank Morrison

Frank Morrison is a noted painter whose works are collected for their artistic value. He brings a canvas alive with beauty.

He is known for his special style with its long, thin, dramatic figures. Although he had an interest in art early in life, he didn't know that was to be his calling. While visiting the Louvre Museum in Paris, he suddenly realized he wanted to paint.

Comedian Bill Cosby, who takes pride in discovering the artistic talents of African Americans, is a collector of his paintings. Mr. Morrison's works have been seen on television shows, and he was commissioned to create a work for the annual music festival sponsored by *Essence* magazine. This work is titled *Duet*.

Mr. Morrison gets inspiration from his mother and his grandparents. He was born in Massachusetts but now lives with his wife, Connie, and their three children in New Jersey.

Here are other books about music.

M Is for Music by Kathleen Krull

Duke Ellington by Andrea Davis Pinkney

Use the *Reader's and Writer's Notebook* to record your independent reading.

Common Core State Standards

Writing 3. Write narratives to develop real or imagined experiences or events using effective technique, descriptive details, and clear event sequences.
Also Writing 3.a., 3.d., Language 2., 2.b.

Let's Write It!

Key Features of a Personal Narrative

- tells a real story about a personal experience.

- uses first-person point of view (*I, me*).

- reveals author's voice through thoughts and feelings.

READING STREET ONLINE
GRAMMAR JAMMER
www.ReadingStreet.com

Personal Narrative

A **personal narrative** tells about something one has experienced, using vivid details. The student model on the next page is an example of a personal narrative.

Writing Prompt In *Sweet Music in Harlem,* a character dreams of playing his clarinet onstage. Think about something you worked hard to accomplish and whether you feel you were successful. Write a personal narrative about this experience.

Writer's Checklist

Remember, you should . . .

☑ communicate thoughts and feelings about an experience.

☑ include details to engage the reader.

☑ use proper punctuation in sentences, including commas in compound sentences.

The School Play

Every year our class performs a play for the entire school, and every year I dread the production. Each student must choose a role. (It can be a large role or a small role, but you must pick something.)

Last year, we did a play about the Old West. I had a choice of the following roles: a rancher, a cowhand, a gold miner, or a storekeeper. I chose to be the storekeeper because I thought the role would be small.

It turned out, however, that the storekeeper was the narrator of the entire play. I had to learn pages and pages of lines. It was very hard, and I was very frightened before the performance. Even though I had studied my lines, I was afraid I would forget them.

However, once the play started, I concentrated on my lines and did not focus on my tense stomach or squeaky voice or my fears. I said my lines loudly and boldly! I overcame my fears; I did fine. I felt relieved and proud of myself when the play was finally over.

Genre A **personal narrative** describes an event in the writer's life.

Punctuation is used correctly.

Writing Trait Author's voice is revealed through thoughts and feelings.

Conventions

Punctuation

Remember Use **semicolons** to join two independent clauses. (*I ran fast; Mom walked slowly.*) Also use **periods** at the end of sentences, **commas** in compound sentences, **colons** to introduce lists, and **parentheses** to set off added information.

Common Core State Standards
Informational Text 2. Determine two or more main ideas of a text and explain how they are supported by key details; summarize the text. Also Informational Text 10.

Genre
Expository Text

- Expository texts contain facts and information about different subjects.

- Some expository texts use cause-and-effect patterns or a series of main ideas and details to explain the relationships among ideas.

- Expository texts can use graphics and illustrations to relate information or give an overview of the contents.

- Read Debbie Taylor's "Author's Note." Think about how organizational patterns and illustrations help you understand the text.

SWEET MUSIC IN HARLEM:
Author's Note

BY DEBBIE A. TAYLOR

Sweet Music in Harlem was inspired by a photograph on a T-shirt my husband was wearing one day. In the photograph a crowd of famous jazz musicians poses on the steps of a brownstone in Harlem, New York, while children sit on the curb. I wondered who those children were and what they might have thought about seeing all those people gathered on their street.

Months later, on the way to a hotel in St. Louis, I passed nightclubs, restaurants, and streets with jazz-related names. They reminded me of that picture of jazz musicians. As I sat in the hotel eating breakfast the next morning, the plot of the story evolved clearly. A boy named C. J. started racing through Harlem, trying to find his uncle's missing hat in time for a photo shoot for a jazz magazine.

The picture on that shirt was taken in 1958 by Art Kane, a young photographer on his first assignment for *Esquire* magazine. He had invited some musicians to a photo shoot in Harlem, not knowing if anyone would show up. Magically, the news spread quickly, and fifty-seven of the greatest men and women of jazz gathered, as well as some curious neighborhood children!

Let's Think About...

What is the main idea of this page? How is it supported by details?
Expository Text

Let's Think About...

What do you think caused the jazz musicians to decide to show up for the photo shoot?
Expository Text

Let's Think About...

Look at the photograph on this page. How does it relate important information?
Expository Text

The jazz greats in the historic photograph above are numbered for your reference:

1. Hilton Jefferson **2.** Benny Golson **3.** Art Farmer

4. Art Blakey **5.** Wilbur Ware **6.** Chubby Jackson

7. Johnny Griffin **8.** Dickie Wells **9.** Buck Clayton

10. Taft Jordan **11.** Zutty Singleton **12.** Red Allen

13. Tyree Glenn **14.** Sonny Greer **15.** Jimmy Jones

16. Miff Mole **17.** Jay C. Higginbotham

18. Charles Mingus **19.** Jo Jones **20.** Gene Krupa

21. Osie Johnson **22.** Max Kaminsky

23. George Wettling **24.** Bud Freeman

25. Pee Wee Russell **26.** Buster Bailey **27.** Jimmy Rushing

28. Scoville Brown **29.** Bill Crump **30.** Ernie Wilkins

31. Sonny Rollins **32.** Gigi Gryce **33.** Hank Jones

34. Eddie Locke **35.** Horace Silver **36.** Luckey Roberts

37. Maxine Sullivan 38. Joe Thomas 39. Stuff Smith
40. Coleman Hawkins 41. Rudy Powell
42. Oscar Pettiford 43. Sahib Shihab
44. Marian McPartland 45. Lawrence Brown
46. Mary Lou Williams 47. Emmett Berry
48. Thelonious Monk 49. Vic Dickenson 50. Milt Hinton
51. Lester Young 52. Rex Stewart 53. J. C. Heard
54. Gerry Mulligan 55. Roy Eldridge 56. Dizzy Gillespie
57. Count Basie

Let's **Think** About...

Reading Across Texts Both selections are about inspiration. Think about what inspired C. J. and what inspired Debbie Taylor.

Writing Across Texts Write a paragraph explaining what inspired C. J. and Debbie and why. Then tell about something that inspires you and explain why.

465

Common Core State Standards

Language 5. Demonstrate understanding of figurative language, word relationships, and nuances in word meanings. **Also Foundational Skills 4.b., Speaking/Listening 2., Language 4.a.**

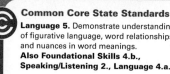

Let's

Learn

It!

Vocabulary

Homographs

Context Clues Homographs are words that are spelled the same but have different meanings. You can use context clues to tell which meaning is being used in a sentence. Think of all the meanings of the word. Then see which one makes the most sense in the sentence.

Practice It! Think of three homographs. Write down the words and trade your words with a partner. Choose one homograph from your partner's list and write a sentence for each meaning of the word.

Fluency

Expression

You can use your voice to bring the characters alive as you read by using expression. Change the pitch of your voice for different characters, and vary the tone to show how the characters are feeling.

Practice It! With a partner, read page 447 in *Sweet Music*. Take turns reading so that one partner reads as C. J. and the other reads as Mr. Garlic. Then switch roles. How are the characters' expressions different?

Listening and Speaking

When you speak in a drama, enunciate your words clearly.

Readers' Theater

In Readers' Theater, a story is presented in a dramatic form. Actors read from scripts but don't memorize them.

Practice It! With your group, prepare a Readers' Theater performance of *Sweet Music in Harlem*. Choose a scene, create a script, assign roles, and rehearse. Present it to the class, and then discuss ways it compares to the original text.

Tips

Listening . . .

- Listen carefully to each speaker.
- Interpret what each speaker says.

Speaking . . .

- When you speak your lines, make eye contact with the audience.
- Enunciate your words and speak clearly so that the audience understands you.

Teamwork . . .

- Take turns playing different roles.
- Consider suggestions from other group members.

Common Core State Standards
Language 5. Demonstrate understanding of figurative language, word relationships, and nuances in word meanings. **Also Literature 5., 10.**

Poetry

- Onomatopoeia is a word that sounds just like the thing it is describing. An example of onomatopoeia is the word *boom*.

- Alliteration is the repetition of consonant sounds at the beginning of words. It's used to reinforce the meanings of important details.

- Rhyme scheme is the pattern of words that sound the same in poems. For example, "The Bat" on page 469 has a distinct rhyme scheme. Notice the words the poet chose to rhyme. Are they important to the poem's meaning?

Colors Crackle, Colors Roar

by Pat Mora

Red shouts a loud, balloon-round sound.

    Black rackles like noisy grackles.

Café clickety-clicks its wooden sticks.

    Yellow sparks and sizzles, tzz-tzz.

White sings, Ay, her high, light note.

Verde rustles leaf-secrets, swhish, swhish.

Gris whis-whis-whispers its kitten whiskers.

    Silver ting-ting-a-ling jingles.

Azul coo-coo-coos like pajaritos do.

Purple thunders and rum-rum-rumbles.

    Oro blares, a brassy, brass tuba.

Orange growls its striped, rolled roar.

Colors Crackle. Colors Roar.

The Bat

by Theodore Roethke

By day the bat is cousin to the mouse.
He likes the attic of an aging house.

His fingers make a hat about his head.
His pulse beat is so slow we think him dead.

He loops in crazy figures half the night
Among the trees that face the corner light.

But when he brushes up against a screen,
We are afraid of what our eyes have seen:

For something is amiss or out of place
When mice with wings can wear a human face.

Let's **Think** About...

How does the sound word "tzz-tzz" in "Colors Crackle, Colors Roar" help you understand the poem's meaning?

Limericks

There was an Old Man with a beard,
Who said, "It is just as I feared!
    Two Owls and a Hen,
    Four Larks and a Wren,
Have all built their nests in my beard!"
Edward Lear

A bridge engineer, Mister Crumpett,
Built a bridge for the good River Bumpett.
    A mistake in the plan
    Left a gap in the span,
But he said, "Well, they'll just have to jump it."
Anonymous

Sunflakes

by Frank Asch

If sunlight fell like snowflakes,
gleaming yellow and so bright,
we could build a sunman,
we could have a sunball fight,
we could watch the sunflakes
drifting in the sky.
We could go sleighing
in the middle of July
through sundrifts and sunbanks,
we could ride a sunmobile,
and we could touch sunflakes—
I wonder how they'd feel.

Glossary

How to Use This Glossary

This glossary can help you understand and pronounce some of the words in this book. The entries in this glossary are in alphabetical order. There are guide words at the top of each page to show you the first and last words on the page. A pronunciation key is at the bottom of page 473. Remember, if you can't find the word you are looking for, ask for help or check a dictionary.

The entry word is in dark type. It shows how the word is spelled and how the word is divided into syllables.

The pronunciation is in parentheses. It also shows which syllables are stressed.

Part-of-speech labels show the function or functions of an entry word and any listed form of that word.

an·ces·tor (an′ses′tər), *NOUN.* person from whom you are descended, such as your great-grandparents: *Their ancestors had come to the United States in 1812.* ❑ PLURAL **an·ces·tors.**

Sometimes, irregular and other special forms will be shown to help you use the word correctly.

The definition and example sentence show you what the word means and how it is used.

Aa

a·ban·don (ə ban′dən), *v.* to give up entirely: *We abandoned the idea of a picnic because of the rain.* *v.* **a·ban·doned.**

ac·com·plish·ment (ə kom′plish mənt), *N.* something that has been done with knowledge, skill, or ability; achievement: *The teachers were proud of the pupils' accomplishments.* ❑ *N. PL.* **ac·com·plish·ments.**

a·dorn (ə dôrn′), *v.* to add beauty to; put ornaments on; decorate: *She adorned her hair with flowers.* ❑ *v.* **a·dorned, a·dorn·ing.**

ar·mor (är′mər), *N.* any kind of protective covering: *The steel plates of a warship and the bony shell of an armadillo are armor.*

armor

at·tempt (ə tempt′), *N.* act of making an effort; endeavor: *an attempt to climb Mount Everest.* (*Attempt* comes from the Latin word *attemptare,* meaning "to test.")

Bb

bass¹ (bās), **1.** *N.* the lowest male voice in music. **2.** *N.* the largest, lowest-sounding stringed instrument in an orchestra or band.

bass² (bas), *N.* North American freshwater or saltwater fish with spiny fins, used for food.

bel·low (bel′ō), **1.** *v.* to make a loud, deep noise; roar: *The bull bellowed.* **2.** *v.* to shout loudly, angrily, or with pain: *He bellowed at the children who were trampling his flowers.*

bi·zarre (bə zär′), *ADJ.* **1.** strikingly odd in appearance or style; fantastic; grotesque: *The frost made bizarre figures on the windowpane.* **2.** peculiar.

bleached (blēcht), *ADJ.* whitened by exposure to sunlight or chemicals: *The animal skulls were bleached by the sun.*

blu·ish (blü′ish), *ADJ.* somewhat blue; somewhat like the color of the clear sky in daylight.

blun·der (blun′dər), *N.* a stupid mistake: *Misspelling the title of a book is a real blunder to make in a book report.* ❑ *N. PL.* **blun·ders.**

breath·tak·ing (breth′tā′king), *ADJ.* thrilling; exciting: *We took a breathtaking ride on a roller coaster.*

Cc

car·cass (kär′kəs), *N.* body of a dead animal. ❑ *N. PL.* **car·cass·es.**

cart·wheel (kärt′wēl′), *N.* a sideways handspring with the legs and arms kept straight. ❑ *N. PL.* **cart·wheels.**

cav·ern (kav′ərn), *N.* a large cave. (*Cavern* comes from the Latin word *caverna,* meaning "hollow.")

cav·i·ty (kav′ə tē), *N.* hollow place; hole. *Cavities in teeth are caused by decay.* ❑ *N. PL.* **cav·i·ties.**

civ·i·li·za·tion (siv′ə lə zā′shən), *N.* the ways of living of a people or nation: *The civilizations of ancient Egypt and ancient Greece had many contacts over the centuries.*

clar·i·net (klar′ə net′), *N.* a woodwind instrument, having a mouthpiece with a single reed and played by means of holes and keys.

cleanse (klenz), **1.** *v.* to make clean: *Cleanse the wound before bandaging it.* **2.** *v.* to make pure: *cleanse the soul.*

com·bi·na·tion (kom′bə nā′shən), *N.* series of numbers or letters dialed in opening a certain kind of lock: *Do you know the combination of the safe?*

a in *hat*	ėr in *term*	ô in *order*	ch in *child*	ə = a in *about*
ā in *age*	i in *it*	oi in *oil*	ng in *long*	ə = e in *taken*
â in *care*	ī in *ice*	ou in *out*	sh in *she*	ə = i in *pencil*
ä in *far*	o in *hot*	u in *cup*	th in *thin*	ə = o in *lemon*
e in *let*	ō in *open*	u̇ in *put*	ᵺ in *then*	ə = u in *circus*
ē in *equal*	ȯ in *all*	ü in *rule*	zh in *measure*	

com·plex (kom pleks′), _ADJ._ hard to understand: _The instructions for building the radio were complex._

cramp (kramp), _v._ to shut into a small space; limit: _Living in only three rooms, the family was cramped._ ❑ _v._ **cramped, cramp·ing.**

crit·i·cal (krit′ə kəl), _ADJ._ being important to the outcome of a situation: _Help arrived at the critical moment._

crit·i·cize (krit′ə sīz), _v._ to find fault with; disapprove of; blame: _Do not criticize him until you know all the circumstances._ ❑ _v._ **crit·i·cized, crit·i·ciz·ing.**

cruise (krüz), _v._ to travel in a car, airplane, boat, etc., at the speed at which the vehicle operates best. ❑ _v._ **cruised, cruis·ing.**

Dd

Dal·ma·tian (dal mā′shən), _N._ a large, short-haired dog, usually white with black spots; coach dog. _N. PL._ **Dal·ma·tians**

de·bris (də brē′), _N._ scattered fragments; ruins; rubbish: _The street was covered with broken glass, stone, and other debris from the storm._

de·cay (di kā′), _N._ process of rotting: _The decay in the tree trunk proceeded so rapidly that the tree fell over in a month._

dem·on·strate (dem′ən strāt), _v._ to show how a thing is done; explain by using examples. ❑ _v._ **dem·on·strates, dem·on·strat·ed, dem·on·strat·ing.**

drench (drench), _v._ to wet thoroughly; soak: _A sudden, heavy rain drenched us._ ❑ _v._ **drenched, drench·ing.**

Ee

e·co·nom·ic (ek′ə nom′ik), _ADJ._ of or about the management of the income, supplies, and expenses of a household, government, etc.

en·a·ble (en ā′bəl), _v._ to give ability, power, or means to; make able: _The airplane enables people to travel great distances rapidly._ ❑ _v._ **en·a·bled, en·a·bling, en·a·bles.**

en·case (en kās′), _v._ to cover completely; enclose: _A cocoon encases the caterpillar._ ❑ _v._ **en·cased, en·cas·es, en·cas·ing.**

en·vy (en′vē), _N._ feeling of discontent, dislike, or desire because another person has what you want: _The children were filled with envy when they saw her new bicycle._

ep·i·sode (ep′ə sōd), _N._ one part of a story that is published or broadcast in several parts, one at a time.

er·a (ir′ə), _N._ a period of time or history: _We live in the era of space exploration._

ex·plo·sion (ek splō′zhən), _N._ act of bursting with a loud noise; a blowing up: _The explosions of the bombs shook the whole city._

ex·tinct (ek stingkt′), _ADJ._ no longer existing.

extinct

Ff

feat (fēt), *N.* a great or unusual deed; act showing great skill, strength, or daring. (*Feat* comes from the Latin word *factum*, meaning "to make or do.")

fidg·et·y (fij′ə tē), *ADJ.* restless; uneasy: *That fidgety child keeps twisting and moving.*

flee (flē), *v.* to run away; get away by running: *The robbers were fleeing, but the police caught them.* ❑ *v.* **fled, flee·ing.**

fo·cus (fō′kəs), **1.** *N.* the correct adjustment of a lens, the eye, etc., to make a clear image: *If the camera is not brought into focus, the photograph will be blurred.* **2.** *N.* the central point of attraction, attention, activity, etc.: *The new baby was the focus of attention.*

for·get·ful (fər get′fəl), *ADJ.* apt to forget; having a poor memory: *When I get too tired, I become forgetful.*

frill·y (fril′ē), *ADJ.* full of frills, ruffles, or ornaments merely added for show: *She wore a frilly dress to go dancing.* ❑ *ADJ.* **frill·i·er, frill·i·est.**

Gg

grav·i·ty (grav′ə tē), *N.* the natural force that causes objects to move or tend to move toward the center of the Earth and causes objects to have weight: *The laws of gravity are essential to life on Earth.*

gym·nas·tics (jim nas′tiks), *N.* a sport in which very difficult exercises are performed.

gymnastics

Hh

head·line (hed′līn′), **1.** *N.* words printed in heavy type at the top of a newspaper article telling what it is about. **2.** *N.PL.* **head·lines,** publicity: *The invention got headlines.*

hes·i·ta·tion (hez′ə tā′shən), *N.* act of failing to act promptly; doubt; indecision.

hid·e·ous (hid′ē əs), *ADJ.* very ugly; frightful; horrible: *a hideous monster.*

high-pitched (hī′picht′), *ADJ.* of high tone or sound; shrill: *a high-pitched voice.*

hy·dro·gen (hī′drə jən), *N.* a colorless, odorless gas that burns easily, combines with oxygen to form water, and is present in most organic compounds: *Hydrogen is a chemical element that weighs less than any other element.*

Glossary

Ii

im·mense·ly (i mens′lē), *ADJ.* very greatly: *We enjoyed the party immensely.*

in·de·pend·ence (in′di pen′dəns), *N.* freedom from the control, influence, support, or help of others: *The American colonies won independence from England.*

in·spire (in spīr′), *V.* to fill with a thought or feeling; influence: *A chance to try again inspired her with hope.* ❑ *V.* **in·spired, in·spir·ing.**

in·ter·i·or (in tir′ē ər), *N.* inner surface or part; inside: *The interior of the house was beautifully decorated.*

Jj

jam¹ (jam), **1.** *V.* to press or squeeze tightly between two surfaces: *The ship was jammed between two rocks.* **2.** *V.* to make music with other musicians without having practiced (slang). ❑ *V.* **jammed, jamm·ing.**

jam² (jam), *N.* preserve made by boiling fruit with sugar until thick: *strawberry jam.*

Ll

life·less (līf′lis), *ADJ.* without life: *a lifeless statue.*

lime·light (līm′līt′), *N.* center of public attention and interest: *Some people are never happy unless they are in the limelight.*

Mm

mon·i·tor (mon′ə tər), **1.** *N.* a television set connected to a computer. ❑ *N. PL.* **mon·i·tors. 2.** *V.* to listen to and check radio or television transmissions, telephone messages, etc., by using a receiver. ❑ *V.* **mon·i·tored, mon·i·tor·ing.**

mu·cus (myü′kəs), *N.* a slimy substance produced in the nose and throat to moisten and protect them.

Nn

night·time (nīt′tīm′), *N.* time between evening and morning.

Oo

ooze (üz), *N.* a soft mud or slime, especially at the bottom of a pond or river or on the ocean bottom.

o·ver·run (ō′vər run′), *V.* to spread over: *Each year, vines overrun that wall.* ❑ *V.* **o·ver·ran, o·ver·run·ning.**

Pp

par·a·site (par′ə sīt), *N.* any living thing that lives on or in another, from which it gets its food, often harming the other in the process. *Lice and tapeworms are parasites.* ❑ *N. PL.* **par·a·sites.**

plunge (plunj), *V.* to fall or move suddenly downward or forward: *The sea turtle plunged into the water.* ❑ *V.* **plunged, plung·ing.**

pre·cious (presh′əs), _ADJ._ having great value; worth much; valuable. _Gold, platinum, and silver are often called the precious metals; diamonds, rubies, and sapphires are the precious stones._

pro·file (prō′fīl), **1.** _N._ a side view, especially of the human face: _She liked her profile from the right side better._ **2.** _N._ concise description of someone's abilities, personality, or career: _That profile identifies the right person for the job._ **3.** _N._ low profile; moderate attitude or position, deliberately chosen in order to avoid notice: _The candidate kept a low profile._

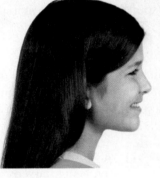

profile

prom·e·nade (prom′ə nād′), _v._ to walk about or up and down for pleasure or for show. ❏ _v._ **prom·e·nad·ed, prom·e·nad·ing.**

Rr

realm (relm), _N._ kingdom.

ro·bo·tic (rō bot′ik), _ADJ._ of or for a machine with moving parts and sensing devices controlled by a computer: _robotic design._

robotic

role (rōl), **1.** _N._ an actor's part in a play, movie, etc.: _She played the leading role in the school play._ **2.** _N._ role model, a person whose patterns of behavior influence someone else's actions and beliefs: _Parents are important role models for children._

roost (rüst), **1.** _N._ bar, pole, or perch on which birds rest or sleep; **2.** _v._ to sit as birds do on a roost; settle for the night.

rus·tle (rus′əl), _v._ to make or cause to make a light, soft sound of things gently rubbing together: _The leaves were rustling in the breeze._ ❏ _v._ **rus·tled, rus·tling.**

Ss

sav·age (sav′ij), **1.** _ADJ._ not civilized; barbarian: _savage customs._ **2.** _ADJ._ fierce; cruel; ready to fight; brutal: _a savage dog._ **3.** _ADJ._ wild or rugged: _savage mountain scenery._ (_Savage_ comes from the Latin word _silvaticus,_ meaning "of the woods; wild.")

scarce • substitute

scarce (skârs), *ADJ.* hard to get; rare: *Water is becoming scarce.*

scrawl (skròl), *v.* to write or draw poorly or carelessly. ❑ *v.* **scrawled, scrawl·ing.**

scraw·ny (skrò′nē), *ADJ.* having little flesh; lean; thin; skinny: *Turkeys have scrawny necks.*

sec·ond·hand (sek′ənd hand′), **1.** *ADJ.* not new; used already by someone else: *secondhand clothes.* **2.** *ADV.* from other than the original source; not firsthand: *The information came to us secondhand.*

sed·i·ment (sed′ə mənt), *N.* material that settles to the bottom of a liquid: *A film of sediment covered the underwater wreck.*

ser·pent (sèr′pənt), *N.* snake, especially a big snake.

skid (skid), *v.* to slip or slide sideways while moving: *The car skidded on the slippery road.* ❑ *v.* **skid·ded, skid·ding.**

som·er·sault (sum′ər sòlt), *v.* to run or jump, turning the heels over the head.

somersault

so·nar (sō′när), *N.* device for finding the depth of water or for detecting and locating underwater objects. *Sonar sends sound waves into water, and they are reflected back when they strike the bottom or any object.*

spe·cial·ize (spesh′ə līz), *v.* to develop in a special way: *Animals and plants are specialized to fit their surroundings.* ❑ *v.* **spe·cial·ized, spe·cial·iz·ing.**

spe·cif·ic (spi sif′ik), *ADJ.* definite; precise; particular: *There was no specific reason for the party.*

spoon·ful (spün′fúl), *N.* as much as a spoon can hold.

sprain (sprān), **1.** *v.* to stretch or tear ligaments in a joint by a sudden twist or wrench: *I sprained my ankle.* **2.** *N.* injury caused by a sudden twist or wrench: *The sprain took a long time to heal.*

star·va·tion (stär vā′shən), *N.* suffering from extreme hunger; being starved: *Starvation caused his death.*

ster·ile (ster′əl), *ADJ.* free from germs: *Bandages should always be kept sterile.*

strat·e·gy (strat′ə jē), *N.* the skillful planning and management of anything.

strict (strict), *ADJ.* very careful in following a rule or in making others follow it: *The teacher was strict but fair.*

sub·sti·tute (sub′stə tüt), **1.** *N.* one who takes the place of another, particularly a teacher: *We had a substitute today because our regular teacher was ill.* **2.** *v.* to put in the place of another: *We substituted brown sugar for molasses in these cookies.* ❑ *v.* **sub·sti·tut· ed, sub·sti·tut·ing.**

sus·pi·cion (sə spish′ən), *N.* belief; feeling; thought: *I have a suspicion that the weather will be very hot today.* ❑ *N. PL.* **sus·pi·cions.**

Tt

throb (throb), *v.* to beat rapidly or strongly: *My injured foot throbbed.* ❑ *v.* **throbbed, throb·bing.**

tun·dra (tun′drə), *N.* a vast, level, treeless plain in the arctic regions. The ground beneath its surface is frozen even in summer.

tundra

Vv

va·cant (vā′kənt), *ADJ.* not occupied: *a vacant chair, a vacant house.*

vi·tal (vī′tl), **1.** *ADJ.* very important; basic; very necessary: *Good government is vital to the welfare of a community.* **2.** *ADJ.* of or about life: *Vital statistics give facts about births, deaths, marriages, etc.* **3.** *ADJ.* necessary to life: *The heart is a vital organ.*

Ww

wince (wins), *v.* to draw back suddenly; flinch slightly: *I winced when the dentist's drill touched my tooth.* ❑ *v.* **winced, winc·ing.**

Word List English/Spanish

Unit 4

Weslandia
blunders / tropezones
civilization / civilización*
complex / complejo*
envy / envidia*
fleeing / huir
inspired / inspiró*
rustling / susurrando
strategy / estrategia*

Tripping Over the Lunch Lady
Dalmatian / dálmata*
frilly / adornado
promenading / paseando
sprained / torcido
substitute / sustituto*

Exploding Ants: Amazing Facts About How Animals Adapt

critical / críticos*
enables / permite
mucus / mucus*
scarce / escaso
specialize / se especializan
sterile / estériles*

* English/Spanish Cognate: A **cognate** is a word that is similar in two languages and has the same meaning in both languages.

The Stormi Giovanni Club
cavities / caries
combination / combinación*
demonstrates / demuestra
episode / episodio*
profile / (mantenerse en) segundo plano
strict / estricto*

The Gymnast
bluish / azulados
cartwheels / volteretas laterales
gymnastics / gimnástica*
hesitation / duda
limelight / centro de atención
skidded / patinó
somersault / dar saltos mortales
throbbing / latía
wincing / haciendo una mueca de dolor

Unit 5

The Skunk Ladder
abandoned / abandonado*
attempt / intento
bellow / vociferar
cavern / caverna*
feat / hazaña
immensely / inmensamente
savage / salvaje*

The Unsinkable Wreck of the R.M.S. *Titanic*
cramped / estrecho
debris / restos
interior / interior*
ooze / limo
robotic / robótico*
sediment / sedimento*
sonar / sonar*

Talk with an Astronaut
accomplishments / logros
focus / atención
gravity / gravedad*
monitors / monitores*
role / ejemplo
specific / específico*

Journey to the Center of the Earth
armor / armadura
encases / reviste
extinct / extintas*
hideous / horroroso
plunged / sumergido
serpent / serpiente*

Ghost Towns of the American West
economic / económico*
independence / independencia*
overrun / rebosante
scrawled / garabateó
vacant / vacantes*

Unit 6

The Truth About Austin's Amazing Bats
bizarre / extraño
breathtaking / impresionante
headline / titular
high-pitched /agudo
roost / percha
vital / esencial

The Mystery of Saint Matthew Island
bleached / decolorados
carcasses / animales muertos
decay / descomposición
parasites / parásitos*
scrawny / escuálido
starvation / inanición
suspicions / sospechas
tundra / tundra*

King Midas and the Golden Touch
adorn / adornar*
cleanse / (te) bañas
lifeless / inanimada
precious / precioso*
realm / reino
spoonful / cucharada

The *Hindenburg*
criticizing / criticando
cruised / navegó
drenching / empapándolo
era / era*
explosion / explosión*
hydrogen / hidrógeno*

Sweet Music in Harlem
bass / bajo
clarinet / clarinete*
fidgety / inquieto
forgetful / olvidadizo
jammed / improvisé
nighttime / noche
secondhand / segunda mano

Acknowledgments

Text

Grateful acknowledgment is made to the following for copyrighted material:

Arnold Adoff Revocable Living Trust

"Under the Back Porch" from *Home* by Virginia Hamilton. Copyright 1992, 2008 by Virginia Hamilton. © 2010 by the Arnold Adoff Revocable Living Trust.

Atheneum Books for Young Readers an imprint of Simon & Schuster Children's Publishing Division

"Desert Tortoise" by Byrd Baylor. Reprinted with the permission of Atheneum Books for Young Readers, an imprint of Simon & Schuster Children's Publishing Division from *Desert Voices* by Byrd Baylor. Text copyright © 1981 Byrd Baylor.

Antheneum Books for Young Readers an imprint of Simon & Schuster Children's Publishing Division & Joanne Settel & Columbia Literary Associates, Inc.

"Exploding Ants" by Joanne Settel, PH.D. Text copyright © 1999 Joanne Settel. Used by permission.

Barry Goldblatt Literary, LLC

"Tripping Over the Lunch Lady" by Angela Johnson. From *Tripping Over the Lunch Lady and Other School Stories*. Copyright © 2004 by Angela Johnson. Used by permission of Barry Goldblatt Literary LLC, as agent for the author.

Candlewick Press, Inc.

"Weslandia" by Paul Fleischman. Text copyright © 1999 by Paul Fleischman. Illustrations copyright © 1999 by Kevin Hawkes. Reprinted by permission of the publisher Candlewick Press, Inc., Somerville, MA.

Caroline House an imprint of Boyds Mills Press

"The Mystery of Saint Matthew Island" from *The Case of the Mummified Pigs and Other Mysteries in Nature* by Susan E. Quinlan. Publishing by Caroline House, an imprint of Boyds Mills Press. Reprinted by permission.

Clarion Books an imprint of Houghton Mifflin Harcourt Publishing Company

"Which Lunch Table?" from *Swimming Upstream: Middle Grade Poems* by Kristine O'Connell George. Text copyright © 2002 by Kristine O'Connell George. Reprinted by permission of Clarion Books, an imprint of Houghton Mifflin Harcourt Publishing Company. All rights reserved.

Columbia University Press

"All About Gymnastics" from *The Columbia Electronic Encyclopedia, 6th ed.* Copyright © 2003.

Used by permission of Columbia University Press.

Curtis Brown Ltd

"Share the Adventure" by Patricia and Fredrick McKissack. Copyright © 1993 by Patricia and Fredrick McKissack. First appeared in National Children's Book Week Poem, published by The Children's Book Council. Reprinted by permission of Curtis Brown, Ltd.

Doubleday a div of Random House, Inc & Faber & Faber

"The Bat" from the *Collected Poems of Theodore Roethke* by Theodore Roethke, copyright 1938.

Edward Blishen

Excerpt from "Journey to the Center of the Earth" by Jules Verne from *Science Fiction Stories,* chosen by Edward Blishen.

Estate of bp Nichol

"A Path to the Moon" from *Giants, Moosequakes and Other Disasters* by bp Nichol, 1985, Black Moss Press. Used by permission of The Estate of bp Nichol.

Farrar, Straus & Giroux, LLC

"The drum" from *Spin A Soft Black Song*, Revised Edition by Nikki Giovanni, illustrated by George Martins. Copyright © 1971, 1985 by Nikki Giovanni. Caution: Users are warned that this work is protected under copyright laws and downloading is strictly prohibited. The right to reproduce or transfer the work via any medium must be secured with FSG.

HarperCollins Publishers

"Keziah" from *Bronzeville Boys and Girls* by Gwendolyn Brooks. Copyright © 1956 by Gwendolyn Brooks Blakely. "King Midas and the Golden Touch" as told by Charlotte Craft, illustrated by K.Y. Craft. Text copyright © 1999 by Charlotte Craft. Illustrations copyright © 1999 by Kinuko Y. Craft. "Sunflakes" from *Country Pie* by Frank Asch. Copyright © 1979 Frank Asch. Used by permission of HarperCollins Publishers.

Henry Holt & Company, LLC

Adaptation of "The Hindenburg" by Patrick O'Brien. Copyright © 2000 by Patrick O'Brien. "The Skunk Ladder" from *The Grasshopper Trap* by Patrick F. McManus. Copyright © 1985 by Patrick F. McManus. Reprint by permission of Henry Holt and Company, LLC.

Houghton Mifflin Harcourt Publishing Company

Text and photographs from *Ghost Towns Of The American West* by Raymond Bial. Copyright © 2001 by Raymond Bial. From *Shipwreck Season* by Donna Hill. Copyright © 2008 by Donna Hill. Reprinted by permission of Houghton Mifflin Harcourt

Illustrations

Photographs

92 (T) Joe McDonald/Corbis; 92 (B) John Cancalosi/Alamy; 93 Michael & Patricia Fogden/Corbis; 95 (T) Steven Hunt/Getty Images; 96 Premaphotos/Alamy; 98 Kevin Schafer/Corbis; 99 (C) Corbis/Jupiter Images; 99 (Bkgd) Getty Images; 99 (B) Stublefield Photography/Shutterstock; 100 (TR) Blickwinkel/Alamy; 100 (C) Dave Watts/Alamy; 100 (BR) Michael & Patricia Fogden/Corbis; 100 (B) Michael A. Keller/Corbis; 101 Wayne Lawler/Ecoscene/Corbis; 103 Premaphotos/Alamy; 104 Westend61 GmbH/Alamy; 105 (R) Randy Faris/Corbis; 105 (B) Nicholas Prior/Getty Images; 108 (T) Image Source/Corbis; 108 (C) FB-STUDIO/Alamy; 108 (B) Jim Naughten/The Image Bank/Getty Images; 130 Cynthia Farmer/Shutterstock; 131 Jupiter Images; 136 Andrey Kiselev/Fotolia; 137 (R) Thomas Fricke/Corbis; 137 (L) Pixtal/SuperStock; 139 Rubberball Productions/PunchStock; 140 (T) Ann Stevens/Alamy; 140 (B) ©Blend Images/Alamy; 140 (C) Artur Shevel/Fotolia; 141 Jeff J Mitchell/Reuters/Corbis; 144 Jupiter Images; 147 Veer; 156 Don Mason/Corbis; 158 (BC) Photos to Go; 158 (BR) PCN Photography/Alamy; 158 (BL) Corbis; 159 PCN Photography/Alamy; 168 Simon D. Warren/Corbis; 169 (T) Moodboard/Corbis; 169 (BR) Jochen Tack/Alamy; 171 (T) Olaf Graf/Corbis; 171 (CR) Shutterstock; 172 (T) Fabrice Bettex/Alamy; 172 (C) Photolibrary/Getty Images; 172 (B) Dlillc/Corbis; 173 (T) Liz Hymans/Corbis; 173 (CR) Michelealfieri/Fotolia; 192 Getty Images; 193 Getty Images; 194 Getty Images; 195 Getty Images; 198 (B) Bill Ross/Corbis; 198 (bkgd) Stephen Frink/Corbis; 199 Zach Holmes/Alamy; 202 (T) Michael Brooke/PhotoLibrary Group Inc/Getty Images; 202 (C) WidStock/Alamy; 202 (B) Tom Stoddart/Getty Images; 203 Ralph White/Corbis; 204 (BC) 1998 from Ghost Liners/Ken Marschall; 206 (BL), (BC), (BR), (T) 1998 from Ghost Liners/Ken Marschall; 207 (CR), 218 Jim O Donnell/Alamy; 207 (BL), (BC) 1998 from Ghost Liners/Ken Marschall; 208 1998 from Ghost Liners/Ken Marschall; 210 (T) 1998 from Ghost Liners/Ken Marschall; 210 (B) Woods Hole Oceanographic Institution; 211 (BL), (BR) Woods Hole Oceanographic Institution; 212 1998 from Ghost Liners/Ken Marschall; 213 Barbara Coutts Kharouf; 214 1998 from Ghost Liners/Ken Marschall; 215 (TL), (TR) Woods Hole Oceanographic Institution; 215 (TC) Michael Freeman/Corbis; 216 (T), (C), (B) 1998 from Ghost Liners/Ken Marschall; 217 (bkgd) 1998 from Ghost Liners/Ken Marschall;

217 (TR) UPP/Topham/The Image Works; 226 (C) 1998 from Ghost Liners/Ken Marschall; 227 (C) 1998 from Ghost Liners/Ken Marschall; 228 (T) GRIN/NASA; 228 (bkgd) NASA; 229 Original image courtesy of NASA/Corbis; 231 NASA; 232 (T) Barry Austin Photography/Getty Images; 232 (C) Jupiter Images; 232 (B) Monkey Business Images Ltd/Getty Images; 234 World Perspectives/Getty Images; 236 (T), 246 (T), 248 NASA; 237 Mark E. Lawrence/Corbis; 239, 246 (C) Corbis; 240 NASA; 243, 246 (B) NASA; 244 Original image courtesy of NASA/Corbis; 247 (B) NASA; 247 (T) AP Images; 250 (T) NASA; 250 (R) Corbis; 250 (L) Getty Images; 251 NASA; 252 Time Life Pictures/NASA/Getty Images; 253 NASA; 256 (bkgd) Macduff Everton/Corbis; 256 (T) Getty Images; 257 John & Eliza Forder/Getty Images; 260 (T) Joel Sartore/Getty Images; 260 (C) Imageshop/Corbis; 260 (B) Corbis; 275 (L) Lebrecht Music and Arts Photo Library; 275 (TR) Corbis; 284 (C) Richard T. Nowitz/Corbis; 284 (bkgd) Dave G. Houser/Corbis; 284 (B) Jupiter Images; 288 (T) FK Photo/Corbis; 288 (C) Photolibrary; 288 (B) WavebreakmediaMicro/Fotolia; 289 Shutterstock; 290 James Nazz/Corbis; 291 Chris Collins/Corbis; 292 (L) DK Images; 292 (C), 311 Raymond Bial; 293 John Cancalosi/PhotoLibrary Group Inc/Getty Images; 294 Bettmann/Corbis; 295, 302 (T) Western History Department/Denver Public Library; 296 (T) , 302 (C) Museum of History & Industry/Corbis; 296 (B), 310 (B) Raymond Bial; 298 (L) Raymond Bial; 298 (R) David Stoecklein/Corbis; 299, 304 Raymond Bial; 301 (T), 302 (B) Lynn Radeka/SuperStock; 301 (BR) Western History Department/Denver Public Library; 303 (TR) Sarah Bial/Raymond Bial; 318 (bkgd) Roger Tidman/Corbis; 318 (TL) Andersen Ross/Getty Images; 319 Somos/Jupiter Images; 321 Wally Eberhart/Getty Images; 322 (T) Frank Greenaway/Getty Images; 322 (C) Aspix/Alamy; 322 (B) Jason Edwards/National Geographic/Getty Images; 323 (TL) Marty Snyderman/Getty Images; 323 (TR) James Hager/Robert Harding World Imagery/Getty Images; 324, 337 (B) Arco Images GmbH/Alamy; 326, 336 (T) Arco Images GmbH/Alamy; 328, 337 (CR), 343 Merlin D. Tuttle/Bat Conservation International; 329, 336 (C) Bettmann/Corbis; 332, 336 (B) Victor Habbick Visions/Photo Researchers; 334, 342 Merlin D. Tuttle/Bat Conservation International; 340 (TR) Corbis; 340 (TC) Getty Images; 340 (B) Getty Images; 341 Getty Images; 344 (bkgd) Paul A. Souders/Corbis; 344 (B) Kennan Ward/

WORDS! | Vocabulary Handbook

Antonyms

An antonym is a word that has the opposite meaning of another word. *Day* is an antonym for *night*.

Smooth

Bumpy

Antonym = Opposite

Strategy for Antonyms

1. Identify the word for which you want to find an antonym.
2. Think of other words or phrases that have the opposite meaning.
3. Use a thesaurus to help you find antonyms.
4. Use a dictionary to check antonyms' meanings so that you use the word that best communicates your ideas.

Synonyms

Synonyms are two or more words that have the same meaning or nearly the same meaning.

Wash

Synonym = Same

Clean

Strategy for Synonyms

1. Identify the word for which you want to find a synonym.
2. Think of other words or phrases that have the same, or almost the same, meaning.
3. Use a thesaurus to help you find more synonyms, and make a list.
4. Use a dictionary to find the word that best communicates your ideas.

Base Words

A base word is a word that can't be broken into smaller words.

Earth

Unearthly

Earth is the base word.

Strategy for Base Words

1. Look for a base word in the unknown word.
2. Determine the meaning of the base word.
3. Guess the meaning of the unfamiliar word. Does it make sense in the sentence?
4. Check your meaning in the dictionary.

Prefixes

A prefix is a word part added onto the front of a base word to form a new word.

Formal

Informal

Strategy for Prefixes

1. Look at the unknown word and identify the prefix.
2. What does the base word mean? If you're not sure, check the dictionary.
3. Use what you know about the base word and the prefix to figure out the meaning of the unknown word.
4. Use the dictionary to check your guess.

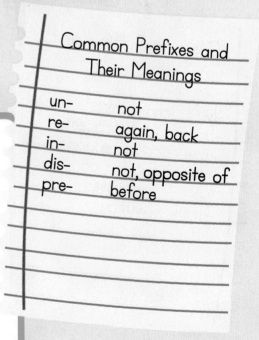

Common Prefixes and Their Meanings

un–	not
re–	again, back
in–	not
dis–	not, opposite of
pre–	before

Suffixes

A suffix is a word part added to the end of a base word to form a new word.

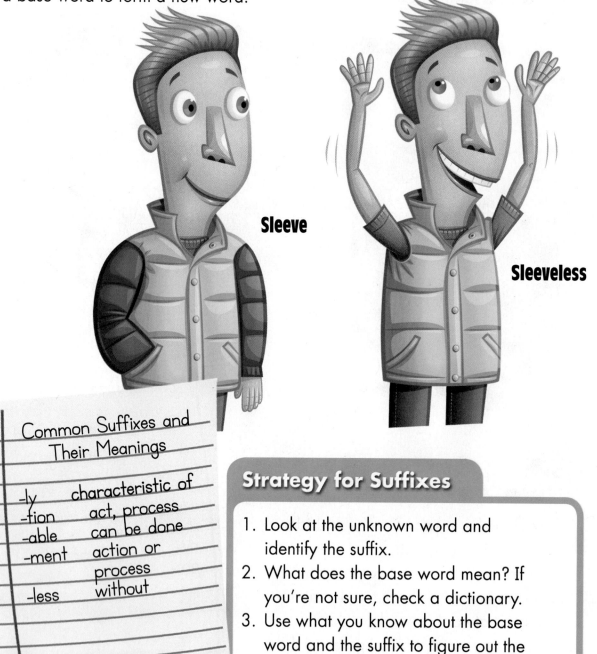

Sleeve

Sleeveless

Common Suffixes and Their Meanings

-ly	characteristic of
-tion	act, process
-able	can be done
-ment	action or process
-less	without

Strategy for Suffixes

1. Look at the unknown word and identify the suffix.
2. What does the base word mean? If you're not sure, check a dictionary.
3. Use what you know about the base word and the suffix to figure out the meaning of the unknown word.
4. Use a dictionary to check your guess.

Context Clues

Context clues are the words and sentences found around an unknown word that may help you figure out a word's meaning.

I saw many animals at the zoo! I saw an elephant, a lion, capybaras, and a monkey.

ROARY

BIG BLUE

Strategy for Context Clues

1. Look for clues in the words and phrases around the unknown word.
2. Take a guess at the word's meaning. Does it make sense in the sentence?
3. Use a dictionary to check your guess.

Related Words

Related words are words that all have the same base word.

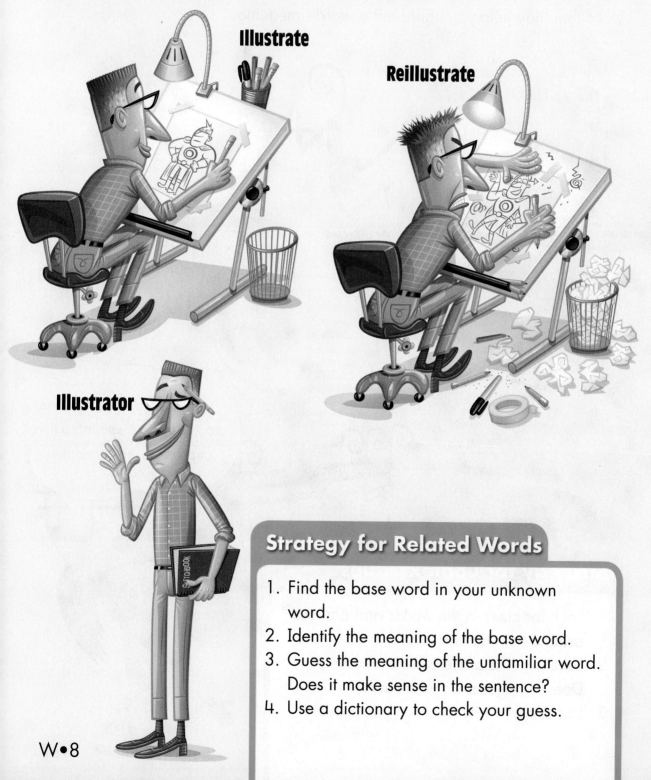

Illustrate

Reillustrate

Illustrator

Strategy for Related Words

1. Find the base word in your unknown word.
2. Identify the meaning of the base word.
3. Guess the meaning of the unfamiliar word. Does it make sense in the sentence?
4. Use a dictionary to check your guess.

Word Origins: Roots

Many English words contain Greek and Latin roots.

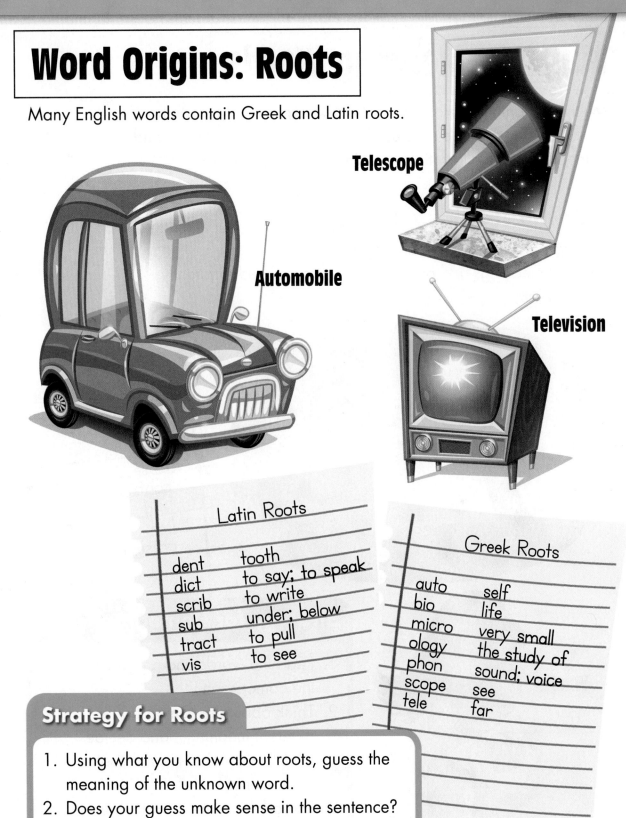

Telescope

Automobile

Television

Latin Roots

dent	tooth
dict	to say; to speak
scrib	to write
sub	under; below
tract	to pull
vis	to see

Greek Roots

auto	self
bio	life
micro	very small
ology	the study of
phon	sound; voice
scope	see
tele	far

Strategy for Roots

1. Using what you know about roots, guess the meaning of the unknown word.
2. Does your guess make sense in the sentence?
3. Use a dictionary to check your guess.

Multiple-Meaning Words

Multiple-meaning words are words that have different meanings depending on how they are used. Homonyms, homographs, and homophones are all multiple-meaning words.

Homographs

Homographs are words that are spelled the same but have different meanings and are sometimes pronounced differently.

Wind

Wind

Some Common Homographs

bass
close
contract
lead
live
present

Strategy for Homographs

1. Read the words and phrases near the homograph.
2. Think about the homograph's different meanings, and decide which one makes the most sense in the sentence.
3. Reread the sentence with your guess to see if it makes sense.
4. Check your guess in a dictionary.

Homonyms

Homonyms are words that are pronounced the same and have the same spelling, but their meanings are different.

Pitcher

Pitcher

Strategy for Homonyms

1. Read the words and phrases near the homonym.
2. Think about the homonym's different meanings, and decide which one makes the most sense.
3. Reread the sentence with your guess to see if it makes sense.
4. Use a dictionary to check your guess.

Some Common Homonyms

pen
duck
mail
ear
bank
bark

Homophones

Homophones are words that are pronounced the same way but have different spellings and meanings.

Eight

Ate

Some Common Homophones

ate	eight
bored	board
brake	break
knight	night
weight	wait

Strategy for Homophones

1. Think about the different spellings and meanings of the homophone.
2. Check a dictionary for the definitions of the words.
3. Use the word that best fits your writing.

This chart can help you remember the differences between homographs, homonyms, and homophones.

Understanding Homographs, Homonyms, and Homophones

	Pronunciation	Spelling	Meaning
Homographs	may be the same or different	same	different
Homonyms	same	same	different
Homophones	same	different	different

address

Homograph

address

Mr. Smith
36 Anytown Street,
Anytown, Ohio

duck

Homonym

duck

Homophone bear

bare

Dictionary

A dictionary is a reference book that lists words alphabetically. It can be used to look up definitions, parts of speech, spelling, and other forms of words.

punc•tu•al ① (pungk′ chü əl), ② *ADJECTIVE.*
③ prompt; exactly on time: ④ *He is always punctual.*
⑤ ✹ *ADVERB* **punc′tu•al•ly.**

① Pronunciation

② Part of speech

③ Definitions

④ Example sentence

⑤ Other form of the word and its part of speech

Strategy for Dictionary

1. Identify the unknown word.
2. Look up the word in a dictionary. Entries are listed alphabetically.
3. Find the part of the entry that has the information you are looking for.
4. Use the diagram above as a guide to help you locate the information you want.

Thesaurus

A thesaurus is a book of synonyms. A thesaurus will also list antonyms for many words.

cute

adjective

attractive, appealing, amusing, charming, adorable, enchanting.
ANTONYMS: plain, ugly

Strategy for Thesaurus

1. Look up the word in a thesaurus. Entries are listed alphabetically.
2. Locate the synonyms and any antonyms for your word.
3. Find the word with the exact meaning you want.